DARING YOUNG MEN

The Story of England's Victorious Tour of
Australia and New Zealand, 1954–55

DARING YOUNG MEN

The Story of England's Victorious Tour of
Australia and New Zealand, 1954–55

ALAN HILL

Methuen

Published by Methuen 2005

10 9 8 7 6 5 4 3 2 1

Copyright © 2005 by Alan Hill

Copyright in the Foreword © 2005 Frank Tyson

The right of Alan Hill to be identified as author of this work has been asserted
by him in accordance with the Copyright, Designs and Patents Act 1988

Methuen & Co. Ltd
11–12 Buckingham Gate, London SW1E 6LB

Methuen & Co. Ltd Reg. No. 5278590

A CIP catalogue record for this book
is available from the British Library

ISBN 0 413 77435 X

Typeset by SX Composing DTP, Rayleigh, Essex
Printed and bound in Great Britain by
St. Edmundsbury Press, Bury St. Edmunds, Suffolk

Contents

To the memory of Sir Leonard Hutton – 'our Len', as he was always known in Yorkshire – and for the joys of his wondrous summers.

Foreword

My love of William Wordsworth's verse tells me that in my life:

> There was a time when meadow, grove and stream,
> The earth, and very common sight,
> To me did seem
> Apparelled in celestial light
> The glory and the freshness of a dream.

For a band of eighteen English cricketers, myself among them, one such halcyon period occurred in the six months between September 1954 and March 1955: a sporting era which enriched us all with the experience of a lifetime when we journeyed with Len Hutton on a tour of Australasia. We returned from that Odyssey with a series 3–1 victory and the Ashes; but more than the result itself, it was the manner in which it was achieved that mattered. Downed by a crushing margin in Brisbane's first Test, we refused to submit but rose Lazarus-like, asserting the spirit of the second Elizabethan age: the zeitgeist of the fifties, which accompanied the accession of Elizabeth II, saw the conquest of Everest, the four-minute mile and breathed a new enthusiasm into English cricket.

It was a time to be remembered and savoured by our captain, Len Hutton: the first occasion he had returned victorious from Down Under. As such it represented the high-watermark of Hutton's personal achievements. The bouquet of certain moments of the tour were to linger long on the palates of our batting tyros, Colin Cowdrey and Peter May who surely never scored better centuries than they did at Christmas in Sydney and New Year in Melbourne. May and Cowdrey epitomised the youthful exuberance of a trans-generational English side, emerging from the wonderful era of

Hutton, Compton and Edrich to set their own personal stamp on the future. Three of England's fast bowlers Down Under in 1954 were only twenty-four years of age and the promise of future performances must have been cold comfort for international batsmen around the world. Indeed, the balanced threat of England's Statham, Tyson, Appleyard, Wardle, and Bailey would have constituted the most potent threat to batsmen of any era and any area of the cricketing world.

The MCC side which visited Australasia in 1954–55 were the 'Happiest Band of Cricket Warriors' I have ever encountered. True there were areas of discontent. Bill Edrich's monopoly of the opening bat position, in spite of a succession of failures made his possible replacements very unhappy. Alec Bedser was jettisoned from the side for the Sydney Test in a most unfeeling and ungracious manner. Hutton's fibrositis and his consequent reluctance to play in the Melbourne Test were a source of uneasiness in the minds of many senior players. But collective strength emerged from the individual discontent as players proved themselves big enough to subordinate their whinges to the general good of the team. And therein lay one of the secrets of the side's success.

Another source of England's collective success was to be found in outstanding individual talents and attributes. If ever one dismissal turned the course of a Test series it was the acrobatic catch taken by Godfrey Evans off a Neil Harvey leg-glance on the final morning of the Melbourne Test. Never has a wicket-keeper covered so much ground, so quickly, at such a crucial moment – in a game and in a rubber. In the Adelaide Test, Bob Appleyard took vital wickets at important junctures. In Sydney, 'the Boil' chipped in with wickets when they were most needed. In every game 'George' Statham plugged away, usually into a breeze and uphill, as I captured the glory and the headlines with the wind behind me and any slope in my favour. But make no mistake, without Statham, there would have been no 'Typhoon' in Australia in 1954–55.

That antipodean summer, 'George' and I took 69 Test wickets in Australia and New Zealand; in first-class matches we claimed 118 victims. Such statistics create the illusion that we monopolised the bowling crease but it could be argued that our slower bowlers, Appleyard and Wardle, played just as great a part in our victory as our speedsters. In the first instance as tail-enders, they scored vital runs with the bat in Sydney and at the bowling crease, they took 21 wickets at 21.57.

They were happy and successful days. I shall enjoy reliving them again in these pages. But the years have passed, so I turn once again to William Wordsworth:

> It is not now as it was of yore; –
> Turn wheresoe'er I may
> By night or day,
> The things I have seen I now can see no more.

Frank Tyson,
Queensland, Australia.
2005.

Introduction

Since the beginning of the twentieth century England had won only four series in Australia: in 1903–4 under Pelham Warner; in 1911–12 led by Johnny Douglas; and in 1928–29 and 1932–33 with Percy Chapman and Douglas Jardine at the helm. Twenty-two years later Jim Swanton observed: 'Some of these teams had great cricketers but the personal performances of none of them, with bat or ball, or both, meant as much to his side as Hutton's contribution did to his team.'

It was a triumph of youth over experience, cunningly devised by an adroit and relentless campaigner. Victory in Australia in 1954–55 was the apogee of Len Hutton's career. As the first professional captain in modern times, he laid the foundations for a rich and exciting chapter in the nation's cricket history. His success in winning two consecutive series against Australia withered the energies of a diligent and conscientious man. 'His tremendous skill and knowledge of the game gave him a great pull with the players,' commented Geoffrey Howard, the MCC manager.

Frank Tyson, one of the precocious young guard in Australia, says: 'The dedication to England winning and the commitment to that end was there before the series began. It was what I had dreamed of as a boy in the 1930s and Len, among all my captains, was able to evince that passion.'

Sir Leonard had to weather a cricketing Dunkirk in the disastrous opening Test. He did not abandon his tactical plan and the emphasis on all-out pace. His response to the defeat at Brisbane was to keep faith with the complementary forces of Frank Tyson and Brian Statham. Statham was the immaculate foil – in his partner's words, 'it was like having Menuhin play second fiddle to my lead' – as Tyson brutally pounded the Australians into submission.

There is one telling illustration of the supremacy of the novice bowlers over their vaunted Australian counterparts, Lindwall and Miller. The Australian fast bowlers were collectively the veterans of 78 Tests. They took 24 wickets in four Tests in the 1954–55 series. A distinguished combination was overshadowed by the ebullience of their younger rivals. Tyson and Statham, with only 18 Tests behind them, captured 46 wickets in the series.

My Australian collaborators include Ron Archer, Arthur Morris and Colin McDonald. They all testify to the menace of Tyson as he ran amok at Sydney and Melbourne to begin England's recovery. 'Frank was something special that year,' is the lingering view. Alan Davidson, a Test newcomer in the series, remembers the 'perfect blend' of the England team and that each one of them had special attributes. Rising above the failures of their seniors as batsmen were the Oxbridge pair of Colin Cowdrey and Peter May. 'You had these young pups,' says Davidson. 'They were the same age as me and I knew I was going to cop it from them in the next decade.'

Davidson also recalls that despite the reverses the series was a special time for him. As part of his apprenticeship, he was a privileged beneficiary of the wisdom of his elders. 'Nobody passes on their knowledge as they did in my day. It gave me a better comprehension of what cricket is all about.'

For my descriptions of a memorable series and the supplementary personality profiles I am deeply indebted to the assistance of England contemporaries, Trevor Bailey, Tom Graveney, Peter Loader, Bob Appleyard, Keith Andrew, John Warr and the late Colin Cowdrey, Geoffrey Howard and David Sheppard.

Frank Tyson, fearsome and inspirational as a bowler, has been another valued supporter, patiently answering my emailed questions from across the world in his Queensland home. I am most grateful to him for providing the foreword to the book. My impressions of Tyson in his formative years have also been enhanced by the recollections of a wise Northampton mentor and his former county captain, Dennis Brookes. Notable assessments of Brian Statham – one of the gentlemen of cricket – have emerged in conversations with former Lancashire colleagues, Roy Tattersall and the late

Geoffrey Edrich. The Rev. Malcolm Lorimer has also kindly given me access to his book, *Glory Lightly Worn*, a compilation of tributes to a revered cricketer. John Woodcock, the former *Times* cricket correspondent who covered the series, has related the events of the 'watered wicket' at Melbourne, a contentious issue at the time.

Walter Hadlee, the former New Zealand captain and administrator, has recalled the undermining experience at Auckland in March 1955 when his fellow Kiwis were dismissed for 26, which is still the world's lowest Test score. Rowland Potter in Auckland, has rendered much appreciated help with researches in his local newspapers. I have also consulted articles by Glenn Turner, Geoff Howarth and Richard Streeton in retracing the progress of New Zealand through to a happier and more successful era.

I am pleased to acknowledge the reminiscences of fellow writers, Jim Kilburn, Alex Bannister, Crawford White, Denzil Batchelor and, especially, the valued impressions of the late Jim Swanton. Praise must also be given to the courteous assistance of the British Newspaper Library staff at Colindale, London. Special thanks are also due to Rob Boddie, the Sussex CCC librarian and archivist and Jeff Hancock, the former Surrey CCC librarian, David Robertson, the Kent CCC librarian, Adam Chadwick, the MCC curator and Ken Daldry, library assistant at Lord's. Each of them has been unsparing in their aid and encouragement. Bernard Whimpress, the historian and librarian, South Australian Cricket Association in Adelaide and Alf Batchelder, Melbourne Cricket Club, were other respected collaborators.

This is, above all, a homage to a great cricketer who advanced the professional cause during his then revolutionary elevation to the England captaincy. Sir Leonard Hutton was the fourth in line of Yorkshire's England captains. The Edwardians, Lord Hawke and the Leeds-born stylist, Stanley Jackson, who held the highest batting average among his contemporaries against Australia, were briefly in command at the turn of the last century. More than forty years elapsed before the gracious South Yorkshireman, Norman Yardley succeeded Wally Hammond in 1947. Yardley, considered the best player on merit to lead his county, dismissed Don Bradman three times in succession in the first post-war series in Australia. Yardley's captaincy was constrained by business commitments and it also coincided with the imperious reign of Bradman's 'invincibles' in England in 1948.

Three other Yorkshiremen from different generations would profit from the campaigning zeal of their distinguished predecessor. Brian Close, in his sadly curtailed and undefeated reign as captain, won acclaim as the best of his time. It was then the turn of his shrewd Yorkshire ally and friend, Raymond Illingworth, whose own appointment coincided with his move to Leicestershire. His astute leadership and tactical skills helped to recover the Ashes and then successfully defend them in the 1970s. The latest in the line is Michael Vaughan, whose young squad face some searching challenges.

Richard Hutton, in another introduction, said that in his childhood, he discovered most about his father from the back page of the daily newspaper delivered to his home. He confessed that he learned to read by picking out his parent's name and score from the scoresheet. As he grew older, he would go to matches and tot up Dad's runs in his own scorebook and anguish over every ball in the dread that the innings would be abruptly concluded.

It is good to know that Richard endorsed my own feelings as another hero-worshipping Yorkshire schoolboy. In Len's big season in 1949, when he scored 3,429 runs, he also registered five ducks. One was woeful indeed for his admirers. He was run out, off the fourth ball of the August Bank-holiday match against Lancashire at Headingley. There was also the disaster of a 'king pair' against Reg Perks and Worcestershire. These were rare moments of torment we had to suffer before we could marvel at the centuries, twelve of them, including three double hundreds in a fantastic season.

At Leeds, against Australia in 1953, the hush that descended on a vast crowd is a stark memory. Len was yorked by Lindwall's second ball after refusing a sharp but manageable single wide of mid-on. Perhaps the worst indignity of all was when he was dropped, for the only time in his career, against Australia at Manchester in 1948. *Wisden* reported that Hutton had been 'plainly uncomfortable' against the pace of Lindwall and Miller at Lord's. It was an affront speedily remedied on his recall at Leeds where he shared two century opening partnerships with Cyril Washbrook. Jim Swanton would later observe: 'I never saw Len flinch again for the rest of his career.'

It was not until Hutton's retirement that I was able to move beyond my boyish adoration. We were just two Yorkshiremen talking together when I interviewed him in his Surrey garden. It was in connection with my book on one of his Yorkshire mentors, Hedley Verity. But I was certainly thrilled again to receive a complimentary letter from him on the publication of the book. Len wrote: 'I am so pleased that you did it.'

Vivian Jenkins, in the *Wisden* of 1950, penned one of the most felicitous of tributes to a great cricketer. 'For Hutton's art is of a garden, tended through the years by fond Yorkshire hands, a pure white rose, all satin and sheen, the beholder's joy, the possessor's pride.'

Alan Hill,
Lindfield, Sussex.
2005.

1

Echoing Fortunes in Australia

'The lessons of Jardine's unyielding command would form the template for Hutton's own pursuit of cricket's holy grail in the years to come.'

The man with the maimed left arm was not pretending when he said that there must be 'a better way of earning a living.' The self-mocking sally was produced at moments of tension, most regularly during two torrid post-war series against Australia. Len Hutton, his arm shortened by two inches in a wartime accident, never forgot the gruelling examinations set in those matches by his great adversaries the Australian fast bowlers Ray Lindwall and Keith Miller.

There were accusations that he was vulnerable to hostile pace. In the 1946–47 series Hutton was goaded into furious action in the second Test at Sydney. Bill Bowes recalled a conversation with his former Yorkshire colleague. 'You know what they're saying, Len?', Bowes had asked, 'They reckon you're *freetened* of fast bowling.' Hutton did not waste words on a reply but his response when it came expressed all the indignation of an affronted man. Neville Cardus enthused about an 'enchanting innings' and how the Yorkshire master 'rippled the sunlit field by stylish drives, quick and wonderfully late.' In less than half an hour Hutton struck six boundaries. England reached 49 in a captivating counter-thrust. 'In the last over before lunch,' added Cardus, 'the cruellest bolt of mischief brought Hutton down to prosaic earth.' He attempted another forcing backstroke off Miller and, after hitting the ball, lost the grip of his bat with one hand and the uncontrolled swing of it broke his wicket. Hutton's 37 took him only 24 minutes. Cardus concluded: 'It is not reckless to assume that a century was nipped in the bud, a rare page blotted in the book of cricket's history.'

The brilliant cameo at Sydney rolled back the years to the blithe batsmanship Hutton had displayed as a cricket prodigy before the second world war. Herbert Sutcliffe, his Yorkshire and England predecessor and mentor, had then described Hutton as 'a marvel – the discovery of his generation.' The record-breaking marathon at Kennington Oval in August 1938 catapulted the slight, boyish and reluctant hero to overnight fame. The painstaking vigil in which he accumulated 364 in 13 hours, 17 minutes – eight sessions of play – ushered the 22-year-old into a demanding realm.

Hutton was one of five Yorkshire players in the England team at the Oval. One of them, Arthur Wood, the wicketkeeper, brought a touch of humour to the determined pursuit of runs, which culminated in a total of over 900 before the declaration. Coming in with 770 on the board, the waggish Wood said: 'I am always at my best in a crisis!' The self-discipline that Hutton displayed on a memorable occasion was sharpened by the presence of his seniors. Hedley Verity was his principal counsellor as he strove to maintain his concentration over the hours.

'I owe him the kind of debt that one can never repay,' said Hutton. 'As my innings developed it was obvious that something out of the ordinary was in the offing, and the ever kindly and wise Hedley made it his duty to stay with me during every lunch and tea break while I nibbled at a sandwich and sipped tea. He sat by my side like a faithful ally to make sure that my thoughts did not wander. His quiet, natural dignity was an immense source of strength to me.'

Fifteen years after Hutton's death in September 1990 at the age of seventy-four, the memories of his exploits are undimmed. Through five series against Australia, the unhurried classicist with a 'bat with no edges' was saddled with expectations that were to tax him at all points in his distinguished career. He disappointed his admirers on only a few occasions. Rarely has a cricketer, particularly one so circumspect and introvert by nature, prospered, as Hutton did after such an auspicious beginning. He was technically unassailable, according to Alan Davidson, one of his later Australian rivals.

For Trevor Bailey, a devoted adherent, Hutton with Denis Compton, Bill Edrich and Joe Hardstaff represented the cream of English batting, whose careers were interrupted by the second world war.

Cricket history – like all history – has a remarkable tendency to repeat itself. The Ashes mission which Len Hutton would later undertake with success closely followed the pattern of England's previous post-war recovery leading on to Test ascendancy under the leadership of Percy Chapman in 1928–29. In 1920–21 and 1946–47 an exhausted and unprepared England were defeated 5–0 and 3–0. In 1921 and 1948 they again wilted against fast bowling and lost by margins of 3–0 and 4–0. The revivals began in 1924–25 under Arthur Gilligan and again in 1950–51 under Freddie Brown. Trevor Bailey, a member of the latter MCC party, believes that the 4–1 defeat in Australia gave a distorted picture of the series. In the Test matches at Brisbane and Melbourne the teams were separated by margins of only 70 and 28 runs. In each of these post-war series England won one Test out of five in heartening fashion, but the 'writing on the wall' was accepted as having more significance than the figures in the scorebook.

It is necessary to roll back the years to examine the changing fortunes. The legend of Douglas Jardine's quest to regain the Ashes in Australia in 1932–33 must have figured strongly in Hutton's cricketing infancy. The lessons of unyielding command would form the template for his own pursuit of cricket's holy grail in the years to come. The firepower of Larwood and Voce bequeathed to Jardine would be replicated in Hutton's discovery of two young men with comparable aggression. There was also the telling message of the pattern of conquest in Australia in the testimony of fellow Yorkshiremen, Herbert Sutcliffe, Maurice Leyland, Bill Bowes and Hedley Verity, all members of the MCC party in a controversial campaign.

'Jardine was a powerful friend but a relentless enemy,' related Bowes. He observed that his captain had so much courage that he would have tackled lions barehanded. 'Players used to say: if it ever comes to fighting for my life, I hope I have the skipper on my side.'

It is beyond argument that no other England captain faced an assignment so formidable as that faced by Jardine in subduing Don Bradman in the 1932–33 series. It was calculated that Bradman scored a century every second time he went to the wicket and that one in two of these centuries became a double century. Someone neatly described him as having a 'single-track mind with no sidings at the crease.' After Jardine's death at the age of fifty-seven in June 1958, Jack Fingleton's obituary tribute was an Australian's recognition that the English captain had succeeded in his objective. 'He saw to it that Bradman was drubbed. Where I think Jardine made his mistake was in thinking that the Australian team was made up of eleven Bradmans.'

Adoration has its pitfalls even for someone as omnipotent as Bradman. Bob Wyatt, England's vice-captain, was on patrol in the outfield during the second Test at Melbourne. He had the last laugh in one verbal exchange with the barrackers in the outer. 'Wait until our Don comes in,' went up the cry. Bradman did make his usual jaunty entrance, only to be dismissed first ball, dragging a delivery from Bowes on to his stumps. Wyatt allowed a suitable interval to elapse before he broke the funereal silence. He turned to the crowd and said: 'Oh, by the way, gentlemen, *when* is your Don coming in?'

Herbert Sutcliffe, in his autobiography published in 1935, placed the emphasis on perfect wickets as the reason for the introduction of leg-theory in Australia. 'There would never have been any need for this method if perfect wickets had not been produced to make good-length fast bowling innocuous,' he said. He added that batsmen had, for years, been given a great and not entirely fair advantage by the preparation of super wickets.

Don Bradman, as the major target of bodyline bowling, agreed with Sutcliffe that it was a reaction against the dominance of bat over ball. He did, however, understandably regard it as the wrong remedy. 'Killing a patient is not the way to cure his disease,' he said. Sir Donald, in a letter to the author in 1986, wrote regretfully of the frost that descended on relations with respected England players in the immediate aftermath of the tour. 'As I get older I appreciate more and more what so many of us missed over the years. Sadly, too, the bodyline era set up an enmity between Australian and English players which didn't really disappear until after the war.'

It could be argued that but for the remarkable reign of Bradman in the 1930s England might have basked in a near supremacy after regaining the Ashes at the Oval in 1926. The period beyond this triumph had witnessed the closing years of some of the greatest of English cricketers – Hobbs, Woolley, Tate, Hendren and Strudwick. Waiting in the wings were Wally Hammond, as the magnificent counter to Bradman, and Leyland, Paynter and Ames as a massively dependable middle order. England's bowling resources were markedly better than those available to Australia. From Maurice Tate and Arthur Gilligan, whose bowling thrusts were soon to be undermined by injury, the opening attack moved to Larwood and Voce supported by Allen and Bowes. The concept of attack was based on shock bursts, first at one end and then at the other. Weaving spells in support was the high-class spin of J.C. White and Hedley Verity, and the accurate medium pace of George Geary, later Peter May's coach at Charterhouse.

The effectiveness of Jardine's leg-theory in Australia was utterly dependent on accuracy. Certainly no one but Larwood could have deployed it with such success. 'I don't think people realise just how accurate Harold was,' recalled Bob Wyatt. 'To bowl short either directly over the leg or off stump required remarkable skill.' Uneven bounce was a major concern for the Australian batsmen. Wyatt added: 'The anxiety arose because you were not sure whether the ball was going to bounce or not. The difficulty was in getting into line to play what might be reasonable length and then finding it up around your armpits. You had to get out of the way or be hit.'

Bill Bowes said that Larwood's bowling acquired what he described as a ricochet effect on Australian wickets. His deliveries did not seem to bounce so much as skim off the pitch. Any ball delivered by Larwood, was quite likely to take off towards the batsman's throat from only just short of a length. Another ball off roughly the same length might just as easily come through below bail height. Bowes attributed this effect to Larwood's tremendous speed, to the hard Australian wickets, and to his low trajectory.

Australia, by contrast, were serviced by negligible fast bowling after the departures of Jack Gregory and Ted McDonald, who had routed England in the series following the first world war. The untimely death of Archie Jackson, at the age of twenty-three from tuberculosis, deprived Australia of a batsman whose light had promised to shine as brightly as that of Bradman. Jackson died at Brisbane in February 1933 on the day that Jardine's team regained the Ashes. It was left to Woodfull, Fingleton and Ponsford, each of them obdurate run accumulators, together with the stylish Stan McCabe, to win a share of the batting limelight.

Australia's bowling, however, really started and ended with the leg-spin of Bill O'Reilly and Clarrie Grimmett and, briefly, the left-hand variations of Leslie Fleetwood-Smith. No attack with such artists, belligerent and cunning by turn, could be dismissed as paltry; but the fact remains that Australia depended heavily on their assorted spinning wares. For searching and penetrative pace they would have to wait for the end of another world war and the arrival of Lindwall and Miller.

Nevertheless the emergence of the 20-year-old Bradman on to the international stage in 1928–29 was a signal to Percy Chapman's triumphant tourists that major troubles lay ahead. One leader writer, while agreeably relieved that England cricket was out of its lean years, prophetically opined that it would be wise to remember that the sun would not always shine.

Victory by 4–1 over Australia was though, he added, an occasion to be savoured. 'In the sad adventure of 1920–21 when an England eleven lost all five matches, it was written that never before had one side showed an overwhelming superiority. Since then the wheel has gone round. Australia has lost many of its matchwinners and we have found the young men to take the places of the old masters.'

One of them was Wally Hammond at his imperious best on his first tour of Australia. Hammond's 905 runs, at an average of 113.12 in the series, included two consecutive double centuries at Sydney and Melbourne and a century in each innings at Adelaide. The aggregate of runs has only been exceeded by Bradman, with 974 in his first golden summer in England in 1930.

In 1928–29, England for the first time, began a series in Australia with three consecutive wins. In the 1911–12 series, Pelham Warner's team, led by Johnny Douglas suffered an initial defeat at Brisbane before taking the honours with four consecutive wins. The opening salvo in 1928 was a record victory by 675 runs at Brisbane. Australia were bowled out for 122 and 66. Jack ('Farmer') White, the Somerset left-arm bowler, took four wickets for seven runs in 39 balls in the second innings. White, then aged thirty-seven, delivered 406.4 overs including 134 maidens and conceded only 760 runs for his 25 wickets in the series. He summoned exceptional control over all the Australian batsmen, not excluding Bradman on his Test debut.

Arthur Mailey was a fellow spinner and humorist with a millionaire's disdain for the concession of runs in luring opponents to their doom. He was well equipped to applaud White's teasing menace. 'His slow innocent-looking deliveries seem to have been created to be knocked about, but we have yet to see an Australian batsman embarrass the Somerset left-hander.' Mailey added that White, with a well-placed field, would bring the greatest driver down to the level of an ordinary batsman.

Major C.H.B. Pridham, writing in *The Cricketer*, said it was White above all who had retained England's hold on the Ashes. He reported on the heroism displayed in the fourth Test at Adelaide. White delivered 749 balls in the match, a feat only surpassed by Verity at Durban in 1938–39 and Ramadhin at Edgbaston in 1957. His 125 overs for 256 runs and 10 wickets were bowled in a temperature of around 100 degrees on a rock-hard wicket. It was an exercise in endurance and precision and endowed with artifice and cricket astuteness in a contest that lasted in those unlimited time matches for a week.

Jack Hobbs, in his 47th year, became the oldest cricketer to score a Test century in the final Test at Melbourne to seal his farewell tour of Australia. Hobbs and Sutcliffe were associated in the last of their valiant partnerships as England retained the Ashes by winning by three wickets in the third Test at Melbourne. The foundations for victory were laid in a perilous period that threatened disaster.

Technically consummate batsmanship on an evil wicket carried the pair to a century partnership and England towards their goal.

England required 332 runs to win and Clem Hill, an illustrious name from Australia's past, remembered a conversation with Percy Chapman at the start of an epic stand after lunch on the Friday. 'How many will we get, Clem?' asked Chapman. Hill replied: 'It will be a good performance if you get 150.' He later wrote that this estimate was a flattering one. 'If I had to prophesy what Australia would have scored under the same conditions, I would have reduced it to 100 – and then they would have had to bat extraordinarily well to do that against England's bowlers. I shudder to think how nasty White and Tate would have been.'

The *Reuters* correspondent expanded on the brilliant manner in which Hobbs and Sutcliffe acquitted themselves. Saucy singles were run with all the old skill. Evident, too, was Hobbs's genius in defence. 'The adroitness in collecting runs where none seemed possible, his calm demeanour while surrounded by difficulties, won him the homage of a record crowd and made the partnership with Sutcliffe one of the greatest ever played in the history of the game.' It was an episode of character in adverse circumstances. The harmony and trust between the veteran and pupil was never better revealed. Monty Noble, the former Australian captain, had earlier officiated in the salutations to Hobbs on his 46th birthday at Sydney in December. He made a presentation of a wallet containing a sovereign for each year of Hobbs's life, and an inscribed boomerang.

Australia, led by Jack Ryder, were left to rue their dependence on veterans in the 1928–29 series. The reluctance of the selectors to bring in new blood prompted one observer to produce the epithet, 'the eternal side.' Longevity among cricketers was not then exceptional but one selection to puzzle Australian cricket followers was the call-up of Don Blackie, the Victorian offspinner from Bendigo. He made his Test debut in his 47th year. Blackie had, in fact, retired from first-class cricket and was spending his Saturday afternoons gardening before teaming up with another veteran, Bert Ironmonger, in grade cricket with St. Kilda.

They so mesmerised local opposition that both were selected for the series against England. Blackie played in three Tests, took 14 expensive wickets, and then went back into retirement.

Ironmonger, a left-arm bowler and one of the most remarkable characters in Australian cricket, also made his debut against England in this series. He claimed his age was forty-one when he was, in fact, forty-six. Four years later he was still going strong and he shared the spinning plaudits with Bill O'Reilly in England's defeat in the second Test at Melbourne.

Sir Donald Bradman, in his later assessment of the series, described the Australian attack as rather inept and ill-supported in the field against Percy Chapman's team. 'Stork Hendry and Ted A'Beckett were just ordinary medium pace, Ron Oxenham, slow medium, and Blackie bowled slow looping off-breaks.' Clarrie Grimmett, the other member of the spin combination, would later reach his zenith as a bowler in tandem with O'Reilly on two tours of England in the 1930s.

Bradman's verdict was endorsed in the reaction of the Australian selectors and the team-rebuilding programme that followed the humbling defeat by England in 1928–29. Amid the euphoria at home the *Daily Telegraph* correspondent laid emphasis on the decline in his postscript to the series. 'It is now clear that Australian cricket is in much the same state as our own after the war. The men who were in Warwick Armstrong's all-conquering side – Gregory, Mailey, Collins, Bardsley and Macartney – are most of them out of the game and their successors have not been found.'

The start of the relentless march of Don Bradman in England in 1930 was, though, only a few months away. His dominion would last throughout and beyond the next decade. As one English bowling rival, Bill Bowes put it: 'Don hit all your bad balls for four and many of your good ones as well.' Len Hutton, as a 14-year-old, watched Bradman's record-breaking 334 at Headingley. Little did he know then that the time would arrive when he would be able to impose his own implacable command.

2

Professional at the Helm

'Hutton won favour as a captain not because he was a born leader but because he was a supreme tactician who planned everything down to the last detail.'

Yorkshire Post.

England emerged from her own years of austerity in a resounding explosion of talent in the 1950s. Len Hutton was chosen to oversee the young guard when he was appointed captain against India in 1952. He was the first professional to lead his country since Arthur Shrewsbury in the 1884–85 series in Australia. It was, as one Yorkshire contemporary says, a decision by the selectors to adopt the Australian method of picking the best player for the post. As England's greatest batsman, Hutton was, in this context, demonstrably the only candidate.

The extent of the departure from tradition can, though, be judged from the names of Hutton's predecessors as captain. They included five Oxbridge men – Percy Chapman, Gubby Allen, Norman Yardley and Freddie Brown from Cambridge – and Douglas Jardine from Oxford. The one exception was Wally Hammond, a product of Cirencester Grammar School. Hammond reverted to amateur status when he captained England against Australia in 1938.

Hutton, to his credit, remained loyal in his promotion to the professional cause. He never officially captained Yorkshire and one of the reasons for this isolation could perhaps be found in the comment of John Nash, the county secretary. 'They shouldn't have done that,' said Nash after Hutton's appointment as England captain. It was hardly a vote of confidence in a fellow Yorkshireman. A charitable assumption would be that Nash felt it was too much of a burden.

It is true that Hutton's pioneering quest was not fulfilled without an immense toll on his stamina. His stewardship began with an undemanding and successful campaign against India. This was but a prelude to a memorable stage in cricket history. His praises were sung throughout the land after the triumph over Australia in the Coronation Year of 1953. The decisive victory was by eight wickets at the Oval. It broke the spell of Australian domination extending back over twenty years to Jardine's mastery in the 1932–33 series.

Jim Swanton, in a later commentary, said that the hurrahs of the excited followers came on a day of unexpected release. 'For those of us, who have been watching the struggle over so many years, the truth was hard to believe until the crowds surged in a multi-coloured mass in front of the pavilion. The country was taken up by the euphoria of the moment to a degree never known before, since the great boom in the sale of television sets occasioned by the Coronation allowed millions to both see and listen.'

The thrilling events at the Oval should have sealed Hutton's own coronation as England captain but the dissenting voices in Establishment circles were not yet stilled. The prevailing view, despite his record, was that Hutton had been given a job for which he had no real training. Cricket expertise, his tactics only coming under serious censure during near defeat at Leeds, scarcely registered in the argument. Here, said his critics, is a man ill at ease socially and lacking the essential graces of a leader.

Jim Kilburn, the Yorkshire historian and a close friend provided a more balanced observation: 'Hutton's captaincy grew in authority, though he always seemed to feel himself on trial, restricted by custom and circumstances.' Another Yorkshire commentator said that Hutton subsequently won favour as a captain not because he was a born leader, but because he was a superb tactician who planned everything down to the last detail.' There was also the competitive urge instilled in him from his earliest days as a cricketer. 'Len did not believe in sparing the opposition once he had got them down on the floor,' remembers one contemporary player.

C.B. Fry referred to the 'humpty dumpty of snobbery' enthroned on the wall in the ensuing deliberations on Hutton's qualifications for the tour of Australia in 1954–55. He described, as absolute bunkum, that there was a supposed party at Lord's so rooted in the feudal past as to object to a professional on social grounds. Fry believed that, other things being equal, professionals themselves preferred an amateur as captain. 'As a rule amateur captains from boyhood upwards have more experience of captaincy and are free from the handicap of knowing that what they do or not do may gravely affect the economic career of a member of their team.'

The august elder did acknowledge Hutton as a shrewd and capable captain and as an almost universal favourite for Australia. But the class distinction he and others espoused presented a threat to Hutton. From his time as a young professional he had been strictly instructed that he must seek to excel in every way above the amateur. He was now called upon to measure up to this creed and justify the honour being dangled before him. The appointment was not a cast iron certainty.

Hutton was still on trial as captain in the West Indies in the winter of 1953–54. He had to cope with menacing crowds and ill temper in the fierce heat of the Caribbean. Alex Bannister considered it a 'sheer miracle that with so many distractions and worries off the field, Hutton was still able to stand head and shoulders above any batsman on either side and to maintain consistency and concentration.' Hutton headed the England batting averages, with 677 runs, including a superb double century to level the series in Jamaica, and averaged 96.71.

The Yorkshire general emerged triumphant though not unscathed; at one stage when he was not in the best of health, as Bannister reported, he lost caste as a captain. Hutton was charged with tactical weaknesses. He was also accused of being less than severe in his condemnation of recalcitrant members of the MCC party. The worst aspect of the vilification was that he was assailed by the stigma of being a professional. 'To a section of people in the West Indies the idea of England being led by a professional was apparently repugnant, as it is to a minority in England,' commented Bannister.

Jim Swanton, as another observer in the West Indies, believed that Hutton's stern assignment would have been rendered easier with a stronger manager as his guide. Billy Griffith was the captain's own choice as manager. The availability of Griffith then an assistant secretary at Lord's, ought to have silenced those critics on the MCC committee who were opposed to the first appointment of a professional captain overseas. In the event, the committee decided that Griffith could not be spared for the tour.

'The most extraordinary part of the business,' said Swanton, 'was the decision not to provide Hutton with a manager at all, but to appoint Charles Palmer, the Leicestershire captain, as player-manager.' He maintained that Palmer, even with full status of manager and for all his personal virtues, would not have been the first claimant as a disciplinarian. 'He did not know the West Indies and had not played in a Test match. He was put in the contradictory situation of being under Hutton's jurisdiction on the field, yet otherwise responsible to the MCC for the administration and discipline of the team, presumably including even the captain.'

David Sheppard, then preparing for his ordination at Ridley Hall, was the Establishment favourite for the England captaincy in Australia. He had deputised for Hutton in two Tests against Pakistan in the home series that preceded the tour. The selectors had taken soundings on Sheppard's availability for Australia. The overtures could not be concealed from the press. Within a short time the captaincy issue was being furiously debated in the media.

News of the discussions at Lord's did not pass unnoticed in Australia. A leader writer in the *Melbourne Argus* rose to Hutton's defence. 'One thing we do hope is that Hutton, whether or not he is chosen as captain, will consent to make the tour. It is sixteen years since this batting genius played his first Test innings against Australia (at Trent Bridge) – and made a century. An England team without Hutton would be like the sky without the Southern Cross.'

Sheppard remembered his dilemma and the unappealing develop-ment, which called upon him to break his training for the ministry for two terms. The other consideration involved offering himself as a rival to Hutton, whom he regarded as a friend and honoured as a master cricketer. The matter was resolved in Hutton's favour. Sheppard, as deputy captain against Pakistan, sensed the changed climate of opinion almost as soon as he stepped on to the field for the second Test at Nottingham.

One of the selectors, Walter Robins, apologetically confirmed this a few days before the announcement of the team for Australia. 'I feel we've been unfair to Len. He was in a very difficult position in the West Indies,' he said. By the time of the rain-ruined Test at Manchester, Sheppard knew that he was out of the reckoning. 'For the only occasion I can think of in Test cricket I breathed a sigh of relief when I was out of it after that match.'

In the end the issue was decided by the restored fitness of Hutton. His illness, a combination of physical and mental fatigue, had impelled an enforced rest for a month during the summer. Hutton expressed his relief at the decision to renew his appointment. It was also cheering news for others in the England camp. Peter May, not given to overstatement, declared his allegiance in one conversation with Geoffrey Howard, the tour manager. 'What a good job we will have Len out there because David would never have done it.' May's appointment as vice-captain was a signal that he was on trial as Hutton's successor.

Jim Swanton returned to his theme of the importance of harmony between manager and captain in the days following Hutton's appointment as captain for Australia. It was his contention that too much should not be asked of someone of frail physique and upon whose shoulders the cares of leadership and control did not rest lightly. The MCC then played one of their strongest cards. They alighted upon a man adjudged to be one of the finest managers ever to manage England on tour. Tom Graveney remembers the devoted services of Geoffrey Howard in Australia. 'He was so good in the way he handled everybody, not just the stars.'

Howard recalled a tour of 'unceasing work' in which he was always conscious that the 'buck stopped with me.' 'Leonard as captain didn't want to be involved with anything off the field. He was fortunate to have such a good collection of players and also myself to attend to his needs as far as I possibly could. I was very fond of Leonard but he was a worrier and I don't think I was.'

One important figure was missing from the MCC party. He was Fred Trueman. Ray Robinson, the Australian writer, regretted his absence: 'A speed attack without Trueman is like a horror film without Boris Karloff.' Peter Loader, another emerging paceman was, it seems, considered a safer ambassador. Trueman, like Surrey's Jim Laker and Tony Lock, had to wait four more years before he toured Australia in 1958–59. Wardle, Appleyard and McConnon were the spinning choices in 1954. One of the ironies of that year was that, after being passed over for the tour, Laker and Lock suddenly found rampant form. In their last ten championship games they took 103 wickets between them, Laker securing 59 and Lock, 44, both for an average of less than nine runs apiece.

Len Hutton was still attempting to bridge the divide consequent upon his new status. He had been judged as too lenient in curbing the coltish transgressions of Trueman and Lock in the earlier tour of the West Indies. Their supposed misconduct effectively excluded them from selection for Australia. Tom Graveney maintains that they were singled out as culprits when other more senior members of the party should have been targeted.

Hutton – and his co-selectors – thus elected to leave out the 'problem boys' who had both played major roles in the defeat of Australia at the Oval in 1953. Alex Bannister was among those disaffected by the omission of Trueman. In his view, the Yorkshireman, as a maturing bowler, had no superior in English county cricket for speed allied to control. Trueman took 134 wickets at fewer than 16 runs each in 1954.

The criticism in Yorkshire found boisterous expression in the *Yorkshire Evening News*. The Editor earnestly attested that Trueman had an incontestable claim to a place in the MCC party. 'We find it incomprehensible that Freddie should pay such a dire penalty for being something of a stormy petrel on his first tour. Maybe he still has a lot to learn, especially off the field, yet we are stimulated by a boy who goes into the attack with such a will to win, and hating every batsman as he hurls down his expresses.'

Another Yorkshireman, Bob Appleyard, had newly returned to first-class cricket after a life-threatening illness in 1954. He regarded his selection ahead of Laker as one of the biggest compliments of his career. One of the most intriguing aspects of Laker's exclusion was that Len Hutton in 1948 was deputed by a prominent member of the Yorkshire committee to enquire, discreetly, whether Laker was settled in Surrey. The answer was that he was perfectly happy in his adopted county. 'Yorkshire went on needing Laker badly,' lamented Hutton. 'We in the post-war Yorkshire team would wince when this gifted Yorkshire exile tied us in all sorts of knots in our matches with Surrey.'

The praise was at variance with the report he submitted as captain to the MCC after the tour of the West Indies in 1953–54. Of Laker he said: 'He is an extremely fine bowler. But he has a tendency to be afraid of certain batsmen instead of adopting the attitude: "I am a better bowler than you are as a batsman. When a good batsman is at the wicket he is inclined . . . to indicate his unwillingness to bowl."'

Another theory advanced by Frank Tyson was that Laker did not always do justice to his immense talents on overseas wickets. 'He did have a reputation, particularly among the Australians, of not having a big heart. Jim failed to take the wickets he should have done on occasions because he did not stick at it.'

Eccentricity mingles happily and sometimes sadly with genius. The enigmatic manner was the cloak into which Len Hutton withdrew to disperse unwelcome questions. There was also a perverse side to his nature, which could be unsettling when it icily descended into ridicule of fellow players. One example was in the then British Guiana shortly before the end of the West Indies tour. Hutton, Graveney, Laker and Brian Statham were sitting in the hotel lounge, sipping cold drinks.

The England captain broached the subject of Australia. 'Now, Brian, how would you like to go to Australia?' Statham replied: 'Not 'arf, skipper, I want to go again.' Turning to Graveney, Hutton said:

'And how about you, Tom?' 'I'd love it. There's nothing I'd like better than an Aussie trip,' said Graveney. A noticeable pause followed before Hutton looked in Laker's direction and enquired: 'Like another drink, Jim?'

Yet, despite all his contradictions, Hutton could display true compassion, as in the case of Colin Cowdrey, one of the most enterprising of selections for Australia. It was his first overseas tour and Cowdrey had to overcome the hugely distressing blow of the death of his father. A telegram announcing the bereavement awaited him when the MCC team arrived in Perth. Cowdrey recorded: 'When I went down to dinner Len Hutton said nothing. It was only after the meal, when I was having coffee in the lounge, that he came round the back of my chair, put his hand on my shoulder and said: 'I'm sorry.' There were tears in his eyes.' Cowdrey added that Hutton never made reference to his father again. Hutton did, however, ensure that for the rest of the tour his junior was not allowed to brood in his grief.

Frank Tyson was regarded as a 'hunch' selection although he tends to refute the argument that he was a speculative choice for Australia. His chances of Test recognition were thought extremely slim. He had just completed his first full county season with Northamptonshire. Alec Bedser, at thirty-six, was making his third tour of Australia and was expected to share the new ball with Brian Statham, with Trevor Bailey in support.

There was, however, one telling and ferocious blast by Tyson that brought a gleam to the eyes of the watching selectors. He summoned all his considerable energy in a duel with Bill Edrich in the County match against Middlesex at Lord's in July. Edrich, attempting to hook, was late on the shot and had his jaw broken. 'I think the selectors thought that if I could do that to such a competitive player as Bill then I was worth consideration.'

Australia had also been alerted to the speed of the novice bowler. Photographs of the 25-yard run from which Tyson generated his eye-blinking pace had been airmailed to newspapers in the major centres. Australian writers had been given one amazing statistic by their English counterparts. It was estimated that when Tyson began his run-up to bowl a distance of 72 yards separated him from wicket-keeper, Keith Andrew. The photographs on the sports desks gave the impression that Tyson and Andrew were playing in different matches! It was above one newspaper photograph that Tyson first acquired his threatening sobriquet. An enterprising sub-editor noted the distance and what could cover it in a blur of pace and in the twinkling of an eye. His headline read: 'It takes a Typhoon!'

The furore could not disguise the fact that Tyson was still a raw and unproven candidate. Furthermore, as Len Hutton intimated on the voyage out to Australia, Tyson, along with Andrew and Peter Loader would be supernumeraries on the tour. 'Don't regard yourselves as likely to be regular members of the team,' they were told. 'Treat the tour as an experience and a learning curve.'

Bill Edrich and Denis Compton, comrades of old, were Hutton's principal batting companions in Australia. Edrich was perhaps one series past his best but, as Geoffrey Howard remembered, Hutton had insisted on his retention in the party. 'Len had a lot of confidence in Bill and wanted him by his side.' The presence of such a stout-hearted and influential ally would serve Hutton well in times of adversity.

Equally important was the service of the irrepressible Godfrey Evans, the first choice wicket-keeper. 'The great thing about Godfrey,' recalls Tom Graveney, 'was that he was never down whatever the circumstances. He was a fantastic cat-napper. He'd come in at tea and go out like a light and sleep for ten minutes.' It was a refreshing rest for a man with a 'marvellous buzz in his cricket.'

There were other surprising selections for Australia, notably Vic Wilson, a good county cricketer but apparently chosen for his fielding skills. Either of Wilson's two Yorkshire colleagues, Willie Watson or Frank Lowson would have enhanced England's batting line-up. Certainly, the battle-hardened Watson, after his match-saving vigil with Trevor Bailey at Lord's in 1953, could have filled the role of opening batsman in Australia. Hutton had four different partners in the Tests, none entirely satisfactory and adding to his burden. This was though, in the main, a time of cricket riches.

Others left at home were simply waiting their turn in the queue. John Arlott thought that the inclusion of another Yorkshireman, Brian Close, blooded too early four years previously and then in prime form, and Allan Watkins, of Glamorgan, would have brought greater all-round strength to the party.

Before the series against Australia in 1953, C.B. Fry had persuaded the BBC to set up a panel to discuss England's prospects of winning back the Ashes. It included three other England captains, Douglas Jardine, Gubby Allen and Arthur Gilligan. 'The upshot of this parliament was that on my proposition that the Australians were the most vulnerable team since the first world war, I was outvoted by three to one.' Fry's fellow panellists took the view that the Australians were always hard to beat. His whimsical reaction was that Allen and Gilligan had both failed to beat them and that Jardine had had the inestimable advantage of Harold Larwood in his team. 'But my inferior hunch was the right one. We did beat them.'

Fry said that what stood out a fathom was that the Australians had only four batsmen of genuine Test match-winning class – Hassett (soon to retire), Miller, Harvey and Morris. Their fielding, he said, was excellent; their close-ups, four behind the wicket on the off, four on the legside, breathed fiercely on the bat and added heat to their two fast bowlers, Lindwall and Miller. 'These two invited an appointment with speed – and perhaps fear; they seemed the real spearhead in the Australian attack.'

The prophecy of the venerable sage was made in a critical year in England's fortunes. It foretold a 'cordial whacking' for the long dominant Australia. Any vulnerability did seem to belong to England when the battle was resumed in Australia. Len Hutton might well have been regarded as a misfit after his monumental blunder in the first Test at Brisbane.

3

Debacle at Brisbane

'I do not think Len was necessarily wrong in putting Australia in
to bat. He would not have expected so many missed chances.'
Ron Archer, Queensland allrounder.

Seven days of unrelenting sunshine transformed the Wooloongabba
wicket into a slumbering idyll for batsmen. The bold gamble by Len
Hutton served only to break his bowler's hearts on the scorched
rectangle at Brisbane, which was, in the words of one writer as
devoid of vice as 'the quilt on your maiden aunt's bed.'

The fateful decision by Hutton to put Australia in to bat was the
act of a man obsessed by speed. Only Johnny Douglas, in those days
of uncovered wickets, had successfully exploited the manoeuvre at
Melbourne in the 1911–12 series. The overwhelming consequence
was a massive innings defeat for the Ashes victor of 1953. It was a
dire overture and Hutton was scorned as a captain for his profligacy.
He had, so it seemed, betrayed the trust placed in him as the
guardian of professionalism.

Trevor Bailey today remembers what was for him an inexplicable
lapse by a normally technically adept captain. Hutton's misjudge-
ment was rendered even more implausible by the selection of a team
top-heavy with pace bowlers, four in all. Bailey was amazed when the
news was relayed to him by one co-selector, Godfrey Evans. 'I
couldn't believe what was happening,' says Bailey. 'You don't need
four seamers, or we didn't at that time. We obviously wanted
balance in the attack and we hadn't got it.' Those watching the
ensuing onslaught were perhaps reminded of the *mot* attributed to
W.G. Grace: 'A captain should never send the other side in though
he should sometimes think very hard about doing so.'

The accent on pace was a rare departure from spin in Anglo-Australian meetings. Speed was also in the thinking of Douglas Jardine in the only other previous example in the bodyline series in 1932–33. England, on that occasion at Melbourne, went in to the field with four fast bowlers – Larwood, Voce, Allen and Bowes. Australia, with the spin of O'Reilly and Ironmonger as their guide, achieved their only victory of the series by 111 runs.

England also paid the penalty for unwise selection at Brisbane. 'If you put the opposition in to bat in a five-day Test (or six days as operated at that time) you've got to take at least three wickets before lunch,' observes Trevor Bailey. The wayward use of the toss on a featherbed pitch ensured a gruelling ordeal for the bowling quartet of Bedser, Statham, Tyson and Bailey. Each of them conceded over 100 runs, as Australia totalled over 600. Frank Tyson maintains, with a quiver of remembrance, that Hutton's decision to field was a logical extension of the team choice, which omitted Appleyard and Wardle, the two spinners. It virtually dictated that England had to bowl first in the hope of quick rewards.

Hutton, however misguided, was intent on pursuing his pre-determined policy of outright speed. It had yielded impressive results in the preliminary passages of the tour. Before Brisbane, Statham had taken nine wickets against Western Australia, admittedly in propitious conditions for fast bowlers, at Perth. Statham, Tyson and Bailey had also shared the honours in the innings victory over a Combined Australian XI, which included Neil Harvey and Graeme Hole from the eastern states. Even more satisfactory, on a slow wicket at Adelaide, were Tyson's six wickets against South Australia in the win by 21 runs.

The exclusion of spin at Brisbane was only partly explained by the inconsistency of England's slow bowlers. The value of Appleyard especially would be shown later in the series; but he was then, by his own admission, having to make a major adjustment to his bowling methods. He was also inconvenienced by a rib injury sustained in the match at Colombo on the voyage out to Australia. Even so, there were substantial wicket hauls for both Appleyard and his Yorkshire colleague, Wardle at Perth and Adelaide.

The evidence of one Australian rival, Ron Archer, the Queensland allrounder, makes apparent Hutton's dilemma in the first Test. He had expert knowledge of the 'Gabba' upon which he played for both the state and his club. Archer says that by Australian standards his home wicket was slow and flat around this time. The situation changed when the new curator, Jack McAndrew decided to prepare wickets with more grass and moisture. It resulted in 'some life' for the first two sessions of play until the drying powers of extreme heat and subsequent rolling crushed the green roots. Archer says that it was not surprising that Ray Lindwall was persuaded by the new conditions to move from New South Wales to Queensland in 1954.

Making capital of the initial advantage was the challenge relished by the state bowlers. In those years, in Sheffield Shield matches, if Queensland had the chance, they invariably asked the opposition to bat first and hoped to gain important first innings' points. Archer concedes that the state games lasted only four days but in principle he does not think that Hutton was necessarily wrong in his action in the Test. 'It is always easy to look at events with hindsight. But Len would not have expected so many missed chances.'

Hutton, though, ought to have considered the change in the weather in the days following the MCC match against Queensland. Brisbane had sweltered in high temperatures with prolonged hours of sunshine in this time. The England captain failed to recognise the change in this early examination of his leadership. *Wisden*'s correspondent was sympathetic: 'The wicket looked a beauty, but Hutton had inspected the wicket most carefully and he carried out his plan . . . Although on subsequent events he could be condemned, the fact remains that England allowed about twelve possible chances to go astray. If the England fielding had approached any reasonable standard Hutton might well have achieved his objective.'

According to Alec Bedser, the nature of the wicket in the previous state game was persuasive in the action taken by Hutton. 'It was very humid and the ball was swinging about all over the place on a green pitch,' recalls Bedser. Interestingly, in a rain-affected fixture, Ken Archer, the Queensland captain, also put the MCC in to bat. It was not an unqualified success as the match ended in a tame draw. Colin McDonald, another Australian rival, refers to the durability of the wickets at Brisbane. 'They invariably favour batsmen and only slightly deteriorate due to wear throughout a match,' he says.

Peter May led the MCC against Queensland. Ominously for England was the bowling of Ray Lindwall, in his first game in the state's colours. He dismissed Cowdrey and Bailey cheaply but both Simpson and Compton scored hundreds in a fourth-wicket partnership of 234 runs. Simpson took the opportunity to press a claim for an opening role in the Tests but, as the *Wisden* observer reported, 'never again on the tour did he reveal the same powers of concentration.'

Queensland replied with 288, a deficit of 16 runs; but it was a laborious affair, occupying over seven and a half hours. The drawn match subsided into batting practice for the tourists, notably May and Compton, in their second innings. The most encouraging feature was that Bedser drew attention to his prospects with lively and economical bowling. 'Throughout the MCC's long stay in the field Bedser bowled splendidly,' enthused *Wisden*.

Reflecting on England's defeat in the Brisbane Test, Trevor Bailey remembers the tourists' fielding display as 'an absolute shambles'. An unbalanced bowling attack was cruelly exposed as a succession of chances were missed. Frank Tyson maintains that the chances missed were not particularly difficult and most 'would have been swallowed by a good Test side.' Bedser was the chief sufferer and Ray Robinson, the Australian writer, reported that five chances were missed off his bowling. Two of Australia's most dangerous batsmen took full advantage of their good fortune: Morris (153) and Harvey (162) between them scored over half of Australia's total. They added 202 runs for the third wicket.

Keith Andrew, deputising for Godfrey Evans, a victim of sunstroke, was severely judged as one guilty party. He reportedly fumbled a catch offered by Morris off Bedser before he had scored. Tyson exonerates his Northamptonshire colleague from blame. 'It was an inside edge and would have demanded superhuman reflexes for him to have taken it.' Andrew was acknowledged by his peers as having the best pair of hands of any wicket-keeper in England. Along with Surrey's tidy and unassuming Arthur McIntyre he was unfortunate that his career coincided with that of the mercurial Evans.

It was said that the acrobatic Evans was safer with the near-impossible than the easy ones, because when he was stationary he tended to make a kangaroo style jump in the air at the moment of catching the ball. For such an extrovert character it would otherwise have been too simple. He did like to play to the gallery; his zest and proficiency noticeably declined away from the big stage.

Les Ames, Evans's illustrious predecessor, was widely credited as being one of the few people able to control the ebullience of his junior. Ames was captain in one match for Kent. He watched Evans plunge into a dive to attempt an impossible catch. The ball just eluded his fingers as he sprawled in front of Arthur Fagg at first slip. Evans picked himself up as Ames, standing at second slip, looked on with disdain. 'Gawd,' said Les, 'another one put down.' He was not unduly impressed with Evans's spectacular but abortive dive. It elicited a typically deadpan rebuke. 'If you are going to put it down, I should let it go to slip,' he said.

Keith Andrew was a complete contrast as a wicket-keeper. 'His lack of fuss,' commented Alan Ross, 'would, in anyone else, be greatly ostentatious; he takes Tyson's thunderbolts as a butler might accept a calling card, with no notice at all. He would not, I think, get near some of the things Evans catches: but greatness and great competence are rarely akin.'

Dennis Brookes, Andrew's county captain, was incensed by the sweeping criticism heaped on the wicket-keeper at Brisbane. Brookes says: 'Keith was so good, we were surprised if he missed a catch.' Brookes, like Tyson, rejected the unfair claim against Andrew at Brisbane. 'It was a ridiculous criticism. They never forgave him for that.' Andrew had to wait five more years before he was selected for another tour under the captaincy of Peter May to the West Indies in 1959–60. Even then it was as reserve to Surrey's Roy Swetman.

The plunder reflected by the final scoreboard was slow to gain momentum at Brisbane. Morris and Harvey, after the dismissals of Favell and Miller, seemed almost bemused to be batting. Tom Goodman, in the *Sydney Morning Herald*, wrote that Harvey was a ghost of the player who had stroked his way to brilliant centuries against England in the previous year.

On the first day Bill O'Reilly reserved his highest praise for Statham, as England spiritedly attacked on the docile wicket. 'Even at the end of a really tough day he was still giving the job everything, by way of energy and enthusiasm. It is not easy to bring to mind a better fast bowling exhibition than this.' Evidence of Statham's control was shown in two spells at the start and end of the day. In the beginning he conceded only 13 runs from his first 10 overs. His stamina was still undiminished in the closing minutes. Statham bowled five overs to Morris and Harvey at a cost of 12 runs, each of them grudgingly surrendered.

Keith Miller, in his most princely vein, produced the batting highlight of the day's play. Denzil Batchelor presented his own flourish to a richly entertaining innings. 'Miller hit a no-ball from Bedser over long-on for a steepling sixer into the outer reserve, the stroke of an exultant golfer. He late-cut Tyson like a beau flicking the snuff from his fingertips. Bailey resorted to defensive tactics; then got his victim. It was a delectable late cut that did it. Miller's most relished stroke was taken too fine for once, and the stumps were askew. Miller made a gesture of disappointment as he left the pitch. There are times when cricket means as much to him as horse-racing.' His forty-nine runs had also included four 4s. The bat was raised high in regret as much as triumph as the pavilion rose to him. It had been an innings of panache, resonant with the flair of a cavalier of cricket.

The catalogue of misfortunes never ceased as England toiled in the field for over two days. The worst of the blows was the injury to Denis Compton. Just before lunch in the opening session he raced around from third man in a vain attempt to prevent a boundary. He tried to steady himself by clutching hold of one of the rungs of the pickets. As he did so, he slipped and lost his balance and dropped to his knees with his hand imprisoned. The result was the fracture of the metacarpal bone of the fourth finger of his left hand.

Australia's innings was marked by the return to form of Arthur Morris. His 153 was his eighth century against England. It gave him an aggregate of 3,197 runs and placed him third behind Bradman and Clem Hill in the list of Australians in Tests against all countries. Morris and Harvey were the beneficiaries of a spate of fielding lapses. The runs mounted because the chances and half-chances were squandered. The most palpable of the errors occurred early on in the innings when Bailey missed a straight to hand catch. Directly after tea Morris hooked Bedser hard and true to deep fine leg. Bailey, near the fence, got right under the ball, had it in both hands but let it drop out. Morris was then on 55 and the total 145. It was an unaccountable blunder by a normally safe fieldsman and would cost England dearly.

Morris, on 89, was again reprieved when May dropped him at slip off the second delivery from Bedser, using the new ball on the second day. The shine was still on the ball when Harvey, having scored 58, was missed by Bedser at short fine leg – a sharp chance to his left hand. At 103 he had another life when a return catch eluded Bedser. Before Harvey was finally out Statham leapt but just failed to take what would have been a remarkable catch at mid-off.

Alec Bedser, after five unaccepted chances off his bowling, did finally take his first wicket, that of Harvey. By then there was the unjust count of 110 runs against his name. Bailey, too late, made amends in a more familiar fielding territory for him. He tumbled to the ground to hold a hard pull at backward short leg. Harvey, after a sketchy start, had finished his innings in imperious style. His 162 was his third and highest against England and also his first century against them in Australia.

The turmoil for England's bowlers was not yet over. It continued with Lindwall and Benaud in a seventh wicket partnership of 81 runs. Lindwall, to huge acclaim, reached his 50, offering further proof of his batting powers down the order. 'He not only blasted the outfield with dynamite drives, but also cut with the lofty assurance of a dowager on church parade,' commented Denzil Batchelor.

Lindwall was unbeaten on 64 when Australia, with two wickets in hand, declared their innings closed.

As Hutton gazed at a scoreboard reading 503 for 6 at the close of the second day, the consequences of his decision were painfully evident to him. He rejected the criticism of the English press, which alleged that he had been tricked by the Brisbane groundsman, Jack McAndrew into believing that he had a fiery wicket at his disposal. He was weary but not downhearted. 'If we had taken all our catches the position would not look nearly so bad now, would it? I sent Australia in because I thought it was the best way to start winning the match.'

In an interview given to the *News Chronicle* later, Hutton said that he had based his move on the experience of playing in five matches in Queensland. 'In the state game and Test in 1946 the ball moved about a great deal until around three o'clock on the first day. Now that wickets are covered in Australia it is more than ever important to take advantage of early liveliness, for on the second and third days the pitches have become easier and easier. I was trying to do just that.'

The besieged captain also asked his critics to be mindful of how England, with what he considered a weaker attack, had bowled Australia out for 228 at Brisbane in 1950. For Jim Swanton the uncapricious excellence of the wicket four years later meant that there could be no repeat of that heartening feat. 'There was not the oppressiveness in the air that had helped Bedser, Bailey and Brown to overthrow Australia.'

Len Hutton, according to Richard Whitington, was misled on more than one count in his captaincy gamble. Whitington referred to the gastric trouble, which had caused Ray Lindwall to withdraw from the Queensland attack in the match against the MCC at Brisbane. 'Hutton allowed Lindwall, whose complexion before the Test was as pallid as an opium addict's, the advantage of a day's rest in the pavilion recovering what remained of his renowned vitality and venom.' Whitington concluded: 'Lindwall was twice the bowler when England's turn came to bat than he would have been in his weakened, convalescent condition on the first day.'

England, as they forlornly sought to salvage pride, perished against a revived Lindwall and his bowling partner, Keith Miller. The alliance was just as fearsome as it had been on the tour of England in 1948. Four wickets, including the precious one of Hutton in Lindwall's first over, were swept aside for 25 runs in the first hour. Miller's first over was similarly imbued with aggression; he unleashed a ball which shattered Simpson's wickets while the batsman remained rooted in his crease.

Stubborn resistance almost inevitably involved Trevor Bailey. He was the stabilising influence in the disarray. His rescuing stand with Cowdrey yielded 82 runs. The highlight of Bailey's top-scoring innings of 88 was uncommon for such a soberly inclined cricketer. Throwing caution to the winds, he heaved Johnson for six over mid-on and out of the ground.

Bailey describes the venture as a 'frivolous moment'; he was unaware at the time that a local businessman had offered a prize of one hundred Australian pounds for the first six to be hit by an Englishman on the tour. Denzil Batchelor whimsically commented that the umpire went up and spoke to the apparently conscience-stricken Bailey. There were some, he said, who believed that he had offered to take the batsman's temperature. Others wondered whether Bailey had infringed his amateur status.

Peter Loader, another member of the MCC party, recalls the brief flight from style by a man who could stay safely at the wicket for hours by simply refusing to be tempted into audacious strokes. Afterwards the England players were reeling for other reasons than astonishment as they celebrated the mighty six-hit. 'Brisbane's Lennons Hotel probably has never forgotten it,' says Loader.

When Bailey was out he took immediate steps to check that he had actually won one hundred pounds. He dashed back to the hotel to trace the notice in the local newspaper and just as quickly received a confirmatory telephone call from the generous donor. 'I invited him to join us,' says Bailey. 'We had a very good party at Lennons.'

It was a refreshing experience at the conclusion of a humiliating match. Bailey, the dissenting voice at Hutton's decision, resumed his defiant posture when England followed on, 411 runs behind. He batted for nearly six hours for 23 to complete a total of eight hours and 40 minutes in the match in a marathon display of concentration. Bill Edrich, too, also brought cheer to the gloomy proceedings. He equalled Bailey's first innings score before hooking too soon and being bowled by Johnston. Rubbing salt into the wounds of defeat was the fact that England's last four wickets fell to the spin of Benaud and Johnson in less than half an hour on the final day. The match ended with a glorious running catch, taken with urchin glee in the deep by Harvey to dismiss Statham.

There was an intriguing sequel to the sorry episode at Brisbane. Trevor Bailey remembers travelling down to the team headquarters at the Windsor Hotel in Melbourne with Godfrey Evans, Denis Compton and Brian Statham. 'As we were going up the stairs, who should be coming down but the Australian Prime Minister, Bob Menzies.' Menzies was well known as a charming host and avid supporter of the game. His welcoming gesture to a group of disconsolate English cricketers went beyond mere pleasantries. 'You boys look as if you could do with a grog,' he said. 'Come in and have a drink.' Bailey recalls that they then spent the next hour in his hotel suite. 'It was a great occasion for us all.'

4

The Typhoon and
Gentleman George

'To me, it felt like having Menuhin play second fiddle to my lead.'
Frank Tyson on Brian Statham.

The Wagnerian tumult of the skies was the signal for Bob Menzies
to elicit roars of laughter from the diners on a stormy night in
Canberra. The Australian Premier playfully dangled the menace of
Frank Tyson before his guests. His sparkling rejoinder foretold the
haunting of his cricket countrymen and conjured a ghostly presence
not unlike Banquo at Macbeth's table.

The speaker at the dinner was Lindsay Hassett, the former
Australian captain. The newly retired Hassett had embarked on a
scathing indictment of his batting successors. He had just reached
the nub of his argument concerning their inadequate technique to
contain Tyson when it was suddenly muffled by a booming crack of
thunder that reverberated around the room. The bombardment
provided the cue for a gleam of wit to match the lightning in the
heavens. 'Hang on, Lindsay, said Menzies, '*he's* just running in.'!

The hilarity that convulsed the assembly at Canberra gave more
than a hint of the dangers to be posed by Tyson, the modest youngster
from England. He was still a novice in international terms, having just
completed his first full season in county cricket. Tyson's raw,
untutored bowling had, though, while he was a university student,
brought him to the attention of Len Hutton. 'You want to watch out
for this lad from Durham University, he's quick,' was the advice
relayed to Hutton during his benefit match at Redcar in 1950.

Tyson recalls that his call-up for the match against Yorkshire occurred while he was studying at Hatfield College. Among his many friends in the colleges and university teams was a Redcar townsman, Dick Hansell, who played for the local club. It was Hansell who recruited Tyson to add strength to the Redcar side. 'My main memory of that encounter was my first spell,' says Tyson. 'I rather surprised Len by hitting him several times on the pads while his bat was still coming down from the top of his backlift.' It was rumoured that Hutton sent a message to his Yorkshire colleague, Fred Trueman, who was playing snooker in the Lobster Pot pub adjoining the Redcar ground. Hutton knew, from experience, how Trueman would react to his goading prompt to cross over the road and watch a bowler who was faster than him!

The rivalry between two great fast bowlers would become one of cricket's talking points in later years. The Yorkshire partisans did, of course, fervently worship the indomitable Trueman. Dennis Brookes, the former Northamptonshire captain, provides a memory of a contest within a game involving Tyson and Trueman at Park Avenue, Bradford. 'The crowd was awe-struck and excited when Fred careered in down the slope from the pavilion end to bowl. But when Frank came on there was a deathly silence. The spectators were absolutely stunned. Fred was a better bowler but Frank was so much faster.'

Ralph Barker, in his book *Purple Patches*, recalled the episode involving Len Hutton, the master and Frank Tyson, the pupil, at Redcar. 'Hutton watched the bowler receding into the distance, pacing out an enormous run. He thought this must be the undergraduate who was supposed to be quick.' Almost immediately he played and missed and was struck on the pad. The delivery was astray, clearly missing the leg stump, but Hutton felt its impact, both physically and mentally. It was rare indeed for any bowler in county cricket to pierce his defence with such violence. He asked for and received confirmation of the bowler's name. The memory of the encounter lingered and was stored for future reference.

Others had watched or had been astonished by the explosive pace of Tyson in his apprentice years. None more so than an early mentor, John Kay, the former *Lancashire Evening News* cricket correspondent and a long-serving member of the Middleton club in the Central Lancashire League. Kay was associated with two other great cricketers, Hedley Verity and Basil D'Oliveira at Middleton. He took great pride in his discoveries. It gave him cause for regret when Tyson and D'Oliveira moved to counties other than Lancashire and went on to represent England with distinction.

Roy Tattersall, the former Lancashire and England bowler, remembers that his interest in Tyson was first aroused because they had both, at different periods, attended the same school – Castle Hill at Bolton. Two other international sportsmen, soccer centre-forwards, Tommy Lawton and Nat Lofthouse were also pupils at this school.

In the late summer of 1947, Tyson was called up by Lancashire for a trial at Old Trafford. It coincided with their match against the South African tourists. Entering the hallowed pavilion was, he recalled, akin to a pilgrimage to a holy shrine. He was then aged 17 and a pupil at Queen Elizabeth's Grammar School, Middleton. He was one of three bowling triallists at Old Trafford. His pace on a 'fast and very rough wicket' so affronted Phil King, a century-maker against Yorkshire in the previous week that he stormed from the net. The intense young Tyson also impressed Harry Makepeace, the county coach. He asked the boy if he would be interested in joining the Lancashire staff. 'You know,' said Makepeace, 'if you come here, I think I can make you an England bowler.'

Tyson recalls: 'I hurried home to break the news to my parents. My father, however, had other less glamorous ambitions for me. He made it abundantly clear that under no circumstances would he allow me to go into professional cricket when it was possible for me to go to university.' Tyson had just sat the subsidiary Higher School Certificate and done well. In June of the following year Tyson was successful in the full examination, winning two distinctions and three credits to receive the award of a bursary at Hatfield College, Durham University. 'You will get your degree and a job qualification before risking your future playing cricket,' was the stern admonition of Tyson senior.

His university studies were delayed by National Service. Lancashire though, had not forgotten him and contacted Tyson while he was in the army. He was invited to play in a pre-season trial match at Old Trafford in 1949. He took the wickets of three first team players, Jack Ikin, Winston Place and John Kelly. Roy Tattersall remembers his own astonishment when Tyson uprooted the stumps of Place, a dour battler in Lancashire's cause over the years. The outcome was the offer of a game for the Lancashire second eleven against Northumberland.

It was destined to be his only appearance for his home county. In the summer of 1949 the country was in the grip of persistent rail strikes. On the day before the Lancashire match Tyson had played for the Army at York. His journey from York to Manchester – a distance of 80 miles – took him eight hours. Shortly after three in the morning he tumbled out of the train and began the walk of five miles to his home, still carrying his cricket bag. He snatched a few hours' sleep before catching a bus to Old Trafford. The Lancashire team was already in the field when he dashed into the dressing room. The harassed youngster was given a stern reprimand from county veteran, George Duckworth. Worse was to follow when Tyson pulled a muscle after bowling only three overs and had to withdraw from the game.

Geoffrey Howard, the Lancashire secretary, expressed his sympathy at the injury. Reassuringly, he told Tyson to write to him when he was fit again. Tyson could not shake free of the gremlins; he sprained an ankle and then broke a leg playing soccer. It seemed to him once he was restored to fitness that Lancashire now held the firm view that he was injury-prone. In June 1951 he made one last effort to engage the interest of the county. He wrote to ask for a game with the Lancashire second eleven.

The reply from Geoffrey Howard in July was a signal that this door of opportunity had been shut politely but firmly in his face. It said: 'Thank you for your letter. I am sorry to say that I am afraid that I cannot be of any help to you this year. We have extended invitations for the remaining second eleven matches this season and this, with our existing professional staff, means that there will be no opportunities for you this season.' Tyson was bitterly disappointed at the rebuff. He never heard again from the county club. While he pondered on his plight, there were others, including a shrewd Australian, Jock Livingston, who would soon introduce him to more welcoming pastures at Northampton.

It was a major part of the heritage of the Northern Leagues that nurseries should exist to provide the opportunities for players to climb to the highest branches of the cricketing tree. For Frank Tyson, his league years gave him a comprehensive education as he was pitted against the cream of the world's cricketers. One week he suffered the plight of many when George Tribe, a future county colleague, bowled him with a googly. The following week Vijay Hazare, the stylish Indian batsman, savaged Tyson's own bowling, as a series of punishing strokes rattled against the boundary fences.

Early in his senior career Tyson played against Rochdale and he was opposed to Australian, Cecil Pepper. Tyson recalls: 'He quickly educated me as to what to expect from Aussie rivals.' The joust with Pepper, a fiercely combative leg-spinner, proved a salutary experience. Tyson came in at number 11 and missed each ball – without being dismissed. At the end of the over Pepper told the bewildered batsman: 'All right, open your eyes, young 'un, I'm finished.' Tyson did not forget the indignity and a few years later had the great satisfaction of bowling the Australian in a local Cup match. In a postscript to the story Tyson says: 'The Aussies may talk a good game, but they are beatable.'

These were stern battles to toughen the apprentice in his time as the youngest player, at fifteen, in the Middleton first XI and later as a part-time professional with Knypersley in the Staffordshire League. The step up to the first-class ranks came as a result of a recommendation by Australian, Jock Livingston. It followed a charity match appearance for the North Staffordshire League against a Commonwealth eleven in 1951. The Commonwealth team comprised several Test players: the Indians, Pahlan Umrigar and Hazare; Frank Worrell from the West Indies; England stalwart, Jack Ikin –

and a strong Australian contingent of Tribe, Livingston, Jack Pettiford, Fred Freer and Des Fitzmaurice.

Livingston, inevitably known as 'Doctor', had recently signed for Northamptonshire and one of his unofficial duties was to act as a scout for his adopted county. He was so impressed by the challenge offered by Tyson in the match that he was prompted to issue an invitation to the young bowler to have a trial at Northampton.

At the beginning of the Easter vacation in 1952 Tyson travelled south from Durham to Wellingborough for this eagerly awaited date. He arrived late for the match and the Northamptonshire team was already in the field. Tyson recalled that his sponsor Jock Livingston was keeping wicket. 'When I was brought on to bowl, he moved a respectful distance back behind the stumps. Not so the slip fieldsmen, who appraised my short run and judged that I could not be all that fast. My first delivery clipped the edge of the bat and ricocheted towards second slip at lightning speed. The rather rotund fieldsman crouching in that position was still motionless when the ball cracked him on the knee. His fellow slips carried Fred Jakeman off the field, then resumed their positions – three yards deeper.

Arthur Morris, a future Australian rival, had noted the burgeoning promise of Tyson at Northampton during his tour of England in 1953. It was obvious, said Morris, that here was a coming bowler. He remembered the first two overs that Tyson bowled to him as the fastest he had faced during the entire tour. Dennis Brookes, Tyson's county captain over four peak seasons, also remembers the ferocity of the young contender. 'Frank was very strong and fast, even off three paces in the nets. Against the Australians in 1953 we reduced them to 10 for two. Graeme Hole, who had a very high backlift, came in. His bat was still going down when his wickets were shattered.'

Tyson's reputation also gathered force against the English county professionals. One instructive story involved George Lambert, of Gloucestershire, who as a night watchman, was called upon to face Tyson. It was a fearful experience. Lambert returned to the pavilion, trembling in every limb. He was greeted by his team-mate, Sam

Cook. 'Here's your pint,' said Sam. 'And there's a double scotch chaser. The bugger will be fresher in the morning.'

The fright of the Gloucestershire players in those helmetless days paled by comparison with the menace of Tyson on a spiteful wicket at Old Trafford in August 1953. He had just qualified to play for Northamptonshire and was determined to show his home county their mistake in rejecting him. The speed he displayed against Lancashire was of such velocity as to foreshadow other eye-blinking exploits in Australia little more than a year later. 'The first ball Frank bowled soared over his wicket-keeper, Keith Andrew, positioned a cricket pitch length back, and thudded into the sightscreen,' recalls Roy Tattersall.

Tyson took three wickets in his first five overs, all the time threatening serious injury as the ball skidded through or reared at the batsman's body. The perils were fearsome indeed on a wicket, moist on top after rain but rock hard underneath. 'Frank was the fastest bowler I have ever faced,' said Geoff Edrich, the one valiant Lancashire survivor amid the ordeal. He remembered that none of his teammates relished the challenge. Ken Grieves, a normally combative Australian, was among the appalled onlookers. He was not looking forward to his turn to bat. 'Ken,' said Edrich, 'was normally ruddy-faced.' His complexion, paling by the second, betrayed his anxiety. 'What is the matter, Ken?' enquired Edrich. Grieves replied: 'I don't like the look of this chap, Tyson.'

Tyson himself remembers a fiery pitch upon which one of his bouncers just fell short of six byes. It was not only the Lancashire batsmen who suffered in the atrocious conditions. Brian Reynolds was struck between the eyes playing forward to a lifting delivery from Statham. It was a worrying moment to freeze all on the field with horror. 'We thought Brian was dead as he was carried off,' says Tyson.

Geoff Edrich recorded what Tyson regards as more an act of heroism than a cricket innings against Northamptonshire at Old Trafford. He was, in fact, playing with a hand badly bruised in a previous game. Early in the Lancashire second innings he took a sharp rap on the left wrist from a Tyson lifter. He did not immediately realise that the blow had broken his wrist. Lancashire were dismissed for 141 but Edrich – 'batting pluckily for three hours' in the report in *Wisden* – was unbeaten on 81 at the end.

At the close of play he motored down from Lancashire to Cheltenham for the next game against Gloucestershire. 'When I went down to the College Ground on the following morning I found that I couldn't grip the bat,' recalled Edrich. An X-ray confirmed the legacy of his steadfast batting vigil against Northamptonshire was a broken wrist.

Two gentlemen of cricket, each of them mild in temper and without the stain of malice, were the pioneers of a new era of fast bowling in England in the 1950s. The concentrated fury engendered by Frank Tyson in action was manifestly absent off the field. Peter Loader remembered how he and other tourists in Australia urged Tyson to abandon his accustomed civility. 'Frank, you've got to get stuck into these bastards,' they told him. Brian Statham, who was to become Tyson's great bowling ally, was in the same mould and a disarmingly equable fellow. Roy Tattersall, eight years older and a 'father figure' at Old Trafford, says that Statham never intentionally set out to harm any opponent. If, by chance, he did hit a batsman, he would call down the wicket: 'Rub it, I know it hurts.'

Brian Statham was almost a complete stranger when he came straight from National Service in the Royal Air Force to Old Trafford. His cricket and keenness to succeed had attracted the attention of his sports NCO, Corporal Larry Lazarus, a Londoner and a Middlesex supporter. He wrote to the MCC asking if they had a vacancy for a promising youngster who would shortly be returning to civilian life. The sequel was a trial with Lancashire and Statham joined the ground staff there in 1950.

It was an amazing first season for the novice whose natural talent was allowed to flourish. In his retirement Statham was a guest on a BBC television programme. This was around the time of the revision of the MCC Coaching Manual. The interviewer complimented him on his successes as an England bowler. He next asked Statham to name the most influential of his guides at the beginning of his career. 'No,' said Brian, 'I was very lucky, I didn't have a coach.' It was not, perhaps, a remark that would have endeared him to the headquarters at Lord's. For general advice Statham was indebted to Roy Tattersall. As a former seam bowler, Tattersall remembers one unsolicited compliment from his friend: 'you are the only one who taught me how to control the ball.'

Within two weeks of reporting to Harry Makepeace, the Lancashire county coach, Statham made his debut against Kent at Old Trafford. He was then blissfully unaware of the celebrities on the county circuit. Cyril Washbrook did know about the prowess of the Kent and England opening batsman, Arthur Fagg. 'Don't bowl short at this fellow, he's a good hooker,' he warned. In his opening spell, Statham did try to follow the advice of his senior colleague but inadvertently he pitched one ball short at Fagg. The batsman rocked on his heels in an attempt to hoist the ball to the boundary but it merely looped off his bat in a gentle arc to be caught by Wharton at silly mid-on. Statham often in later years used to laugh about his first scalp in county cricket. 'I'd no idea who Arthur Fagg was,' he said.

Statham's debut season with Lancashire in 1950 coincided with a fierce battle with Surrey for supremacy in the county championship. The title was ultimately shared with the southerners but it was Lancashire's best season for sixteen years. The triumph in 1934 was their fifth title in nine seasons. It ended the most successful period in the club's history. The pursuit of honours in 1950 owed much to the spinning combination of Tattersall and Malcolm Hilton, whose exploits became the talk of the country. Together they bowled over 2,000 overs and shared 288 wickets in the championship. Tattersall, having reverted from seam to spin, took 193 wickets in all matches to head the first-class averages.

Lancashire also turned profitably to Statham after the retirement of Dick Pollard. The decision to omit Pollard, then aged thirty-eight, from the Roses match at Whitsuntide marked the turning point in the county's fortunes. Pollard, flame-haired and with a temperament to match, was known as 't'owd chainhorse' at Old Trafford. Along with Eddie Phillipson, he had been the lynchpin of the Lancashire attack in the seasons before and immediately following the second world war. He played in four Tests and his bowling feats, as he paddled down his long run, included the dismissal of Don Bradman on three occasions in 1948. In the fourth Test against Australia at Headingley he took the wickets of Hassett and Bradman in three balls. The accomplishment earned national acclaim. The sight of Bradman's reeling offstump was one to savour and England's supporters rejoiced with him.

The departure of Dick Pollard left a vacancy which many thought would deprive Lancashire of the required pace to sustain their championship challenge in 1950. Then, reported *Wisden*, along came Statham, still only twenty years of age, to provide a real tonic. Inside a few weeks he had solved the problem of a successor to Pollard but he was not without severe critics. His windmill-style action did not please the purists, who considered that it lacked rhythm. John Woodcock, the former *Times* cricket correspondent, has commented on the fact that Statham was so double-jointed that he could wrap both his legs around his neck until they formed a kind of scarf. Woodcock said that the associated loose-wristedness led inevitably, to the occasional, though never convincing, charge of throwing.

Peter Loader, a key member of the Surrey attack in the 1950s, forged an inseparable friendship with his rival from Lancashire. Statham's even disposition did, he says, have a sobering effect on his hair-trigger temper. 'Brian nearly always bowled at the middle or off stump, a reason why some batsmen felt more at ease when facing him. But he was unorthodox, making an open-chested approach to the wicket and his extraordinary suppleness gave him a graceful motion.'

Trevor Bailey, as a leading swing bowling exponent, observes that Statham's body action was a shade too open for the purist. The high right arm and the way it chased his left arm across his body until checked by his left hip was copy-book but it did mean that he was always more of a seamer than a swing bowler. Statham was helped by his double-jointedness in producing the whippy delivery moving unexpectedly fast off the pitch to confound unwary batsmen.

Bailey remembers the tendency to inward movement to right-handers, another result of Statham's action, but occasionally he could make a ball leave off the seam. 'Brian bowled an utterly bemused Jeff Stollmeyer with just such a ball on a perfect pitch in a Test in the Caribbean. It pitched around middle and leg and clipped the top of the off-stump. It would have bowled anyone in the world.'

Neville Cardus maintained that the truth about Statham's action was that it was so elastic and balanced that there was no forward shoulder rigidity possible; his movement from the beginning of his run to deliver, to the final accumulated propulsion, had not an awkward angle in it. One lissom movement, unconnected with his action, was the act of removing his sweater as he prepared to bowl. Statham would reach the back ribbing by coiling his right arm over his right shoulder more than half way down his spine. Tom Graveney also remembers another example of the indiarubbered suppleness of his Test colleague. Statham would occasionally lose his balance at the point of delivery, turning his foot like a skater on ice. Serious injury was averted by his ability to go limp as he tumbled to the ground.

Lancashire's novice fast bowler silenced his critics in the best possible manner in 1950. *Wisden* said of Statham's opening spell in his first Roses match at Old Trafford in August that it 'bordered on the sensational.' Yorkshire lost half their wickets for 47 runs. Statham dispatched Lowson, Lester and Watson for 13 runs and took two more wickets, those of Halliday and Coxon, in two balls. Len Hutton was in the Yorkshire team and his shrewd eyes swiftly appraised the young executioner. The ball that accounted for his opening partner Frank Lowson, had been rather special, ripping off the seam to hit the middle stump. Hutton an observer at the non-striker's end was already earmarking Statham as a future England prospect.

The satisfaction of taking Yorkshire wickets watched by a rapt full house at Old Trafford was a major source of pride for Statham but in his first imposing season he enjoyed another devastating spell against Somerset at Bath. Lancashire won by an innings and Statham's wickets, three of them clean bowled, included another England opener, Harold Gimblett. Somerset, in fact, were hustled to such an extent that they lost five wickets for eleven runs, all to Statham. His analysis in this opening salvo was five for five in five overs. *Wisden* remarked on his 'skill and determination in attacking the stumps', soon to be confirmed as a trademark approach, as Somerset were bowled out for 72.

Dennis Brookes, Northamptonshire's experienced batsman and later captain, watched Statham take other top order wickets, including his own, at Wellingborough and was prompted to recommend the Lancastrian as a future England candidate to Freddie Brown, his captain and the MCC captain in Australia in the following winter.

Statham later reflected on an eventful season. 'I was chucked in at the deep end but it did not bother me. I was just having fun and I was successful. I think I was just mesmerised by it all. I was lucky to be playing cricket for a living and there were such a lot of nice people around.'

Roy Tattersall, who was to enjoy a lifelong friendship with Statham, remembers a 'very placid lad, never boastful, who took things in his stride.' In his early days with Lancashire Statham's preferred refreshments were a sherry or a shandy. He cultivated a taste for ale when his Lancashire team-mates told him: 'If you want to be a fast bowler you'll need to get a few beers down you.'

The 'deceptively pacific' Statham, in the words of Neville Cardus, was fortified in another way by the belated invitation to join the MCC party in Australia in 1950. Five months after his Roses match triumph he made a four-day journey in a four-engine propeller driven Constellation aircraft. His companion was Roy Tattersall, also selected to bolster the injured forces in Australia. Cardus wrote: 'These two Lancashire lads arrived in what must have seemed to them a truly foreign climate; for they had been rushed out of an English winter, still unnourished in a post-war rationed environment to a land of plenty. They came to Sydney looking as if each had escaped from a Lowry canvas, lean and hungry.'

Tattersall took on the role of chaperone when the pair later teamed up with the rest of MCC party in Melbourne. The sudden accession to the ranks of first-class cricket meant that Statham had had no chance to establish friendships. 'I had to introduce Brian to more than half the England team because had never played against them, such was his rapid success for a twenty-year-old.'

Trevor Bailey, out of action with a broken thumb, was the first to offer his greetings when Tattersall and Statham arrived in Sydney. 'Both the new recruits were understandably pale, nervous and excited while Brian seemed very shy.' They shared their first drinks together that evening. In a later tribute Bailey said: 'Since then I have supped ale with Brian in various parts of the world and there are few better companions, cheerful, thirsty and never dull.'

The endorsement of Sir Matt Busby, the legendary soccer manager, gives emphasis to the fact that Statham was keen on the 'big ball' game as a teenager. One of Statham's close friends was a Busby protégé, Roger Byrne, the Manchester United and England full-back, who was killed in the Munich air crash in 1958. Busby remembered how Statham first came to his attention as a soccer prospect. Byrne and Statham had played in amateur league football together. United at the time were short of wingers and Byrne recommended his friend as a candidate. Statham was invited to the other Old Trafford for a trial but he decided his priorities lay with cricket and did not take up the offer. Busby said that he often wondered whether Statham would have found distinction as a top class footballer. 'His graceful running, fighting spirit and his sportsmanship are all assets which would have qualified him for professional football.'

'He was a great cricketer but a greater father,' was perhaps the finest tribute paid to Brian Statham, coming as it did from his own children on his death in June 2000. Statham was at his happiest with his family. He was proud but never overstated his many triumphs. Away from cricket his favourite hobby was carpentry, and on this he did sometimes indulge in a little self-congratulation. His wife, Audrey remembers the time he built fitted wardrobes at their home. 'He lay in bed looking at them and said, "I did a good job there." That was the only achievement I can recall him mentioning.'

Statham also brought his culinary expertise into play as a cricket tourist. His kitchen party piece, remembers Trevor Bailey, was an accomplishment that was decidedly unusual and considerably more wholesome than most. It involved the cooking of scrumptious pancakes at any hour of the night. 'Brian tossed these with the nonchalance of a super chef and his drops were even fewer than on the cricket field.' Bailey cherishes the memory of these feasts. 'For the moment supreme I would choose an evening in Australia when he was given the freedom of any army kitchen with scores of eggs and gallons of milk at his disposal. He went on for hour after hour and must have produced enough to satisfy a battalion. I have never eaten quite so many pancakes at one sitting!'

There was always a 'George' in the Lancashire dressing room. It has a nice homely ring and it was in keeping with a fair-natured man that Statham should receive this nickname in succession to the previous designate, Winston Place. The origins of the naming went back to the 1920s. Many Lancashire players regarded the presence of George Duckworth in the championship winning teams in the three seasons from 1926 to 1928 as a talisman. It was thought that these successes would not be repeated until Lancashire had another George in the side. The tradition ended with Statham since all agreed that it would be impossible for anyone to follow this particular 'George.'

John Woodcock commented, perhaps a little exaggeratedly, in an article in *The Times* that Statham trained on beer and cigarettes. 'He could have run up to bowl in a blindfold the first ball of the match and still put it on the spot.' Peter Loader also subscribes to a rare talent. 'It was incredible how he could retain his steadiness of delivery without slavish practice. Brian hated nets. He could be out of cricket for months, then resume and put the ball down with the same fire and accuracy as before.'

Alan Wharton, a Lancashire colleague, remembered an instance of the stranglehold Statham exerted on his opponents. 'I once stood with Stan Worthington (the county coach) behind the bowler's arm at Stanley Park, Blackpool. In the course of his opening spell we saw Brian send down 78 deliveries. The batsmen had to play 77 of them.' Statham's target as a bowler was the off-stump or marginally just outside it. He would have rejected the avenue of containment; the so-called corridor of uncertainty for batsmen, employed by some of today's highly regarded Test bowlers. 'If they miss I hit,' was Statham's unarguable philosophy. 'I'm not going to run in all that way and watch a batsman shoulder arms. It's a waste of energy.'

Peter Loader believes that if Statham had had a mean streak he would have been an even greater bowler. The bouncer was rarely used but when he did yield to the impulse it could be a destructive weapon. 'The ball reared around the neck and was launched as straight as an arrow. You had to take action to avoid them,' recalls another Test colleague, Tom Graveney. The reluctance to operate in this style placed Statham as the opposite of the fast bowler stereotype. 'The bouncer was anathema to a gentleman of the game,' says another former Lancashire partner, Colin Stansfield Smith. 'Brian did not need them in his repertoire. If he was coerced into using one it was truly deadly. The batsmen were mesmerised, not knowing which way to sway.'

Statham was deterred from such intimidatory tactics because, it was said, he could be overcome with physical sickness if he struck an opponent. Frank Tyson related the sequel to an incident in the Caribbean when one West Indian bowler hit Jim Laker over the eye. When the offender came in to bat and reluctantly took guard, someone asked Statham to retaliate in kind. 'No,' he said, 'I think I'll just bowl him out.'

More orthodox methods, as on that occasion, generally succeeded. Alongside the fast off-cutter, as recalled by Roy Tattersall, was the proven yorker, trimming the toes of opponents before crashing into their wickets. Tattersall remembers one match against Surrey when Statham nominated Peter May for a yorker dismissal. 'Brian was as good as his word as he breached the defences of a great batsman.'

The early judgement on the slimly built Statham was that he was ill-fitted physically to withstand the demands of regular first-class cricket. They called him the 'Whippet' or 'Greyhound' – 'when he stripped you could count his ribs,' recalls Roy Tattersall. Yet here was a bowler whose wiry strength prevailed, notably in one marathon spell for England against South Africa at Lord's in June 1955. Statham bowled unchanged from the Pavilion end, apart from a rest during a rain interruption, throughout an innings that lasted for three and three quarter hours.

Peter May, his captain, recalled the extraordinary feat at Lord's. 'I realised that our only hope of victory rested on his shoulders. Whenever I asked him to bowl just one more over I knew how exhausted he was, but there was never a word of complaint from him.' England, having trailed by 171 on the first innings, won by 71 runs. Statham dismissed McLean, Endean, Waite and Keith at a personal cost of 17 runs. His final analysis confirmed his endurance. In 29 overs he took seven wickets for 39 runs. Trevor Bailey rated the performance as one of the greatest sustained spells of fast bowling. It was, though, one time when Statham's powers of recovery failed him. 'It won us the match but a year went by before Brian was quite himself again,' says Bailey.

Statham was always unselfishly prepared to take the more taxing end as the immaculate foil to his partners, Frank Tyson and Fred Trueman. He thrived in fitness by bowling and would not have become a great bowler without the discipline imposed by his work-load. After returning from Australia in 1951 Statham spent three full English seasons, as well as a long tour of India learning his craft. In this time he bowled nearly 3,000 overs. His weariness after his toils was illustrated by a recollection of Tyson. 'I shall remember your pep talk to your poor blooded feet propped up on the dressing room table at the tea interval: "Come on lads, just another two hours to go and I can put you up for the night." '

Only eleven days separated Brian Statham and Frank Tyson in age but it was the Lancashire player who, in 1954, was by some stretch the senior in experience. Statham, at twenty-four, had represented England in 17 Tests and had played in at least a part of six series in the intervening years. He was now an established member of the England team. His credentials were reinforced by the high regard of the Australians who had faced him in 1953. The garlands of esteem had blossomed since Len Hutton's glowing report on the apprentice after his first Roses match three years earlier.

Tyson was partnered for the first time with Statham on his Test debut against Pakistan at the Oval in August 1954. He took four wickets for 35 runs in the first innings and it could be termed a satisfactory start except that England's experimental side was beaten. It was England's first defeat at home since South Africa won at Nottingham in 1951. Jim Kilburn in the *Yorkshire Post*, noted the promise of the newcomer at the Oval: 'Tyson plunged the Pakistan innings into a landslide and returned to finish it off and, for all the untidiness of his run-up, he did look the most threatening feature of the attack.'

It was a commendable introduction but Tyson was still a beginner and his chances of playing in the forthcoming series in Australia were minimal. He was expected to occupy the role of understudy alongside others such as fellow Lancastrian, Keith Andrew, the deputy wicket-keeper in the MCC party. Andrew was also the beneficiary of the diligent scouting of Jock Livingston. He was recruited by Northamptonshire to replace Ken Fiddling who had just retired and was an immediate success. Dennis Brookes recalls: 'Keith went straight into the first team. He was a great 'keeper, especially against our spinners, George Tribe, Jack Manning and Michael Allen. Day by day I would rate him as the best in England at that time.'

Tyson and Andrew were the first Northamptonshire professionals in the county's history to be selected for a tour of Australia. Andrew's selection might have been jeopardised had he not followed the advice of Wilf Wooller, the Glamorgan captain. He had sustained a broken finger immediately preceding the announcement of the MCC team. Wooller was told about the injury during the match against Northamptonshire. He warned Andrew not to divulge the problem as it might lead to his invitation being withdrawn. The presence of Godfrey Evans in Australia restricted Andrew to one Test as his deputy at Brisbane. His talents were shamefully disregarded with the emergence of a new breed of batsman-keepers. Jim Parks was one early example of the trend to dispense with specialists and favour those with batting abilities. A key position has been devalued.

Andrew ought to have been an obvious choice as Evans's deputy on the tour of South Africa in 1956–57. This marked the high point in the career of Johnny Wardle. Wardle unfurled his prowess as a wrist-spinner on the South African veld. He took 26 wickets in the series at a cost of 13.80 runs each. Andrew, with his wealth of experience against left-arm bowlers of varying styles, had considered himself certain to gain a place on the South African tour. He had noted the discomfort of Essex wicket-keeper, Brian Taylor in keeping to George Tribe in a benefit match in the previous summer.

Taylor, chosen ahead of Andrew for South Africa, was said to have spent most of the voyage out tussling with Wardle's spinning secrets. 'Missing the South African trip was one of my biggest disappointments in cricket,' says Andrew. 'I would have loved to have kept to Johnny at the height of his powers as a wrist-spinner. Brian spent hours on deck, practising with Johnny who tried to teach him how to pick his spin. But he couldn't keep to Johnny at all.'

The steely determination of Frank Tyson to succeed on his first overseas tour is recalled by Bob Appleyard, another member of the MCC party in 1954–55. 'Frank is an intelligent chap; he was so full of confidence and he had obviously set his stall out for the Australian trip.' There had been, as Tyson's mother said, an emphasis on physical fitness. In his teens he had put on weight rapidly and by the age of nineteen he topped 13 stone. He grew to manhood during the austerity years of food rationing. He did not drink or smoke and he now says that his lifestyle was far more spartan than youngsters of today. The luxury of cars as a mode of travel was unknown; he and his friends walked or rode bicycles. It had the effect of producing mental resilience and an independence of mind.

Tyson's fitness regime included swinging Indian clubs at home. Later, as a means of building upper body strength, he worked on a willow farm managed by Stuart Surridge, the Surrey captain. The tree-felling labours in the winter of the 1953–54 were undertaken on the recommendation of Ken Taylor, the Northamptonshire secretary, and Jack Mercer, the county coach and former Glamorgan bowler. 'Frank came back as a very strong man next season,' recalls Dennis Brookes.

One observer at Sheffield University had earlier noted the growing menace of Tyson. It was the occasion of the Universities

Athletics Union semi-final against Durham University. 'I wondered what sort of a fellow he would be,' said his rival, as he waited to greet Tyson in the hall of residence allocated to the visitors. 'Here was a bowler who had wrought havoc among club and university cricketers in the north country; and for whom one England captain had prophesied an interesting future.' The Sheffield host discovered him stuffing a 'Combined Services' cap (a souvenir of Tyson's army days) into his cricket bag. 'He was tall, well-built, with a strong but cheerful face, and his hair was thinning and receding. He looked a person of determination.'

At that time Tyson had failed his BA examination at Durham – a lapse he remedied at the second attempt. It was in English that he had been unable to satisfy his tutors. 'A pity,' his mother said, 'for he likes English.' Tyson reputedly murmured couplets of Wordsworth as he walked back to his mark, and as he stuttered his feet and moved in to bowl.

'After the first over,' said the Sheffield man, 'I reflected that Wordsworth was decidedly inappropriate for the meditation of a man of iron. Far too romantic. He punched the ball into the pitch from whence it leapt eagerly to the bat's edge, as one endeavoured to thrust it down from under the armpits. Adding to the discomfort was the "Carmody" field of short-legs and slips, all in fearful symmetry, waiting to clutch the flying ball.'

A selection panel of two former England captains, Walter Robins and Norman Yardley and their fellow judges, chairman, Harry Altham, and Les Ames watched Frank Tyson on an auspicious July evening at Lord's in 1954. It amounted to an audition and the chance to press his claims before a distinguished assembly. He was now thrust into a contest with Bill Edrich, at thirty-eight a veteran of bumper duels. Edrich had triumphed in the heat of battle against Australia's Lindwall and Miller. 'He had a small man's aggression, never terrorised by bouncers, only inspired by them,' wrote one observer.

Northamptonshire had batted first on a rain-affected first day and were all out for 409, just before the close of the second day. Tyson recalled: 'The Lord's pitch was lively in those days, with the ball lifting off the ridge and moving up and down the hill.' The situation of the Middlesex openers, Jack Robertson and Harry Sharp, was also imperilled by the dwindling light. The first casualty was Keith Andrew. 'Keith always insisted on standing up to the left-arm medium-pace of Bob Clarke,' says Tyson. 'For his pains he was struck under the chin by a lifting ball, which gashed him and sprinkled the crease area with blood which we soaked up with sawdust – but not before he had caught Robertson behind off Clarke.'

Tyson now took up the attack for the last over of the day. Edrich strode jauntily to the wicket. His demeanour reflected his purpose – to quell the newcomer. As he took guard, he noted the retreating wicket-keeper and slips, all well beyond conversational distance. Tyson, vigorously rubbing the ball, was a barely discernible silhouette at the start of his long pounding run. 'I had heard of Bill's reputation as a hooker,' related Tyson, 'and I decided to test him out with a bouncer. He accepted the challenge willingly but had only moved marginally across the pitch to the offside, when my very fast bumper caught him square on the cheek, and broke it. He went down in a welter of blood and was carted off to hospital.' Tyson believes that his wounding assault won him his spurs. 'The selectors thought that if I could do that to such a competitive player as Bill then I was worth consideration.'

Denis Compton, not having expected to bat that evening, had bathed and watched the downfall of his friend and batting partner. From the comfort of the bar he looked down on the new bowling discovery. 'This bloke will be fast in Australia next winter,' he said. The laconic aside was prophetic. It would soon be fulfilled in the testing arenas across the world.

As a boy in the 1930s, Frank Tyson had grown up in thrall to the deeds of another great fast bowler, Harold Larwood. His ambitions had been stirred then to emulate the devastating speed of his hero. In the months ahead his boyhood dreams would assume nightmare proportions for his opponents. He would shrug his burly shoulders and say: 'For those of us who have bowled quick, really quick, there is no comparable feeling in the world.'

5

The Spur of Youth at Sydney

'It has been a victory for the younger generation of cricketers for whom long search has been made, so that the burden on the more senior might be lessened.'

E.W. Swanton.

Incredulity mingled with gratitude in the Australian camp when England took the field without Alec Bedser in the second Test at Sydney in December 1954. Bill O'Reilly, a champion in his own right, thought it was an ill-timed blow to an admired rival. 'It was tantamount to lowering the team's flag in memory of a bowler who had taken 39 Australian wickets in Tests in England in the previous year.'

Trevor Bailey has since expressed his regret at the omission of Bedser and how he languished in the shadow of the 'big fella' as a bowler. 'The conditions were tailor-made for swing bowling. I was quite useful but not nearly as good as Alec. If he had bowled at Sydney, I swear he would have got at least six wickets.'

The fitness of Bedser was the key factor. Frank Tyson, the beneficiary of the demotion, wholeheartedly agrees that the senior bowler in prime health would have been irresistible in the prevailing conditions. But Len Hutton and his fellow selectors were faced with the sad truth that Bedser was far from well. His immense powers of endurance had been eroded by a severe attack of shingles. Stricter medical attention to what is now known to be a debilitating virus would have produced an order to return home. With hindsight he should not have played in the first Test at Brisbane.

Bedser had contracted the illness on the voyage out to Australia. He had complained to the MCC masseur, Harold Dalton, about unceasing back pains. Intensive massage was thought to be the best treatment to reduce his discomfort. By the time the team arrived in Perth an ugly rash disfigured his back. Bedser was not one to be concerned with trifling injuries but this was a serious matter. The apparent indifference to his condition stemmed from a loyal and strong man's attitude towards minor ailments. He was not an invalid by nature.

Bedser was far from fit when he bowled for the MCC in the match against Queensland in late November. At Brisbane, as he recalls, he had tried 'to bowl at 95 in the shade, with my back full of sores.' Before the match he told the selectors: 'I'll battle on and try to play.' He was, even then, unaware of the severity of his plight. 'I'd played in so many matches when I'd stuck it out. I didn't realise the effect that shingles had had on my constitution.'

It is beyond question that had Bedser's fortitude at Brisbane been justly rewarded with a few wickets it would have taken a brave selector to leave him out at Sydney. Len Hutton on the first morning investigated the wicket and foresaw a 'greentop' But he was still disinclined to use Bedser even though all the omens pointed to a renewal of his senior bowler's mastery over Australia. His critics pressed Hutton hard on the forfeiture of an old and valued campaigner. He was asked at a crucial juncture in the Sydney Test whether he missed the presence of Bedser. His answer verged on the apologetic. 'I always miss Alec,' he said.

Bedser was nowhere more venerated than in Australia. His hosts could not understand the summary exclusion of one of their favourite visitors. Hutton coloured with embarrassment when asked for an explanation at a Christmas party on the Saturday night of the Test. One former Australian bowler introduced his wife to the England captain. 'Who are the awful people who dropped poor Alec?' she asked. Hutton struggled for an appropriate and courteous response. 'Well,' he said, 'a good young 'un is always better than a good old 'un.'

It was saddening that circumstances in Australia should combine to portray a great bowler in decline. Lessons in the management of attacking resources had been assimilated after the misadventure at Brisbane. Morale remained high among the unchastened party. The reappraisal did not deflect Hutton in his belief that outright fast bowling was the key to victory. Alec Bedser was one of the casualties of this quest. Aged thirty-six, he lost out to the challenge of younger men.

Hutton had been given notice of the potential of these challengers soon after the MCC party arrived in Perth. In Western Australia Tyson administered a stinging blow on the leg to one of his opponents. He subsided like a pack of cards, then dragged his pad off to discover the weal of a rapidly growing bruise. The unfortunate batsman took no further part in the game. As Hutton reminisced later, he knew then that he had in his ranks two bowlers in Tyson and Statham who might cause 'the Aussies to jump a bit.'

One surprising revelation by Geoffrey Howard, the MCC manager, was that the selection of Frank Tyson for the second Test at Sydney was a unanimous decision. The choice of the final bowler lay between Bob Appleyard and Bedser. Appleyard, a self-confessed learner at this stage in Australian conditions, was favoured despite nearly a month out of action. His only appearance had yielded a crop of cheap wickets on a sandy showground at Rockhampton in Northern Queensland. It meant a forlorn and perhaps unwarranted exit for Bedser. He did not play again in the series and thus surrendered his place to the explosive talents of Tyson. But before long the burly newcomer would induce in Australia the kind of tension that England's batsmen experienced when Lindwall and Miller were in their prime.

Tom Graveney believes that Bedser's exclusion from the team at Sydney was primarily due to the improvement in Tyson's bowling following the change to his run-up. Back home in England this had been a regular topic of conversation at Northampton. Dennis Brookes recalls: 'Frank used to disappear on to the old football pitch – the cricket outfield at Wantage Road.' Brookes once told Tyson: 'Don't you think you ought to change to a more sensible run and not take so much out of yourself?'

Len Hutton had also broached the subject during Tyson's first

Test against Pakistan at the Oval. 'Don't you ever bowl off a shorter run?' he asked. Hutton did not then pursue the matter; but the decisive intervention came from Alf Gover, the former Surrey and England bowler and a revered coach to whom Tyson had often turned for instruction back home in England. His bowling mentor, then in his capacity as a journalist in Australia, also advocated the change. Tyson did not disagree with him. He was still smarting from one fruitless exercise – the torment of pounding through 29 overs in the heat of Brisbane.

One story on Tyson's long run-up illustrated the comedy of the Australian barrackers. As he trudged back within sight of the boundary fence, one Sydney wag called out: 'If you're looking for the gents it's over here!' The best of these masters of the impromptu remarks was the Sydneyite, Stephen Gascoigne, otherwise known as the 'Yabba'. To unsuccessful bowlers, he would adjure: 'Your length is lousy, but you bowl a good width.'

Others also took up the wit of the 'Yabba'. Trevor Bailey relates with amusement the response of one barracker after he had batted for three hours at Brisbane. He was hailed: 'Why don't you drop dead, Bailey? Or are you?' Frank Tyson captured respect and support by his speed and power. When Neil Harvey played and missed in perilous fashion throughout one over, the cry went up: 'Oi, Tyson, why don't you bowl him a piano; perhaps he could play that.' Later, when a tailender had trouble in closing the pavilion gate behind him, he was told: 'Leave it open, you won't be long.'

The jokes fell on deaf ears for those in the firing line. Tyson revelled in the pace he generated even in the nets. Peter Loader remembers how his colleague on arrival in Australia made practice a nightmare for batsmen facing him. 'Frank could not restrain himself. He took three strides at practice and was still frighteningly quick.' Trevor Bailey very soon excused himself from the ordeal and settled for more orthodox practice against Statham or Loader.

After Brisbane, England's recovery began in the match against Victoria at Melbourne in early December. It also coincided with

Tyson's reversion to the shorter run, which he had successfully employed during his army and university days. Bowling in this style he took six wickets for 68 runs in 21 overs. His victims included Test batsmen, Colin McDonald, Neil Harvey and Ian Johnson. It was then his best analysis in first-class cricket. Tom Graveney remembers the benefits that Tyson's remodelled approach brought him 'It became more compact and more accurate. He frightened the Victorian batsmen to death.'

Watching Tyson in action against Victoria was George Hele, one of the finest of Australian umpires. He had officiated in matches involving Harold Larwood and Australians, Jack Gregory and Ted McDonald in the 1920s. Hele ranked Tyson's speed as just below Larwood's, slightly faster than Gregory, the equal of McDonald and appreciably faster than Lindwall.

Tyson himself remembers the main reason he employed a long run-up. 'I had pulled a leg muscle and felt that I hadn't maintained the impetus in my delivery stride carrying me forward. I was not moving fast enough when I delivered the ball and it was that that caused me to overstretch.' He explains that the longer run was adopted to give him the required driving force. 'Unfortunately, it got out of hand and went up to 30 yards.'

The reversion to 15 yards in the Test at Sydney was basically a return to his original method. 'I still maintained the acceleration within my run, which kept me moving sufficiently quickly in my delivery stride. So I still achieved a full momentum and my control was better.' *Wisden* described the change as an experiment that had begun at Brisbane. 'Tyson reduced his run to 15 yards, beginning with six shuffling steps and finishing with ten deliberate raking strides.'

After the defeat in the first Test at Brisbane Geoffrey Howard declared that the worst thing he had had to do in his life was to go into the Australian dressing room and say: 'Well played.' Howard added that he earnestly wished that he would never have to perform the courtesy again. On the first day of the second Test at Sydney things looked pretty bad for the MCC manager.

England were put in to bat by Arthur Morris, who was deputising for the injured Ian Johnson and were quickly reduced to 111 for nine. England recovered to score 154 all out thanks to some boisterous hitting by Johnny Wardle who, with Brian Statham shared a last-wicket partnership of 43. Wardle was top scorer for England with 35. Their partnership was the best of the innings and Arthur Morris vividly recalls Wardle's aggression in the match. 'I blame Johnny – and blame is very much the operative word – for our loss at Sydney. On a green, moist and uneven wicket we were well on our way to dismissing England for a very low score when Wardle came to the crease.'

Wardle's aggression was particularly directed against Bill Johnston's fast-medium bowling. He took 30 runs off two overs and three balls. His innings salvaged some pride for England and had a demoralising impact on the Australians. Len Hutton reflected on the batting improvisations of his fellow Yorkshireman.

'For four or five balls in each over he would fail to connect by anything from two inches to two feet. Then with the others he would make contact and scored runs from them, often in boundaries.' Hutton recalled with some amusement that Wardle had one particular shot which baffled the Australians. 'Johnny would retreat towards the square-leg umpire and at the same time advance towards the bowler. He fooled them into thinking that he was about to unleash a straight drive but in fact he nearly always hit the ball clean over the heads of the slip fielders.' Wardle was nothing if not an advocate of the 'if you're going to flash, flash hard' philosophy.

When Wardle was at the crease it was usually a vastly entertaining interlude, especially if you were an England supporter. It had been enacted many times before for the benefit of his adoring supporters in Yorkshire. Wardle's cricket was endowed with a careless rapture and he was never too overawed by the occasion to display his own brand of cricketing buffoonery. On a more serious note, Jim Swanton said Wardle was not just a six-hitting cavalier. 'Johnny had a very fine eye. He was a dangerous hitter in the lower order and a decisive batsman for Yorkshire and England.'

Wardle could not manage another act of piracy in the England second innings, but Statham did, this time in company with Bob Appleyard. The pair more sedately added 46 vital runs in fifty minutes. The last-wicket contributions in both innings were invaluable in the context of the match, and says Appleyard, indicated the team spirit prevailing in the MCC party. His own partnership with Statham was punctuated with regular consultations on setting a respectable target for Australia. 'It wasn't classic stuff but we did get important runs.'

Bill O'Reilly, writing in the *Sydney Morning Herald,* said that there had been a tendency to underrate the batting abilities of England's tailenders. There was now cause to revise the opinions. 'Appleyard batted with the *sang-froid* and the business-like technique of a man who has made his big scores on big occasions with little effort. Statham makes up for his lack of finesse with a virile enthusiasm which takes no time to size up the possibilities of a half-volley.'

England were never more indebted to their young men in a stirring rally at Sydney. The real turning point was the fourth wicket stand between Peter May and Colin Cowdrey. Theirs was a stern responsibility; if they had stumbled, as Jim Swanton reported, 'England would have been as good as beaten inside three days.' He added: 'The Ashes challenge would then have gone up in smoke and Hutton's captaincy would have been written off as a failure. It was as close as that.'

None of their future triumphs exceeded in value this redeeming partnership. May and Cowdrey came together after England had lost three wickets, those of Hutton, Bailey and Graveney, for only 55 runs. 'Slowly but surely against bowling and fielding that gave nothing away they righted the ship,' wrote the *Cricketer* correspondent. 'Their magnificent partnership of 116, spread over three and a quarter hours, brought England back into the game with a vengeance.'

It was a day of absorbing cricket filled with character, patience and attrition. Bill O'Reilly wrote: 'Australia's ace bowler Lindwall, within range of 100 wickets in Anglo-Australian Tests, sent down 19 overs without a scalp – not a good omen for England's speed men. O'Reilly observed that 'it was May and Cowdrey who restored order to the sizzling melodramatics of this great match.' May struck ten boundaries, all of them superbly executed, in his stay of four hours and 20 minutes. The England vice-captain also observed the maxim of 'missing the field' with his adroit leg-side shots, stroked with finesse, and each remarkably late in execution.

'England's "baby" cricketers showed their veteran team-mates the kind of poised, shrewd and patient batting that can win Test matches,' reported the *Sydney Morning Herald*. 'The umbrella fieldsmen, so close together on other days, scattered to distant parts as if they had quarrelled in committee.' Crawford White, in the *News Chronicle*, noted a 'happy blend of relentless defence and devouring power which set May's performance on a pinnacle.' 'He hammered Lindwall, Archer and Benaud hard against the far rails. Never for one second did he show a lapse of concentration. Rarely did he allow a loose ball to go unpunished.'

Bill O'Reilly also applauded the concentration of England's saviours as the outstanding feature of a heroic performance. The batting of May, he said, mirrored the purpose of the gladiators in his own heyday in the 1930s. 'His strength has been his resourcefulness in footwork and his splendid on-side play, The innings stamps him as one of the leading players of this era.' May, en-route to his first century against Australia, lost Cowdrey just when the pair appeared likely to remain undefeated.

The appointment of Cowdrey once again to rescue duty was considered likely to stifle his array of strokes if he had to perform this function too often. After the tea interval Cowdrey withdrew into the inexplicable caution that was to beset him at other times in his career. 'With Benaud bowling,' reported the *Sydney Morning Herald*, ' the few square yards in front of the bat might well have been a minefield so reluctantly did Cowdrey stretch forward into it, bat extended like a detector.'

'Poor Cowdrey' commiserated the *Sydney Morning Herald*. 'His was a valiant innings. Like the boy on the burning deck, and not very much older, he fell victim to his own devotion to duty.' After his earlier sparkle, Cowdrey was dragged down into a defensive battle that locked up heart and spirit. He was overcome more by inaction than anything else, mistiming a foxing and highly flighted googly from Benaud. Archer took the catch at long-off. It was a sickening and needless dismissal at the end of a long hard day. Tom Graveney recalls: 'Colin came in and cried his eyes out. He thought he'd lost the Test match.'

Peter May, despite the praise that greeted his century, was also distraught when he finally succumbed to the new ball and a swinging yorker from Lindwall. England, with five wickets left, had scored 222, a lead of 148. The total had advanced by a further 28 more runs when Statham joined Appleyard in what was to prove a conclusive last-wicket stand. Of England's second innings, Frank Tyson recalls: 'Peter May was very disappointed to get out when his side depended upon him. He was almost emotionally upset and annoyed with himself. He had this innate sense of responsibility to keep going in the most difficult of circumstances – as he did on this green wicket with the ball moving around.'

The distress of both May and Cowdrey was relieved by a shattering spell of fast bowling from Frank Tyson who had taken something of a bump himself in England's second innings, and Brian Statham.

Alan Davidson remembers the consternation of his Australian colleagues when Tyson hurriedly ducked but failed to avoid a blow on the head from a Lindwall bouncer. There were howls of dismay among the watching fieldsmen. 'Lindy', they said, 'don't forget this fella's got to bowl at us yet.' Davidson adds that he and his fellow Australians knew what was in store for them. 'Frank was quick before but he was an extra three yards faster afterwards.'

Len Hutton thought it was possible that the delivery from Lindwall contributed to Tyson's emergence as England's fastest post-war bowler. 'When he came out of his concussed state I swear there was a new light in his eyes, as if a spark had been kindled deep down in him.'

Tom Graveney was one of the anxious Englishmen who thought,

'the game has gone' when Tyson collapsed at the crease. Fortunately, an x-ray examination at the local hospital revealed no serious damage. On the following day, the fifth of the match, Tyson recalled his headache had almost gone but his pride demanded swift retribution. It would not be long in coming.

Soon it was Lindwall's turn to bat and accept his fate. An expectant hush fell upon the crowd. 'Tyson fooled everyone by not trying an equaliser with a bouncer of his own,' says Peter Loader. 'Instead he ripped Lindwall's leg stump out of the ground with a yorker.' It was another example of a bowler who did not bear malice; he had other ways of extracting revenge.

'Australia has a winning position in the Test', was the exultant headline in the *Sydney Morning Herald* on the Wednesday morning. The situation was that Australia needed only 151 more runs to win with eight wickets still intact. The pitch, according to Tom Goodman, was behaving well and all the signs pointed to a comfortable victory. Bill O'Reilly sounded a warning note: 'England has set up a score which will have the Australians keeping their noses right down in heavy batting concentration.'

The final stages of this fascinating Test match undoubtedly belonged to Neil Harvey and England's destroyers, Tyson and Statham. Australia should have won the match and would have done so had the brilliant Harvey found any support. Of the whole Australian team, only he showed the class to counter the blistering pace of Tyson and Statham. His unfaltering command deserved the seal of victory. He was the epitome of audacity as a cricketer, never a man intent on records, his resolution thrived when confronted by a crisis. Ron Archer, a former Australian colleague, says: 'Neil would often throw his wicket away when it didn't matter but he loved making runs in tough conditions.'

Harvey, in appearance, resembled a pocket-sized Clark Gable. At Sydney he displayed a nerveless disdain for bowlers to match the hauteur of Gable on the picture screen. Denzil Batchelor recalled Harvey on tiptoe like a 'bristling fox-terrier', determined single-handedly to win the game for his side if this could be done. 'He was good enough to hook Tyson towards the echoing boundary; to drive and glance like a cool genius at net practice with a favourite nephew.' Alan Davidson remembers an 'incredible innings' and in particular, one stroke off Tyson, which took the ball in a skimming arc under the awning and straight into the visitors' dressing room.

Harvey came to the wicket with Australia on 34 for two and well over four hours later he was still there, unbeaten on 92, in his bid to secure victory. For Frank Tyson the valiant innings was a masterpiece not just of shot execution but of 'farming' the bowling. Prospects for an Australian victory had sunk deep below the horizon when Bill Johnston joined Harvey in a stubborn last-wicket stand of 39 runs. When Johnston came in Australia still needed 78, which seemed a monumental task but there was a suspicion that the game was not yet over. Johnston, like many number 11's, cherished his 'not-outs' as a means of achieving batting respectability. As Jim Swanton wrote, he was not nearly such a duffer as a batsman as indicated by his general deportment and expressions of comic bewilderment.

Australia's chances of victory did, of course, rest heavily on Harvey's shoulders. So cleverly did he marshal the strike that during Johnston's 37 minutes at the wicket he faced just 16 of 80 balls bowled, while his more accomplished partner added 27 runs to the score. Excitement mounted as the partnership grew and the gap narrowed. England's bowlers were visibly tiring when Evans ended the agony with a diving catch to dismiss Johnston off Tyson.

England's victory margin was a mere 38 runs but in a game where neither side exceeded 300 runs in an innings, it was comfortable enough. Frank Tyson was England's match-winner. He bowled without respite for ninety minutes and took three wickets for 41 runs in 60 balls. Heaving his shoulders into the attack and swept along by a strong, following southern wind, Tyson was a man of fury. 'Few bowlers – fast, medium or slow – have dominated a match as Tyson did this one,' commented Bill O'Reilly. Tom Graveney remembers the terrifying speed which none of the Australian batsmen, with the notable exception of Harvey, was able to counter.

'I was 50 yards back at slip and nearer the pavilion gate than the wicket. It was like fielding tracer bullets.'

'Throughout an unflagging spell,' wrote O'Reilly, 'Tyson plugged away with inspiring intent that one tried in vain to remember the last time that an England side had looked so formidably certain of victory.' Tyson remains eloquent in praise of his partner, Brian Statham. 'I owed so much to his relentless accuracy – line and length – which induced desperation in the Australian batsmen.'

The herculean effort of Statham, bowling into the teeth of the southerly gale, is also recalled by Alan Davidson. 'Frank and Brian really made a mess of us at Sydney.' Admiringly, he also pays tribute to the pinpoint accuracy of Statham. 'Brian was the bloke who made it impossible for us to score. In all my years in cricket I didn't have a partner like him.'

On the eve of Christmas, England, in winning their first Test at Sydney since the 1936–37 series, ended a drought of eighteen years. The festive greetings were extended especially to the young guard – May, Cowdrey, Tyson and Statham, all of them under twenty-five. It had been a triumph for youth. Jim Swanton enthused: 'The match has made a scintillating new reputation, that of Tyson, whose ten wickets were the reward of as fine a display of sustained speed and stamina as I have ever seen in an English fast bowler.'

Amid the euphoria there was at least one writer who spared a thought for the discarded Bedser. 'There will be many,' wrote Crawford White, 'who will be prepared to argue until their dying day that victory would have come sooner and more convincingly had Bedser been there to bowl at Sydney. But not even Bedser at his best could have bowled better or given more than Tyson.'

Tyson, tagged as a 'four over wonder' in his apprentice years, demonstrated a greater depth of endurance in a thrilling encounter. He shared his success with all his team-mates but it is fitting that the last words are his own; 'It was what I had dreamed of as a boy in the 1930s and Len Hutton was the captain able to evince that passion.'

Tyson joined an elite group of English fast bowlers at Sydney. In the entire twentieth century only two others – Maurice Tate and Larwood – had taken ten wickets in a Test match on this ground against Australia. George Lohmann (twice) and Tom Richardson achieved the feat in the nineteenth century. Andrew Caddick also took ten wickets in England's victory in 2003. Neither Lindwall nor Miller, for all their great exploits, could boast the distinction.

A rendezvous with his boyhood hero, Harold Larwood, sealed Tyson's celebration at Sydney. It linked one architect of Australia's downfall with another. Larwood had been the villain of the piece in the controversial events twenty-two years earlier. It was also a reunion for another England hero, wicket-keeper, George Duckworth, who had kept to Larwood when he first toured Australia in 1928. Duckworth, now the MCC baggage master, arranged the meeting at the suburban bungalow home of Larwood at Kingsford.

At this convivial gathering Larwood reminisced about his part in the bodyline tour and vigorously denied allegations of intimidation of Australia's batsmen. There was recollection too, of his score of 98 as a 'night watchman' at Sydney and Jardine's understated compliment, 'I knew you could bat a bit.'

Before the party broke up, Larwood proudly offered a prized souvenir for Tyson's inspection. It was a silver ashtray inscribed with the words, 'To Lol for the Ashes, Douglas Jardine.' Fittingly, Larwood, still a 'Pom' at heart in his adopted country, reserved one parting shot to excite his young visitor. 'When you hear 50,000 Aussies shouting at you, you know you've got 'em worried.'

6

The Challenge of the Young Pups

'Peter and Colin were the same age as me and I knew I was going
to cop it from them over the coming years.'

Alan Davidson.

Peter May and Colin Cowdrey, both former schoolboy prodigies
established their own careers in Test cricket in 1954–55, on their
first tour of Australia. The batting of both May and Cowdrey pulsed
with an uncommon resolution. They eagerly took the responsibilities placed on them and demonstrated to an admiring public
the virtues of their pedigree. The hurrahs which greeted their arrivals
also acknowledged the bridging of the amateur-professional divide.

Peter May, Len Hutton's heir-apparent as England captain, was
the finest apostle of the new creed. Like-minded in spirit was his
great comrade, Colin Cowdrey. Many observers have judged that
Cowdrey possessed more natural ability than May. If he could have
fused the precise timing, which was his hallmark, with the
ruthlessness of May, cricket connoisseurs might have hailed him as
the perfect batsman. As Frank Tyson tellingly remarks, Cowdrey
lacked iron in his soul, which his friend was endowed with in
abundance.

Colin Cowdrey was a phenomenon who also enjoyed a boyish
relish for the fun of cricket. He only ever forgot this philosophy
when he succumbed to the dark clouds of introspection. He seemed
then to be affected by the cricketing equivalent of writers' block. The
game was either incredibly simple or bafflingly complex, depending

on his mood. As Neville Cardus related, you could never be quite sure whether he was about to thrill and delight you, or cast you into a doldrum of inquiry and frustration. The heart of the matter was that Cowdrey did not realise just how *great* he was as a player.

Alan Gibson cited the uncertainty of Shakespeare's Brutus as one explanation of a gentle monarch who did not realise the enormity of his talents. 'The fault, dear Brutus, is not in our stars. But in ourselves', declared Cassius. Gibson wondered if Cowdrey would have been a happier or better man had he heeded these words. 'Colin was never an assassin, nor a schemer. If you had put a dagger in his hand, placed him behind a cosy pillar in the forum, and set somebody loose before him in an imperial toga, he would be merciful and stay his hand.'

The bestowing of the initials, MCC by his father might have been designed to bolster expectations while Cowdrey was still in his cradle. The cricket world would become his oyster if not quite in the way that his own son, Christopher, would later interpret it. As a seven year-old, there was the special treat of a visit to Lord's. He was informed that this was the home of cricket. Christopher was suitably awe-struck by the wonders of the scene. His young mind, though, could not grasp the distinction between the two sets of initials, one borne by his father and the other by the club. 'Just think,' he pondered, 'one day all this will be mine!'

The inheritance of the elder Cowdrey lay in gifts that encompassed an even mightier estate. At times he almost disowned the riches at his disposal. The riddle of a gifted cricketer, who could become unreasonably becalmed, was a source of amazement. Geoffrey Howard, the MCC manager in Australia, maintained that the inaction was Cowdrey's own choice. It was a strange paradox that someone technically without peer or fault should be so sensitive or too much of a theorist to destroy mediocre bowling.

R.L. Arrowsmith said Cowdrey was a far greater player than most of the bowlers he faced. 'Too often he allowed them to dictate to him when he should have been dictating to them. His natural gifts were wonderful and his technique irreproachable. No bat could be straighter or closer to the leg and he could force the ball with equal ease off the front foot or back. He was the master of the straight drive, a stroke neglected by many batsmen.'

Cowdrey did show his true colours in situations that demanded it, or when faced with a challenge to exercise his fertile mind. He once confessed that he used to fret during an innings if he thought that he had lost, albeit temporarily, the timing that was crucial to him. On such days he would retreat into a shell and consider whether to experiment with his batting grip or stance. 'Batting has always fascinated me,' he said. 'Life becomes a bore if you've nothing left to prove, if you're not stretched.'

Doug Insole, who played in nine Tests including a whole series with Cowdrey in South Africa in 1956–57, confirms Cowdrey's occasional lack-lustre performances that so puzzled his admirers. 'When he wasn't absolutely on song, Colin tended to allow bowlers to dictate to him. He was a little circumspect and unsure of his tremendous ability, but that was in character.'

In his youth Cowdrey was a dazzling success and was quickly identified as someone destined to play for England. When he was still a student at Oxford there was a school of thought that considered Cowdrey ready for Test cricket.

Cricket for Colin Cowdrey began at Tonbridge School – the most eminent of Kent's cricket nurseries – where as a precocious youth his exploits attracted the keen interest of Surrey County Cricket Club. Ironically, Peter May might well have been preceded by Cowdrey as a recruit at the Oval but Surrey's audacious overtures to attract Cowdrey to their cause were unsuccessful and history now records that May joined Surrey and Cowdrey joined Kent. May found security and prospered amid the multi-talented ranks with Surrey whereas Cowdrey joined Kent when their resources were meagre to say the least. However, with Les Ames as manager, Kent and Cowdrey forged a new beginning, and the county slowly climbed from the lowlands to the crest of a championship in 1970.

Colin Cowdrey's success on his first tour of Australia in 1954–55 was final confirmation of the talents he had shown as a boy at

Tonbridge. In 1946, at the age of thirteen, he was in the school's first eleven. In the same year, he became the youngest player to be selected to play in a Public Schools' XI when he played against Clifton at Lord's. He hit 75 out of the first innings total of 156 and 44 out of 175 in the second innings. He also took eight wickets bowling his leg-spin and in a thrilling finale he claimed the last five wickets for 33 runs to wrest victory for Tonbridge by two runs. For five years, the last two as captain, Cowdrey was an irrepressible force and in that period he scored 2,894 runs and took 216 wickets.

He was only seventeen and still at school when he made his debut for Kent at Derby in August, 1950. In the following year he scored 71 against the touring South Africans and was awarded his county cap. At Oxford there was an instant recognition of his merits. Peter Blake, his captain, watched him in only three matches before conferring the next honour, the award of his university Blue. Trevor Bailey watched Cowdrey score a century for the Gentlemen against the Players at Scarborough and considered his batting resembled that of a seasoned professional rather than an 18 year-old.

Len Hutton was also at Scarborough to see Cowdrey's century and was suitably impressed. He would surely have endorsed one of Cowdrey's batting maxims – 'hard enough for four is hard enough.' Hutton, above all the celebrated senior batsmen, was Cowdrey's role model. For the Kent boy there was the anxiety of batting against Alec Bedser and Tom Pritchard in front of a packed house at the North Marine Road ground. 'Stand up and play straight,' was Hutton's message between the overs. Cowdrey believed that it was his innings – and the way he reacted to advice – that helped propel him into the MCC party in Australia three years later.

Interestingly, Hutton took four wickets with his leg-breaks, which were far from negligible assets during his early days with Yorkshire. Cowdrey was one of the victims of his spin, stumped by Dawkes, at Scarborough. Another Yorkshireman, Brian Sellers, did not ignore the dismissal. As Cowdrey, who missed the final match of the festival, was leaving to return home, he was given a brusque reprimand as a farewell. 'Judging by the shot you got out to', said

Sellers, 'I'm not surprised that you are not playing in the last match up here.'

It was a typical piece of Sellers' lacerating criticism directed not just at young aspirants but also, when he saw fit, at Yorkshire's Test men under his command. The broadside was followed by more soothing words. 'Hey, coom back, coom back. Listen, lad, I'll tell thi' something. If you're not playing for England soon, there'll be only one person to blame. You'll be the one to blame. It'll be your fault and nobody else's'. As Cowdrey realised much later, the curt remarks were a Yorkshireman's way of paying a compliment.

It was a bracing time for Colin Cowdrey and Scarborough in 1952 was an appropriate venue for the start of his magnificent partnership with Peter May. May, three years his senior had already begun his Test career, scoring a century while still a Cambridge undergraduate on his debut against South Africa at Headingley a year earlier. Young and old shoots blossomed as the waves pounded against the seashore at Scarborough. The festival crowds enjoyed the customary feast of runs. Hutton, for Yorkshire, and May, for the MCC, each scored separate hundreds in the match. Tom Graveney joined May in a stand of 187 runs and Cowdrey then entered the lists to add 106 with his Surrey partner in 45 minutes.

The flurry of runs beside the sea was just an enjoyable interlude and sterner tasks lay ahead for the two young champions. They would seize the time to observe a unity of purpose to match their great predecessors, Denis Compton and Bill Edrich. Colin Cowdrey would later recall Peter May as a man with a 'gracious, gentle streak' but easily the toughest cricketer with whom he was ever associated throughout his career. May and Cowdrey rejoiced in each other's triumphs. 'I am most proud of the fact that we were not jealous or ever concerned with rivalry,' said the later Lord Cowdrey. 'There was never a hint of a row. No hang-ups at all.'

Peter May, the 'unusually retiring man' in the words of his friend, seemed to undergo a metamorphosis at the wicket. The passion of his command as a batsman held him as if caught in a vice of self-hypnosis. 'You could almost see the flames bursting out of his nostrils,' said Cowdrey. Frank Tyson reinforces the memory of

May's intense concentration. 'Peter really was a tiger, a driven man forced to intrinsic perfection by his own determination. The power of his shots was ferocious. I have never seen anyone hit the ball as hard as Peter.' Like many great players May was intolerant of those who failed to measure up to his own high standards. 'If we could have had a team composed of Peter Mays,' says Tyson, 'we would have been unbeatable.'

Colin Cowdrey related that May's outlook was shaped by his upbringing in Reading in a heavily regimented household. He believed that the regime carried the legacy of a meticulous and well-organised mind when May ascended to the cricket stage. 'There was a gracious demeanour but Peter didn't play the game for fun. We were total opposites as batsmen. I waited and used the pace of the ball whereas Peter, with his exceptional strength, would whack it. He was one of the best of on-drivers, and terrific off the back foot, hitting through extra cover.'

There was a memory, too, of May's homework in his preparations as a batsman. 'Peter was so intelligent at cricket. He had shrewdly appraised bowlers over a period. So his shots off a particular bowler were all pre-selected. The physical strength was backed up by an astonishing single-mindedness.' Like a highly trained artist, May was not immune to tension before the big games at the Oval or Lord's. He would find relief or distraction in other tasks.

'Peter was highly nervous in some ways,' recalled Cowdrey. 'He didn't watch play before going in to bat.' May's business hours at cricket permitted no intrusion. Prolonged bouts of physical training would have irritated him. His fitness was exemplary, but such a needless drain on his energies would have been rejected with disdain. 'Don't ask me to do that,' would have been his response. 'I've got to make a hundred today.'

Peter May first demonstrated his terrific potential as a batsman at Charterhouse School on the crest of the steep slope that rises above the Surrey town of Godalming. Waiting for him was a vigilant tutor and school cricket coach, George Geary, the former Leicestershire and England allrounder. 'George,' said May, 'was an adviser and guide rather than a coach. He picked out natural ability, and encouraged it. He did not stifle and smother it with a maze of technicalities to baffle the impressionable young mind. He never said too much, but whatever he did say demanded an attentive ear.' Geary, for his part, quickly recognised the qualities of his pupil. 'You get some boys who are useful cricketers but they never seem to sort it out. Peter was different. I could see that he had a real cricket brain.'

In his four years in the Charterhouse XI May scored 1,794 runs for an average of 54.36. May had his best season in 1947, his final year at the school, when he scored an aggregate of 651 runs with a highest score of 183 and an average of 81.38. A contemporary at Charterhouse said that May turned cricket into a kind of one-man show. 'When he played in house matches, scoring as many runs as were needed to bowl out the opposition, it was as if an Olympian had deigned to play skittles with mortals.'

Geoffrey Howard said that anyone who spent any length of time at the crease with May or Cowdrey received an object lesson in batsmanship. Towering strength was the keynote of May's cricket. The one-day game might have offended his instincts but those who today pursue a negative leg stump attack would have been made quickly aware of his onside strengths. 'If they had bowled at him in that fashion,' said Howard, 'the ball would have whistled over mid-on time after time.'

May did exult in his right hand – his guide and master – and the source of his power as a batsman. 'How is your right hand today?' was a regular morning greeting at the Oval. He came to maturity as cricket developed into a largely onside game in the 1950s. He recorded his thoughts at the time in an individual batting thesis. 'In the nature of things, I have found many of my runs on this side which has meant bringing my right hand into play. In fact, I would say that I am essentially a right-handed player. That inevitably means a slight occasional dragging of the ball from off to leg, and hitting across the ball a shade. Probably this has got me out a few times – but it has also brought me lots of runs.'

Roy Tattersall, a Lancashire rival, provided an instance, amazing to him at the time, of May's lightning reflexes and ability to realign his strokes. It occurred in a match at Old Trafford. 'Peter played two shots off me, neither of which I had seen before. I had my usual legside field. I was bowling well. The instant before I delivered the ball he adjusted his stance, turned round completely, and hit me square through the covers.' Tattersall shook his head in disbelief. May looked down the wicket at the puzzled bowler. 'It's a good wicket – and I'm seeing it quite well today,' he explained. May then repeated the stroke to show it wasn't a fluke.

Simon Raven, the novelist and a fellow pupil at Charterhouse also noted the audacity of the school star. 'So far from being a robot programmed to select the most efficient and possible stroke, Peter had an individual brilliance which often led him to play the most satisfying and beautiful, even spectacular, shot in a manner that was sometimes in direct defiance of the circumstances.'

John Warr thought Vivian Richards, the West Indian, was the nearest in style to May. Warr, the former Middlesex and England bowler and a close family friend, provides an interesting technical analysis. 'They both appeared to favour the onside but in fact any bowler attacking them on or outside off stump would find plenty of strokes in their repertoires in this area. They both had brilliant foot movement to position themselves for their intended shots, keeping batsmanship as one-dimensional as possible. They seemed also to possess a sixth sense which told them where the ball was going to be bowled.'

Geoffrey Howard, from his time as Lancashire secretary, vividly recalled May's mastery in a duel with Brian Statham at Old Trafford. Statham was a bowler held in the highest possible esteem by May when he succeeded Len Hutton as England captain. The Surrey maestro chose this day to reveal a spectacle of conquest with few parallels. Howard remembered one remarkable shot off Statham. 'Peter, on the back foot, hit him straight over mid-off for six.'

Denys Rowbotham in the *Manchester Guardian*, graphically described an innings as peerless as any witnessed in this famed cricket arena. Surrey had lost three wickets for 64 before May and Barrington came together in a fourth wicket stand of 145 runs. They did save Surrey from humiliation as is shown by one revealing statistic that nine other batsmen scored only 63 runs between them. May's scintillating 174 (out of a total of 314) shone forth like a beacon amid the disarray.

Rowbotham reported: 'When May came to the crease he looked as if he had already been batting for an hour. His judgement seemed well-nigh infallible. His feet moved so swiftly that he was positioned perfectly with time to spare for every shot. Howsoever Statham cut the ball repeatedly away from him, May's front foot was flawlessly planted. It seemed as if the ball's movement had been plotted clairvoyantly and the middle of the bat found by some mysterious act of magnetism.'

'From the start of the innings,' wrote Rowbotham, 'the majestic young man was attacking. Let Statham only once drop slightly short and the right foot was back and the stroke through the covers was punishing to see. The room and time which May had to play these shots was as astonishing as it used to seem with Hammond.'

The exhilarating innings ended in a carnival of strokes. May opened his shoulders with a vengeance. He drove Higgs mightily over mid-off for six and then hit him high to long-on for four. The Lancashire bowlers reeled giddily in the face of the onslaught. Statham stood, hands on hips in bewilderment, as one thunderous stroke, driven scarcely credibly off the back foot, hurtled past him, and over deep mid-off. Statham, at last gained the prize which had eluded him throughout a long and gruelling day. May drove once too often and was bowled. In five hours of savage batsmanship he had held everybody's attention with an innings of spell-binding brilliance.

Dread is not a word that features strongly in the Australian vocabulary but Peter May and Colin Cowdrey, the 'young pups', as Alan Davidson described them, gave notice in Australia that he and other bowlers would 'cop it' in the years ahead. Cowdrey, a hunch selection despite his faltering form in England in 1954, did not neglect his opportunity. May was only marginally more experienced but the grand manner of his cricket excited all who watched him. The savagery of his driving in the Melbourne Test compelled Ray Lindwall to disperse his field in a vain attempt to stem the flow of runs. 'When an Englishman does that to the greatest fast bowler of his time,' wrote Alan Ross, 'it registers, if nothing else, an exchange of domination.'

One Australian correspondent, with memories of the great batsmen over fifty years since the second world war, recalled the tremendous impact May had on the series. 'I have never before, and seldom since, seen such powerful and stylish driving of fast bowlers.' As a privileged young boy in the members' enclosure at Melbourne, he had watched, with awe, May's unbeaten 105 against Victoria. 'He quite destroyed our fast men, John Power and Sam Loxton. 'I was close enough to the dressing room afterwards to note that his bat was unmarked except for a vivid red circle, grapefruit size, in the middle of the blade.'

Len Hutton watched the two young men come thrillingly of age and expressed the view that May and Cowdrey, aged twenty-four and twenty-one respectively, were the best batsmen in the world at their ages. Their authority at the crease masked the decline and varying form of the senior players. May and Cowdrey between them scored 670 runs in the Tests and each scored over 1,000 in all first-class matches on the tour.

The Australian sunshine and faster wickets served to whet Cowdrey's appetite as a batsman. *Wisden* reported: 'From the moment the ship stopped for a day at Colombo he rarely knew failure.' In the tropical heat of Ceylon, Cowdrey immediately displayed the command which he would repeat in more exacting assignments in Australia. A flurry of boundaries, eleven in all, resulted from his mastery over the island's bowlers and he was unbeaten on 66 in a stay of 80 minutes.

Cowdrey batted for the first time with Len Hutton against Western Australia at Perth. They put on 127 runs for the fourth wicket. 'It was a partnership which forged our relationship for the tour,' said Cowdrey. 'He treated me almost as if he had been appointed my guardian.' There were protracted discussions, amounting to a tutorial, during the match. Hutton twice assessed one problem and called upon Cowdrey to adjust his guard against a left-arm bowler coming over the wicket. Eventually he was satisfied that his pupil was middling the ball well.

Cowdrey, easily the youngest of England's touring party, was again batting with Hutton against a strong New South Wales side in November. He faced an attack that included three Test bowlers, Miller, Davidson and Benaud. Cowdrey scored a century in each innings – 110 and 103 – to join three other Englishmen, MacLaren, Rhodes and Sandham who had achieved this feat at Sydney. The distinction came before Cowdrey had scored a century in county cricket.

In the first innings, Cowdrey went in to bat when MCC had lost four wickets for 38 runs. He then shared in a rescuing stand of 163 with Hutton. In his modest version of events, he claimed that his achievements were dwarfed by Hutton's mastery on a turning wicket. It was so slow that Davidson, normally a fast medium bowler, reverted to bowling spinners. An expectant smile greeted this change. Cowdrey was asked to take Benaud at his end, while his captain embarked on a duel with Davidson.

'His performance deserved an Oscar,' recalled Cowdrey. What followed was the apparent dilemma of a great batsman in trouble. Affecting to struggle was a deliberate ploy to mislead Davidson. Throughout his innings Hutton repeatedly showed signs of fallibility that encouraged his Australian rival. While rooted in implacable defence, he was almost goading Davidson in his futile attempts to penetrate it. At the end of the morning both batsmen were undefeated. As they walked off Hutton turned to Cowdrey and asked : 'How are you then?' Cowdrey wearily replied: 'It is hard work.' Hutton nodded in agreement and, as if the thought had suddenly struck him, said: 'Aye, and what's more you're not getting paid for it, are you?'

Hutton was in a relaxed mood at Sydney but he was also expressing his quiet pleasure at the growing confidence of the young amateur. Cowdrey's batting in his first major assignment in Australia prompted some observers to compare him with Wally Hammond. 'For sheer, calm correctness,' commented one Australian writer, 'this youngster led the batting world. While scoring two centuries in this match he batted with the studied concentration of a master sculptor working on a statue. To find his equal for certainty and poise you had to go back to Hammond in the 1928–29 series.'

The exploits at Sydney were just a gathering of early fruits before the harvest at Melbourne. Few players could have survived the ordeal there on an ill-behaved pitch. In scoring 102 of England's total of 191, Colin Cowdrey kept vigil when defeat loomed like a yawning abyss. He belied his years with a serene spirit and batting technique more akin to a veteran. Bill O'Reilly in the prevailing euphoria said it was the finest innings he had seen in a Test match. It was Cowdrey's finest hour, allowing him against all the odds, to claim an honoured place in cricket history.

7

The Watered Wicket at Melbourne

'All Victoria scorched yesterday in temperatures ranging up to 110 degrees. Searing northerly winds exceeded 50 m.p.h. in many parts of the state.'

Melbourne Age, January 3, 1955.

The hottest night on record in Melbourne preceded a chain of events that would decide the outcome of an astonishing Test match. It seemed certain the extraordinary weather would endanger an already crumbling pitch. When play resumed on Monday morning, the players were amazed to discover that the pitch had undergone a remarkable transformation, which would lead to allegations that the Melbourne groundsman had flouted the laws of the game and watered the wicket.

'They had left it desiccated and friable,' reported Jim Swanton, 'but now the sprigs on their boots, which on Saturday had slid over the baked, shiny surface, cut lines in the turf.' In the centre of the field two groups of English and Australian players stood and joked about a 'local shower'. Trevor Bailey, one of the bewildered onlookers, looked at his glistening studs and drew the attention of his colleagues to their own footwear. They were just as wet as they came into contact with the newly softened ground.

The surface was now more hazardous for bowlers than batsmen. Frank Tyson remembers his partner, Brian Statham coming in to bowl at the northern end. 'He had put his foot down about three paces from the pitch when – whoosh – he skated for another three yards, scouring out a great piece of mud.'

Bob Appleyard described the change in conditions as a kind of 'divine intervention'. He had spent the previous rest day at a barbecue at the home of friends from Bradford, who had emigrated to Australia. At the MCC team's headquarters at the Windsor Hotel there was no air-conditioning and the heat was intense. 'We got into the car and, as we were driving off, I wound down the window.' A current of hot air had immediately engulfed them. 'It was more uncomfortable than sitting in the heat in the car.'

Appleyard said that by Monday the weather had cooled. It had, in fact, shown a swift and dramatic change during the early hours after a sweltering night when thousands of people slept on the beaches. The temperature in Melbourne at midnight was registered at 96.2 degrees fahrenheit. Just over eight hours later it had plummeted by over 30 degrees. 'The wicket had looked like crazy paving on the Saturday night. But now the cracks had all sealed up. Our studs made marks in the moist ground.'

John Woodcock, the former *Times* cricket correspondent, confirms that the wicket had shown signs of rapid deterioration, with shooting balls scuttling over the ever-widening cracks. The heat on the Sunday was breathtaking, as a strong northerly wind blew across the continent. Woodcock had not ventured outside his hotel all morning but when he did at lunchtime it was like being struck by a blast of heat.

The fury of the bush fires on Sunday ravaged a besieged state. The fires blazed across a 29-mile front, sweeping through 30,000 acres of grazing country and scrub. They destroyed homes and trapped fire fighters in their trucks on isolated roads. One local police constable said that the country for 50 miles around was 'black everywhere you looked.' Violent winds tore down trees and fences in many Melbourne suburbs. On all the main highways from the city, hundreds of cars were stranded with overheated engines.

In the early afternoon the temperature stood at 105 degrees, the highest reading for 13 months. It was 27 degrees above the normal January temperature. Even more daunting were the record night-time temperatures that exceeded the previous high of 93.9 degrees in 1942. Back in England Roy Ullyett, the cartoonist, wryly depicted a vastly different scene. There was snow piled up against a window. Inside there was a scarf-muffled and shivering couple at the breakfast table. Father was earnestly checking the Test scores. Mother said: 'Don't worry about the score, read me the bits about the baking sun.'

But in Australia, attention was focused on the danger to life posed by the extreme weather conditions. Sport was a side issue in such circumstances but the tumult of accusations did threaten the reputation of Australian cricket. The Melbourne Cricket Club and the Victorian Cricket Association rallied to the defence of the ground curator, Jack House. They jointly denied reports of watering the wicket on the Sunday in violation of the laws of cricket. The authorities expressed their deep concern that the allegations should have gained circulation. A statement read by Albert Cuttress, the club's assistant secretary, was dismissive of the reports and maintained that a searching inquiry had been held and reached the conclusion that no watering of the pitch or any portion of the ground had occurred since the start of the match on Friday, December 31.

The man under suspicion, Jack House, was employed at the Albert Ground at St. Kilda, which was controlled by the Melbourne Cricket Club. House had been brought specially to the MCG to plan and supervise the preparation of the Test wicket. His contribution was supplementary to the work of the regular curator, Bill Vanthoff and was especially important because wickets at the MCG had been criticised recently as of mediocre standard. Some improvement had apparently been made as there were no complaints during the preceding match between Victoria and New South Wales, which started on Christmas Day.

House was interviewed by Richard Whitington on the eve of the Test. He expressed his reservations about his task. 'It was unfair to ask me to take over the preparation of the pitch at this stage. The soil in the pitch is rotten and laminated'. Asked what he meant by laminated, House explained: 'The soil for inches down from the surface is a mixture of rotten earth and grass-cuttings, which have become blended in the years since the war.'

Vernon Ransford, the Melbourne club secretary, put on a bold front. He expressed his confidence that all would be well for the Test. He did, however, express caution should the match be prolonged. 'There should be a packet of runs in it on the Friday and Saturday but I wouldn't go further than that. If conditions are cool over the weekend it may last until Monday. But if they are hot it will crack badly.'

Jack House was well aware of Melbourne's unpredictable and fluctuating climate. But he resolutely defended his work in another interview in the *Sydney Morning Herald* on the Monday of the match. He said: 'The Test pitch has not been touched by water since play started on Friday. In accordance with the laws, the covers were taken off the pitch at 7 a.m. on Sunday and were replaced at 6.15 p.m. During that time the pitch had no treatment except the sun.'

The alleged hosing of the wicket, which was pitched in the centre of the square, would hardly have escaped attention in broad daylight and would have been clearly visible from the adjacent Jolimont Park because of the demolition of two of the members' stands. New stands were in the course of construction in readiness for the Olympic Games in the following year. House seemed to have dispelled any possibility of tampering when he said that the wicket had been under constant supervision during the day and watchmen had kept a close guard during the night.

He continued: 'The wicket sweated because of the humidity on Sunday night. When the covers were removed at 7 a.m. today it was quite damp.' The conditions so mystifying the players were the consequence of the tendency of the tarpaulins covering the wicket to draw moisture and close the cracks. His assessment – and confident prediction – was that it would last the scheduled six days and would soon be in the batsmen's favour.

Percy Beames, a former captain of Victoria and then cricket correspondent of the *Melbourne Age*, had the advantage, as a journalist, of being a good friend and confidante of Bill Vanthoff. According to Gideon Haigh, another Australian writer, the MCG curator alerted Beames to the impending controversy. At his Collins

Street office on the Monday morning he received a telephone call from a clearly worried man. Vanthoff said: 'Percy, something terrible has happened. Jack House has flooded the square. He's put too much water on it.' It was a sensational disclosure and instantly communicated to Beames's editor, Harold Austin. Having ascertained that no evil intent was involved, Austin at first decided against running the story. He had no wish to harm Anglo-Australian relations. His decision was proof that he was more interested in the game than in an exclusive for his newspaper.

It was, however, a story that could not be suppresed. Attempts by the two umpires, Col Hoy and Mel McInnes to douse speculation were doomed to failure. Margaret Hughes, writing in the *Sydney Daily Telegraph*, described the pandemonium in the press box. 'Pressmen could be seen rushing here and there, chatting together, or in groups, snatching phones – the inexplicable feather-bed state of the wicket had been explained – it had been watered.'

Percy Beames could no longer stand back from the fray. He categorically stated that the pitch had been watered on the Sunday. In his report on Tuesday, January 4, he wrote: 'The pitch was watered before the covers were replaced on Sunday evening, thus violating the rules of cricket. At the time the pitch was showing extreme cracks. They extended over the surface of the wicket and in many cases were half an inch wide.'

At one stage amid all the hints and insinuations the Australian Board of Control was reported to have considered a suggestion that if Australia won the Test it would offer to replay it because of the suspicions about the wicket. Beames also believed that the match should be declared void if the cause was a malpractice. Other Australians thought that the Test should be replayed on February 11 to replace a state match at Melbourne on that date.

As late as 1987 the state of the MCG wicket was attracting widespread criticism. Every spring the curator was faced with the same problem: how did he transform the square from wear and tear of football into a surface for the world's best batsmen? He said the task was never easy, but in the wet weather six years earlier the grass roots had rotted. It had become impossible to prepare a flat wicket on the 'stagnant, gooey mess' that lay below the surface.

After a few hours' cricket, cracks and – far worse from the batsman's point of view – dimpled indentations appeared, causing the ball to shoot at ankle height or rear dangerously. The pitch was dug up and relaid with sand and rocks under a thinner layer of clay to improve drainage. Despite this work, the curator said he was still unable to protect the grass on the square during the football season. If he covered it, the grass died; if he did not cover it, the footballers kicked it out.

Experiments were made with different types of new couch grass before the installation of under-wicket heating and overhead lamps to promote rapid growth in the spring, regardless of the climate. The square has since responded to these initiatives and shown an improvement in recent seasons.

Over thirty years earlier the Melbourne authorities were just as preoccupied with the problem of adverse ground conditions occasioned by the clash between cricket and football. The episode of the watered pitch added to their burdens. Various theories were advanced, including the possibility that an underground spring had been activated. One Australian, Colin McDonald, gave credence to this in a recent letter to the author. His conclusion was that 'it was a very poor wicket.' McDonald said that the deterioration had begun with cracks which then subsided into canyons. 'The underground rain affected an area in the exact location of the cricket pitch, thus proving that even a lowly curator's earnest supplications can sometimes be answered.'

Outside cricket circles there was also evidence that appeared to show that the Melbourne curator was being unfairly blamed. Keith Dunstan, in his book, *The Paddock that Grew*, recorded the hilarity of greenkeepers and bowls players in Mildura, the hot border town on the Murray River. 'They thought it was a great joke and couldn't understand why nobody had realised that dew could have been responsible for the condition of the wicket following the great fall in temperature.' Dunstan added that night playing of bowls at Mildura had taught greenkeepers that an amazing amount of water came out of the turf when there was a sudden change after a hot period.

There were also the opinions of two leading soil experts from the Department of Civil Engineering at the University of Melbourne. In a letter to the Victorian Cricket Association, they agreed that the reason given for excessive sweating under the covers appeared to be correct. They explained that with the hot sun of Sunday the top of the wicket had dried to a hard crust, and the sealed moisture underneath tended naturally to go down to colder, lower regions.

The letter continued: 'Then, early on Monday morning, when the cool change came, a reversal of the temperature conditions occurred, so that vapour movement was towards the surface. With the covers over the wicket, moisture loss by evaporation would have been restricted: thus an accumulation of moisture in the soil surface would result and the dry crust would disappear. The consequent swelling of the clay and the closing of the cracks led to the recovery of the wicket.'

'It is for these reasons,' the letter added, 'that we may conclude that the sweating of the wicket was due to a natural phenomenon, the extent of which was aggravated by the abnormal climatic conditions which appertained in Melbourne last Sunday and the use of unventilated covers on the wicket.'

Frank Tyson, with his close knowledge as a former Director of Coaching at Melbourne, offers another climatic explanation as a factor retarding wicket preparation after the use of the ground for football. He cites the colder weather prevailing in early season in the city. 'Not many cricket matches are played at the MCG before Christmas for this reason. In those days before the wicket block was relaid after the 1956 Olympic Games the pitch was basically rolled mud.' Tyson, along with Trevor Bailey and Bob Appleyard, believes that real answer to the riddle of the watered wicket was that the Melbourne curator panicked because he feared the inherent dangers of the situation.

Tyson says: 'He saw the ground on the Sunday when amid the searing heat the pitch was disintegrating. It was just as well that it was watered because it wouldn't have lasted another day. It would have been reduced to a dust heap.' Ron Archer, an Australian rival, agrees that the Melbourne wicket was a disgrace and not fit for Test cricket. 'It would have been unplayable if it had not been "treated" on the Sunday. Someone might have been killed. The cracks were inches wide on the Saturday and the Tuesday when we batted again. Balls would either fly head high or shoot low depending on which side of the crack they hit.'

John Woodcock has said that he is as sure as it is possible to be that Percy Beames did not err in his verdict on the controversy. There were clearly qualms from the outset on the state of the wicket, which prompted the recruitment of Jack House to oversee arrangements for the Test. As events unfolded he was presented with an impossible burden. The case against him was not entirely proven. If he was deemed guilty, he had still carried out his duties with good intentions. It was a logical step on the Sunday to water the wicket. His aim was not just to protect his job but those others quite literally in the front line on the field. It was demonstrably a poor wicket at Melbourne but the intervention of extreme and freakish weather did contribute to his dilemma.

England would become the beneficiaries of the attempted rescue operation. They batted on what Alan Davidson has described as virtually a 'brand new pitch' before the drying sun once again released its devils. The reputation of Australian cricket was salvaged but its players were reduced to helpless passengers in a brutal finale.

8

Humbled by Tyson in Cracking Affair

'Frank was phenomenal. He was so quick, the quickest I've ever seen before or since that time.'

Bob Appleyard.

On the opening morning of the crucial third Test at Melbourne, Len Hutton had reason to despair at the aggression of the mercurial Australian, Keith Miller. 'The bugger's done us,' he moaned. It was the response of a sick man who was mentally drained by the demands of captaincy. Recurring bouts of sciatica had also taken a huge toll of his physical strength. His discomfort was intensified when Keith Miller brushed aside England's top order batsmen in an inspired bowling thrust.

Miller, as Hutton well knew, was a dangerous opponent when in the right mood. He had returned to the Australian team after injury. His rest had given him an extra spur and he was now fully committed to the task in hand. Any lingering doubts about his fitness, expressed in a pre-match conversation with Sir Donald Bradman, were soon dispelled in characteristic manner.

With his right knee heavily bandaged, Miller bowled unchanged for ninety minutes before lunch. England lost four wickets for 41 runs and Miller took three of them for five runs, in a spell of nine overs, eight of which were maidens. Only two scoring strokes were made from those 72 balls – a cover drive for three by Compton and a push square of the wicket by Bailey for two. Miller's attack overwhelmed England and he punched a great hole in the innings when he dismissed Hutton, Edrich and Compton. At the other end,

Lindwall performed with equal fervour. Uncharitably he dismissed May for a duck on his 25th birthday.

Miller's achievement was such as to rank with another stunning performance on the same ground 43 years earlier. On December 30, 1911, the Melbourne crowd had been silenced when S.F. Barnes, then a veteran at 38, took the wickets of Bardsley for a 'golden duck', Kellaway, Clem Hill and Armstrong for just one run in five overs. His opening spell of eleven overs yielded figures of five wickets for six runs.

Miller was three years younger than the incomparable Barnes but on his great day had just recovered from injury. His performance was all the more impressive because his captain, Ian Johnson, had expected to bowl him only in an emergency. Bill O'Reilly, in the *Sydney Morning Herald,* enthused about one of the 'longest and toughest efforts' of Miller's career. 'Basing his attack on a well-directed outswinger, which moved late, Miller exacted full value from the liveliest Test wicket Melbourne has produced in years.'

Frank Tyson still considers Miller as the supreme all-rounder, capable of turning a match on its head with bat or ball in the space of a few overs. At Melbourne, he says, he witnessed one of the best bowling spells in his experience. Ian Peebles viewed Miller as the most threatening bowler of the series with the new ball. It was an unreserved tribute although he did admit that he might be censured for disloyalty to England's own men.

Miller, debonair and dashing, was an entertainer above all. The handsome Australian, with his sleek dark hair, had the presence of a matinee idol. He was held to be a chivalrous opponent. Crowds loved him because he communicated with them and made them part of the show, said John Warr. Dulcie Gray, the actress and wife of cricket devotee, Michael Denison, once confided that she became a convert to the game after watching Miller on television.

Peter Loader believes that Miller was at his best as a fast bowler when fired by a challenge. At other times, when none existed, he could subside into indifference. The former Royal Australian Air Force pilot had first come to the attention of his future English rivals in the 'Victory Tests' in 1945. He scored three centuries, including one for the Dominions XI, at Lord's. The manner in which he played cricket in the immediate post-war years signalled his relief at coming unscathed through a terrible war. He always displayed a sense of theatre in his flamboyant approach to the game. Attrition was alien to his nature; his impulsive spirit was coupled with a desire never to be bored in any circumstance. He embraced life passionately because, as Michael Parkinson remarked, he had seen the alternative.

Miller was the staunchest of Anglophiles and socially at least, a favourite Australian in the English camp. His long friendship with Bill Edrich led to one or two nocturnal escapades. During a match between Middlesex and the touring Australians at Lord's in 1953 the two companions had dallied until the early hours out on the town. On the following morning Miller had almost literally to be helped into his pads. Edrich was gently guided out to his customary position at first slip. He called out to the bowler, Alan Moss: 'Pitch it up; he hasn't been to bed.' Miller tossed back his hair in a familiar gesture. He glared through blood-shot eyes at the Middlesex bowler. 'You think I'm pissed, Mossie; I could play you with the bat handle.' He stumbled into position and smartly glided the first ball to the boundary. He might have played this delivery from memory; but his brain rapidly sharpened as he went on to score a brisk 71. Edrich, watching the reeling bowlers at slip, rocked with laughter.

Peter Loader says that the image of Miller as a bohemian party-goer is less then accurate. There was another facet to his character, little known and rarely, if ever, publicised. He recalls that on one occasion the Australian was an absentee from a cocktail party for cricketing guests. Someone said: 'Where's Miller? I expect he's out on the town tonight.' Loader knew at that precise moment Miller, a lover of classical music, was in the audience at a concert at the Festival Hall in London. 'This revealed to me his versatile personality and his need of release from the demands of cricket through cultural pursuits. It was a relaxation, perhaps, that pushed into the background the memories of his grim experiences in the war.'

It was Colin Cowdrey, at 22 years of age, England's youngest player, who cheered the disconsolate Hutton after his side's batting collapse, with a maiden Test century at Melbourne. He began his innings at the height of Miller's bowling onslaught, and stood firm against the fiery pace. Cowdrey scored 102 out of the 160 runs registered while he was at the wicket. England finally reached 191 and Cowdrey equalled Bradman's record in achieving three figures in the lowest total in Anglo-Australian Tests to contain a century. He was the youngest Englishman to make a Test hundred in Australia since J.W. Hearne on the same ground in the second Test of the 1911–12 series.

Cowdrey, in tandem with Trevor Bailey, arrested the Australian advance after four wickets had fallen in the first hour of the day. They resisted for another two hours in adding 74 for the fifth wicket. Then Godfrey Evans joined his Kent partner in an alliance that lifted England's score by a further 54 runs. *Wisden* reported: 'For four hours Cowdrey batted without a mistake, getting his body and bat behind short rising balls which Lindwall and Miller were able to bowl off this pitch almost at will.'

Tom Graveney was among the fellow tourists who marvelled at Cowdrey's poise in a dire situation. 'It was the most amazing innings. Colin played as though he was batting on a flat 'un.' The major feature for Frank Tyson, who was at the wicket when Cowdrey reached his century, was the unruffled composure at the heart of the innings. 'It was quite remarkable for one so young. His timing was so sweet and his strokes effortless.' Tyson now reflects upon the imperturbability, which characterised Cowdrey's batting then and later. 'It was never more revealed than at Melbourne when the veterans of England's line-up failed again.'

The acclaim of the vast crowd of 64,000 for a masterly 100 had barely subsided when a freak ball bowled Cowdrey. It was delivered by off-spinner, Ian Johnson. The ball pitched six inches outside the off-stump. Cowdrey elected to leave it and raised his bat high. He was dumbfounded as the ball broke across his legs, hitting his leg stump. Johnson, not a great spinner of the ball, had hitherto managed only minimum turn. The delivery, as Tyson recalls, ricocheted off one of the cracks now beginning to disfigure the wicket. Johnson wryly acknowledged the deviation and said: 'I don't usually bowl when the wicket is good.'

Bill O'Reilly, in the *Sydney Morning Herald*, considered that Cowdrey at Melbourne had superseded the failing Hutton in the ranks of world-class batsmen. Classic offside play came under O'Reilly's scrutiny. 'When he plays his now famous cover drive, the fieldsmen are left almost disinterested in the job of cutting it off.' He added: 'Apart from his great ability, still not fully exploited, Cowdrey has such a fine temperament that tough spots and hostile bowling tend to make him concentrate all the more.'

Geoffrey Howard, the MCC manager, remembered that an innings of astonishing maturity dragged Len Hutton out of his depression. 'Len was upset after getting out so quickly. He did not take his pads off and just sat at the back of the pavilion, staring glumly at the wall. Then suddenly those of us who were watching the game started to clap and cheer. It was, of course, Colin. He was quite unbelievable. It was a magical innings. He was making Lindwall bowl with two mid-offs.' Hutton's mood underwent a swift change when he realised from the commotion on the balcony that his pupil was ensconced in a state of batting bliss. 'Len came out to have a look and soon he was sharing our enthusiasm,' said Howard. 'It worked like a charm and pulled him out of his misery.'

The dread, which afflicted Hutton in that episode, was evidence of a tired man beset by anxiety. Earlier he had been greatly troubled by his decision to omit Alec Bedser again. As a considerate man, he was worried about the impending demotion of his senior professional who had been one of England's most loyal and successful players. Melbourne was also one of Bedser's favourite venues. He had taken 22 wickets in three Tests there. Bill O'Reilly was vexed about the exclusion. 'This not only smacks of wanton tempting of providence but also is unhappily like piling petty indignities upon a bowler who should sail comfortably into either of the two teams in this match.'

It now seems certain that Bedser was not fully fit when he was asked to bowl in the first Test at Brisbane. Trevor Bailey and Jim

Swanton both believed that he should have been allowed more time to recover from a severe attack of shingles. Swanton did though find it inexcusable that Hutton was not prepared to ease the pain by giving an explanation beforehand. 'Bedser has played in some 50 Test matches. He has bowled more overs and taken more wickets than anyone who has ever played. If he were to be left out the occasion surely called for some sort of accompanying statement – not a mere dropping half an hour before the start – and that on a ground where he has recorded some of his greatest successes.'

Len Hutton had to be persuaded to play at Melbourne. He was in a low state and had scored only 75 runs in four innings in the two preceding Tests. Geoffrey Howard remembered that Hutton was so overwrought that he asked to see a doctor on the night before the Test. Bill Edrich and Godfrey Evans joined Howard when the examination was carried out on the morning of the match. The doctor announced a clean bill of health and urged Hutton to take a shower, have breakfast and go to the ground. It later transpired that Hutton's 'illness' was psychosomatic. 'Len was devastated; he wanted to be told that he was unfit,' said Howard.

More significantly, the feigned illness was an attempt to escape from the problem concerning Bedser's exclusion from the side. 'Len didn't want to hurt Alec but he refused to delegate the task to Edrich, who was prepared to convey the sad news,' recalled Howard. 'Len had actually taken Alec out to inspect the wicket,' said Howard. 'With all the other problems pressing on his mind, he still couldn't face communicating his decision to Bedser.' To make matters worse the Surrey bowler had already changed for the match, and then was dumbfounded to discover that his name was not included on the team sheet pinned up on the dressing-room notice board.

Bill Edrich, however irrational as a romantic, was a steadfast cricketer. Len Hutton was deeply indebted to a generous companion and cricket adviser. His vitality and strength as a fellow tour selector were of inestimable value to the England captain on an exhausting tour. As boys more than twenty years earlier, they had first taken measure of each other as Norfolk and Yorkshire rivals in a Minor

Counties match at Lakenham. The humanity of Edrich, the former farmer's boy, contrasted with his amorous fol-de-rols. He was still falling in love well into his fifties and beyond.

Geoffrey Howard remembered that Edrich was involved in a shipboard romance with an Australian girl on the voyage out to Fremantle. The 'affair' was revealed to the touring party when Howard discussed with the players what hotel expenses each had incurred that were defined as 'personal' in their MCC contracts. On this occasion Johnny Wardle was first to be interviewed. The session lasted more than 15 minutes, with the Yorkshireman disputing every item in his personal total of eighteen shillings.

Next was Edrich who had overheard Wardle's arguments. 'I wouldn't like your job, Geoffrey,' he said. Howard replied: 'Stop being sorry for me and start feeling sorry for yourself. You owe £38!' Edrich did not raise an eyebrow. He was unabashed by the enormity of the sum. 'If you say so,' was his response. He smilingly appended his name as if signing a mess bill and departed. It later transpired that his substantial bill was largely comprised of costs of long distance telephone calls he had made to his new girl friend in Australia.

Godfrey Evans recalled that it was largely at Edrich's instigation that Len Hutton was prevailed upon to play at Melbourne. 'We had levelled the series after being beaten by an innings and plenty at Brisbane. Psychologically Len had to be out there with us at Melbourne.' Evans and Edrich shepherded the England captain into a cab and travelled with him to the ground. 'We don't care a bugger what you do Leonard, but you must go out on to that field,' was the exhortation.

Len Hutton, as he pledged himself once more to duty, did not have the strident chorale of today's 'Barmy Army' legions to encourage him in his quest. There were only two Englishmen, one named Sam Stott, a friend of George Duckworth, the MCC baggage master, and a Lancashire member. Joining this slender group was an American, 70-year-old Henry Sayen, who had become, in Hutton's words, 'England's good mascot'. Sayen was a member of the last

Philadelphia team to tour England in 1908 and had won com-
mendation as a privileged supporter at Lord's in 1953. He had made
a special journey from Philadelphia and was a spectator when
England fought a sterling rearguard action against Australia to save
the game and make possible the recovery of the Ashes. On the last
day but one when England's fortunes were at low ebb, Sayen
requested an opportunity to meet the England team, and his interest
and encouragement did much to cheer them up.

The veteran, looking on from the pavilion, had been in at the start
of a renaissance of English cricket. From his day at Lord's he had
become a most welcome visitor to any England dressing-room. He
undoubtedly possessed talismanic qualities, for he watched England
in four Tests and never saw them lose. He made another special trip
to Kingston, Jamaica, to see England square a rubber against the
West Indies. Then, despite ill-health, he flew to Sydney in 1954 to
watch the vital second Test. In 1955, he travelled to England this
time to witness another triumph in a keen contest against South
Africa at Lord's.

Henry Sayen, a distinguished ambassador and author of a book
on American cricket, forged a bond of friendship during those few
short years. He regarded himself as the luckiest of mortals to have
become a friend of England's great cricketers. In turn, the players
under Len Hutton's command were happy to share the relaxing
company of a friendly American in times of stress in Australia.

A temporarily benign wicket served England well at Melbourne.
Kickers and shooters had followed each other with exasperating
frequency on the first two days of the Test. Australia, with
Maddocks and Johnson also taking advantage of the changed
conditions, recovered from 115 for six to total 231, a lead of 40 on
the first innings. Maddocks was top scorer with 47 and he and
Johnson put on 54 runs for the ninth wicket. Even the arrival of the
new ball did not check the 'penny dreadful' hitting of the Australian
tailenders, commented one observer.

The question now facing England was whether the previously
villainous pitch would remain in its present condition long enough

to strengthen their position. Peter May reacted with urgent aggression to impose his mastery on a wicket now beginning to worsen. He dominated the scene as commandingly as Cowdrey had done in the first innings. May dealt easily with all the Australian bowlers and scored freely all round the ground.

May was dismissed nine runs short of his fifth century of the tour but before he was out he took full revenge on Lindwall who had had him caught for a duck on his birthday on New Year's Eve. Bill O'Reilly noted: 'One classic boundary hit straight past Miller flashed through the field, leaving two fieldsmen close to the bowler open-mouthed. The fact that the impact of bat on ball was almost noiseless was proof enough that the stroke had been timed to perfection.' May's driving on the offside was so spectacular that Lindwall was compelled to position mid-off, extra cover and cover deeper than where the fieldsmen stood for Australia's slow bowlers.

While May was on the rampage, Len Hutton was fighting a battle for form and confidence at the other end. He did realise that the longer England batted the more likely it would be that the Australians would be batting on a deteriorating wicket in their second innings. Hutton's 42, watchfully compiled, was his best in the series thus far. Crawford White, in the *News Chronicle*, thought it could be properly described as the canny knock of a captain more afraid of getting out than getting in. Bill O'Reilly expressed the same sentiment but couched it more diplomatically. 'It was easy to see from the manner in which Hutton set about his opening job that he was just as keen to spend lots of time at the wicket as he was to score runs.'

The diehard spirit of Trevor Bailey was one to be cherished, even if his obduracy, like Hutton's, brought ironic cheers from the crowd. As England strove to build up a winning advantage, one Melbourne columnist ruminated on the questioning voices of the barrackers. 'There was jeering applause when Bailey simply stopped the ball. Somebody kept calling out: "Too little and too long." After Ron Archer had offered a couple of fiery overs to his obstinate rival, I heard a tired voice murmur: "Get a bulldozer."'

Bailey was unbeaten on 24, having defended stoically for two and three quarter hours. Richard Whitington wrote: 'Bailey must have been seeing the ball through a magnifying glass long before he was left unconquered and alone.' The merry hitting of Johnny Wardle was a more appealing spectacle. Wardle hit 38 out of 46, taking 16 runs in an over from Bill Johnston and 14 from the next by Johnson. 'These were valuable runs for England,' observed the Melbourne writer. 'The crowd loved his daring, and when Ian Johnson bowled him up went the regretful chorus, "Pity it was Wardle." Only the 11 Australians on the field seemed really relieved.'

Down in the catacombs of Melbourne Cricket Ground on Test match days an army of tradesmen caters for the thousands of spectators. Pie and sandwich stalls, soft drink counters and temporary bars stretch round the outer ring of the great sporting amphitheatre. The vendors know less of what is happening above than people at home beside the radio or television. The cacophony of sighs, groans, cheers and howls from up in the stands each have different interpretations among the tradesmen beavering away in the dark. The grapevine became ever more vital as a source of news on the enthralling final day at Melbourne.

Australia, with two wickets down for 75, required 165 runs for victory. It was almost a repetition of their position on the last day of the second Test at Sydney. Lindsay Browne, in the *Sydney Morning Herald*, thought that the spin of Bob Appleyard posed a greater threat than the speed which had destroyed Australia in the second Test. Australia's overnight batsmen were Richie Benaud, tactically promoted above Miller, and Neil Harvey. On the previous evening they had played as if haunted by the delivery from Appleyard that had cut back to bowl opener Les Favell. 'The ball was a beauty,' said Browne, 'and one to nibble wormholes through any incoming batsman's confidence.' So, by this account, Appleyard was the key man in England's attack. 'His friendly hand had a dagger in it, the sharp break of the sudden fast ball that swooped into the batsman's blockhole before he could be halfway with any yawn too carelessly begun.'

The rout of Australia on an extraordinary morning began with an amazing catch by Godfrey Evans off the seventh ball of the first over to dismiss Harvey. Evans described it as perhaps the finest catch he had ever taken standing back. Certainly it resulted in the removal of a batsman who posed a major threat to England's hopes of victory. Jim Swanton said the catch was taken from a genuinely fine glance. 'Evans moved across to the legside not on a prearranged plan but on a hunch that Harvey would play the stroke, and he took the ball after the most prodigious leap at the fullest stretch.'

The Melbourne wicket, said Swanton, had mysteriously come to life again. In the first few overs Tyson and Statham regularly succeeded in hitting the newly opened cracks from which the ball either shot or kept hideously low. Alan Davidson recalls: 'Frank was unplayable. The ball would not only deviate off the edges of the cracks but also scoot. Every now and then you would get one that stood up. Against someone as fast and accurate as Frank it was an impossible situation.'

Bob Appleyard who had been expected to take wickets was never asked to bowl. Nevertheless, as an otherwise gratified observer, he says: 'Frank was phenomenal. He was so quick, the quickest I've ever seen before or since that time.'

A cartoon in the *Melbourne Age* was captioned 'Frank-Enstein-Tyson'. It expressively communicated the despair of the Australian batsmen. England's new strike bowler, who had emerged at Sydney, now proved unplayable. In 79 minutes Tyson took six wickets for 16 runs in 51 balls. His final analysis of 7 for 27 had never been bettered in a match between England and Australia. It was an explosion of an elemental force that rendered technique irrelevant. 'Sheer speed through the air coupled with a shooter at any moment left the batsmen helpless. Tyson blazed through them like a bush fire,' reported *Wisden*. E.M Wellings wrote: 'Not even an auctioneer could have dealt more rapidly with the assorted batting lots than Tyson.'

Such was the dominance of the English pace attack that during the abbreviated passage of play only 22 scoring strokes were made from 91 balls. Australia's last eight wickets went down for just 36 runs and England won by 128 runs. Australia's total of 111 was the lowest for a completed innings by Australia since the 58 and 80 at Brisbane and Sydney respectively in 1936.

Few Test collapses have been so dramatic in execution. Australia's last man, Bill Johnston was dismissed 11 minutes before lunch. 'I wonder now who would have withstood Tyson as he bowled on this pitch on this January morning,' enthused Jim Swanton. 'In little more than an hour 50,000 people were applauding him in and then wending their way home, chattering adjectivally, I expect, in profane disbelief.' Robert Menzies, the Australian Prime Minister, was one of the first people to congratulate Tyson. An important meeting had detained him in his office. 'I listened surreptitiously to the radio once or twice – and discovered that Tyson had deprived me of an afternoon's cricket.'

Frank Tyson contends that it was never contemplated that the spinners would do much work on the last morning. The rapid fall of Australia's wickets against his thunderbolts probably exceeded his own expectations. Fifty years on Tyson still expresses astonishment at the way the Test match ended.

'Every so often the ball would do some extraordinary things. It started off when Neil Harvey got one from me that pitched middle and leg. Neil took it off his stumps and flicked it down to fine leg. But Godfrey was there, three yards down the legside and took a wonderful catch. Benaud tried to hook me only to get an under-edge on to his stumps. Miller came in and got one that reared at him. He gloved the ball to first slip. Len dived as far as he could but only managed to "tip it over the bar". Bill Edrich, at second slip, ran back about ten yards to complete the catch. Hole was caught by Evans, flashing outside the off stump. Brian then bowled Ron Archer. This was all happening in a matter of minutes. Next I bowled one at Len Maddocks well up in the blockhole. He came down on the ball hard and it spun away like a billiard ball and knocked his leg bail off. It was a remarkable episode.'

It was bowling of formidable and concentrated fury that rocketed Tyson to fame on the horror pitch at Melbourne. Bill O'Reilly, watching Tyson's demoralising spell, said: 'He rode roughshod over our full batting strength. Batsmen whom we had regarded as sanely practical had no answer to offer the England speedster. Not since the eight wickets fell for 35 runs at Manchester in 1953 had Australian cricket been so dreadfully humiliated as it was today. Butterfly backlifts have never looked so ludicrously incongruous as they did facing Tyson and Statham.'

C.B. Fry, the octogenarian writer and famed Test cricketer, presented his summary in the *Cricketer*. He reflected that there was little to compare with real speed. 'The genuinely fast bowler is on to you too quickly. You have to be as keen as a razor and swift as a snake in order to counter him. The batsman who does not lift his bat from the blockhole in good time, who does not stand tall and commanding, finds himself snatching a save-me-somehow stroke, edging or missing the high-riser and too late to stop the ball that keeps low.'

Fry concluded on the heroics – the alert determination – required in this fearsome battle between bat and ball. 'No wonder the young Australian batsmen found the need of more study when they had to face Tyson and his mate on the tricksome creek-soil. He added: 'As for our "Typhoon", he is a young treasure we shall do well to nourish with much pleasure and no silly adulation.'

The shrill criticism in the Australian media railed at the complacency of the selectors. It rose above the protestations about the consequences of the crumbling wicket. Instead the judgement was that the signs of frailty had been ignored. Percy Beames in the *Melbourne Age* was among those enraged by a woeful capitulation. 'After two consecutive defeats – both of which followed an identical pattern – it is patent to every Australian cricket follower that changes must be made to restore prestige and determination.'

The discards, said Beames, should be Richie Benaud and Graeme Hole, both of whom had had full opportunity to prove their worth. He advocated the selection of Colin McDonald, the Victorian opening batsman, and Jimmy Burke, the New South Wales's all-rounder, in an attempt to bolster the batting strength. Another candidate was the strangely ignored Ken Meuleman, formerly from Victoria and now domiciled in Western Australia. Meuleman had scored a chanceless century at Perth in October against the full weight of the MCC attack. The heavy scoring of Test regulars, Sid Barnes, Arthur Morris and Bill Brown had denied him a deserved chance. He was twelfth man once in the series against England and would be restricted to only one Test against New Zealand.

The true measure of Meuleman's ability lay in his footwork. It led one former Australian player, Arthur Mailey to describe him as the 'Pavlova' of the crease. Tom Graveney remembers that the West Australian batsman played the quick bowlers better than anyone. 'Ken was a good player and should have played instead of Graeme Hole. We, as a team, were relieved at his omission. We did not want him to be picked.'

The scholarly marauder, who had provoked such outrage in Australia, was dignified in his hour of glory. Frank Tyson quietly but firmly insisted that his share of the spoils at Melbourne owed much to the assistance of his partner, Brian Statham. 'I just had the luck to get the figures,' he said. In his supporting role Statham bowled six miserly overs in taking two wickets for 19 runs. Crawford White, in the *News Chronicle*, regarded Tyson's acknowledgement as a due tribute, if erring in modesty, and laid emphasis on the twin-pronged assault. 'Victory was ours because England could maintain sustained speed at both ends and this was why Australia's brittle batting cracked so badly.' Just how well Tyson and Statham operated together can be gleaned from the fact that they took 31 of the 40 wickets to fall at Sydney and Melbourne.

Back home in England it was also 'Tyson's day' at his home town of Middleton. His mother, Violet Tyson was awakened at 6.30 a.m. by neighbours anxious to relay the news of the triumph. Before long she would also hear that the match-winning ball was to be flown to England for presentation to her. It was to be specially mounted and inscribed with the figures of a devastating analysis. To the reporters who laid siege to her home she sternly claimed that 'Frank was not really ferocious.' There were, it is certain, at least seven Australians who would argue that, in this instance, a mother did not know best.

A Test match that had begun on a note of scandal ended with England counting their blessings in establishing a 2–1 lead in the series. Len Hutton's catchphrase, 'Are you all right, lad' was the rallying call for his praised young men. At the end of the game crowds raced out to the middle and snatched precious heaps of the controversial wicket to keep as souvenirs. Then the groundsmen grimly emerged, and while the excited supporters stood about, they turned on the hoses. Soon the centre of the ground was a vast lake. It could be said by all who saw it that this time the wicket was well and truly watered.

9

Accomplices in Supporting Cast

'Appleyard as a bowler was under-used on this tour. He could
have bowled to tremendous effect had he been given the chance.'
Frank Tyson.

Bob Appleyard came late to first-class cricket and even later to the
international scene. He was brought into Yorkshire's team in 1951
when already 27 years of age as a replacement opening bowler. The
county had lost two senior professionals, one through injury and
another to league cricket.

Appleyard had an astonishing first full season with Yorkshire
when he took 200 wickets at an average of 14.14 runs each. It was
the best for the county since 1925 when George Macaulay reached
the milestone and it also enabled Appleyard to share with Rhodes
and George Hirst the distinction of attaining the figures solely in the
White Rose colours.

But Appleyard's success was to be short-lived because soon
afterwards he was struck down by tuberculosis and lost two seasons
of his career. Few thought he would ever play cricket again but
Geoffrey Wooler, the surgeon who had saved the life of Lord
Woolton, the Conservative Party chairman, was the man who came
to Appleyard's rescue.

'He gave me encouragement right from the start of my illness.'
When asked by his patient about the seemingly forlorn prospect of
resuming his career, Wooler replied: 'Yes, you will, and I shall come
and watch you play.'

Appleyard today says: 'I was lucky in having the skills of a
remarkable surgeon at my disposal. I was also fortunate in that they
had got the surgical techniques and drugs sorted out by this stage.'

It was a long haul back to fitness, spanning eleven months, six of them in bed in hospital, at the end of which he had to learn to walk again. His convalescence was helped by a stay in Switzerland, arranged at Yorkshire's expense. Food rationing was still in force in Britain but one local butcher was able to help his recovery with additional supplies of meat.

Appleyard's return to first-class cricket in 1954 was an exceptional feat against all the odds and he immediately set out to make up for lost time. He bowled well enough to claim 154 wickets that gave him second place in the national averages. He made his Test debut against Pakistan at Nottingham and showed that he was back to his best. In his first bowling spell he took four wickets – those of Hanif, Maqsood, Waqar Hassan and Imtiaz Ahmed – for six runs. Pakistan collapsed from 37 for one to 53 for five. Appleyard finished with figures of 5 for 51 and England won the Test by an innings.

Appleyard always acknowledged the debt he owed to Norman Yardley, his first Yorkshire captain, and Len Hutton, his leader in Australia. 'Both Norman and Len were extremely knowledgeable apart from being top-class cricketers. They'd studied the game and that was very useful for any young cricketer, or an inexperienced one as I was in 1951. My career developed rapidly under their direction. I was able to put three to four years' learning into one year.'

Yardley was the man who helped to establish Appleyard as an off-break bowler. In an early match against Surrey at the Oval, Yardley took his bowler to task after he had first bowled spin. 'I realised I wasn't good enough as a fast-medium bowler. After about five overs I ran up and bowled a slow spinner. The batsman had a tremendous swipe at it. It pitched and turned and knocked his middle stump out. The dismissal was amazing to me and even more so to my own side as no one had seen me bowl off-spinners before.'

The Yorkshire captain was among the bewildered observers of the change. 'Make your bloody mind up,' he told Appleyard. 'How can I set a field when you're bowling like that? Your best bet is to stick to off-breaks and slip in the odd seamer.' Yardley encouraged Appleyard to practice his spinners in the county nets in the following year. The new recruit showed his application to the revised method when he sustained a blister on his first finger. He changed to bowl his off-spinners from the middle finger. 'I found I could bowl it a lot quicker, almost at full pace, and with greater control.'

The second phase of Appleyard's career after the operation, which had reduced his lung capacity, required a readjustment in his technique. It called for a reversion to bowling his off-cutters off the index finger, and a greater emphasis on flight and changes of pace. Jim Swanton, in his appraisal of Appleyard, said he had a distinctly individual talent. 'He had a deadly accuracy and the ball was sharply spun and cut.' Appleyard himself cherishes the compliment of Emmott Robinson, an early mentor and one of the shrewdest of Yorkshire advisers. 'I've seen bowlers with two paces, sometimes three,' said Emmott, 'but never anyone with five like this lad.'

Appleyard's selection in the party to tour Australia in 1954–55 was a defining moment in his career thus far and it signalled his complete recovery from the life-threatening illness he had suffered two years previously. But on the stopover in Colombo he had yet another setback. At the end of the match against a Singhalese eleven an excited crowd surged on to the field. After a collision with one boisterous spectator, Appleyard was left struggling for breath from a sickening blow to his ribs, on the spot where he had undergone a lung operation.

When the MCC party returned to the ship, Appleyard underwent a preliminary medical examination but that proved inconclusive. But Appleyard was in considerable pain during the remaining five days of the voyage to Fremantle. He insisted on an immediate x-ray when the team travelled on to their headquarters in Perth. The diagnosis was a cracked rib, only to be cured by a natural healing process. A cherished tour had had a dispiriting beginning and a month went by before he was fully restored to fitness.

Appleyard regarded his selection for Australia ahead of the vaunted Jim Laker as one of the biggest compliments of his career. 'But I did have an additional string as a seamer. I wasn't just relying on spin.' He always recognised the importance of the two roles to exploit varying wickets. 'It never made much sense to me just to have one style because pitches are always different and you need to deploy various resources to take wickets.' In the first section of his career he shared the new ball with Fred Trueman before reverting to his off-spin mode. 'If the atmosphere and the pitch were responsive to seam bowling I would operate in that style. On the other hand, if it was wet, I wanted to get on to the spinners as fast as possible. It was all a question of assessing the situation.'

Trevor Bailey, as one ally in Australia, says that Appleyard, at medium pace, was entirely different to the ousted Laker. 'Bob was a very good and accurate off-spin bowler. He spun his off-break but he also made the ball *dip* at the last moment. I faced him in the nets. The difficulty was that you often thought he had bowled a half-volley and then found that the ball had dipped at pace.' Bailey adds: 'I don't think I've ever come across anyone else who bowled like that.'

The Australian tour united Appleyard with fellow Yorkshireman, Johnny Wardle. His skills more thoughtfully employed on hard wickets overseas gained him preference over his England rival, Tony Lock. Wardle's stock-in-trade was his wrist spin. It was a commodity, which many believed, could have been linked with Lock's orthodox left-arm spin in England's ranks. Their rivalry which was at its height during Lock's 'throwing' phase, might have been neutralised had it been harnessed in a common cause. Wardle strongly resented his demotion in England and the choice of Lock more particularly since the Surrey spinner's bowling action was considered illegal.

One of the sad aspects of Wardle's career was that his brilliance as a wrist spinner was denied its full flowering in Yorkshire. The county elders expected him to conform to the orthodox methods of his predecessors, Hedley Verity and Wilfred Rhodes. Peter May was one of Wardle's most fervent admirers and his later captain at home and overseas. 'Johnny was a high-class bowler and he had the great gift of being able to bowl his chinamen and googlies without seeming to practise them,' May had said. 'It was a quite extraordinary accomplishment. I cannot recall Johnny bowling his wrong 'uns to me in county cricket.'

The reason, as Frank Tyson reiterates, was because Yorkshire regarded his 'funny stuff' as an unnecessary luxury in their attacking blueprint. Tyson says that Wardle's competency was hard-earned. On board the *Orsova*, carrying the team to Australia, the Yorkshireman could be seen every morning bowling his spin, hour after hour, against the bulkhead.

Keith Andrew, with his vast experience in keeping to the spin of George Tribe at Northampton, also referred to an under-used asset. He recalled that Wardle, like Tribe, had immensely powerful hands. 'Johnny and George both employed a vigorous body action in bowling their wrist-spin.' Jutting determined chins were thrust down the wicket in an intimidating manner.

'Johnny was a great bowler to have on your side,' says Andrew. 'I know that Yorkshire did not want him fiddling about and he did enjoy tremendous success as an orthodox slow left-arm bowler. But he was a brilliant and accurate wrist-spinner; his googly was difficult to spot; and, in my opinion, he did not bowl it enough.'

Godfrey Evans, like Appleyard, believed that Wardle became the complete bowler when he switched more frequently to the unorthodox style in the later stages of his career. 'Johnny was in a different category by that time,' says Appleyard. 'He enjoyed bowling his chinamen and googlies more than his orthodox slows. And he was better in this style once he had mastered the form of attack.'

Brian Close, another Yorkshire contemporary, has paid tribute to Wardle as a bowler of genius, a master of variations of flight and pace, and a cricketer who always thought soundly and responsibly about his plan of action. Wardle appraised his own merits in the following words: 'Four and five overs, me with the stock ball so that I could bowl one a little slower and get a batsman caught in the covers. That's why he could not be allowed to get a single to relieve the tension. We had to stop that single. When I thought the batsman was sizing me up and getting ready for the charge I would toss the ball a little higher, dropping it a foot shorter at the same speed, and hope to get him caught – a caught and bowled or a catch in the covers.'

Wardle remembered how he used to study the opposition all the time and how he bowled at seven or eight different speeds. 'It's all done by body action and the position of your hand at the top determines whether the ball comes out quick or slow. You've got to bowl with a quick action to deceive the batsman.'

He expanded on the enticing strategy: 'You can release the ball at the same speed and you can bowl six different deliveries. You let the ball go at the same pace but you release it a little further back. Then you go a bit further through with it and it's still the same pace. But it is bowled at six different trajectories.'

Wardle generally had to obey the well-tried Yorkshire brand of orthodoxy. In his early days with the county he wheeled away for over after over and was regarded as 'perpetual motion Johnny' by his fellow players. In one season he pounded through 1,800 overs and wore out three pairs of boots. One marathon effort, astonishing even by his own standards of endurance and accuracy, was his stint of 53 consecutive overs for 66 runs and five wickets against Middlesex at Lord's. 'He bowled without rest except for lunch for four hours,' reported the *Yorkshire Post*.

Wardle wore sombre garb as a bowler but he was arrayed in the shining robes of an entertainer as a batsman. Everyone, boys, girls and adults alike, moved forward on their seats in expectation of another glorious feast of hitting whenever Wardle came to the crease. If he was in tempestuous mood, wielding his bat with his immensely powerful forearms, run-making was a fast and furious affair. He was as unpredictable (and disconcerting to opponents) as Ian Botham. On those occasions his batting had a careless rapture.

Wardle was not just a six-hitting cavalier. Jim Swanton remembered him as a dangerous and decisive batsman for Yorkshire and England. 'The virtue of Johnny's cricket did not end with his bowling at all.' Wardle's career figures of over 7,000 runs were achieved in critical as well as hilarious moments. Indeed, there were many good judges who felt that he had the potential to become an all-rounder of merit.

In 1950 he demonstrated this potential with 733 runs and 174 wickets. He is, though, best remembered as a dasher at the crease. Against the MCC and Jim Laker at Lord's he crashed two sixes into the Grandstand and another into a neighbouring garden. In the pavilion there were murmurs of disapproval at such levity. One MCC member remarked: 'Agricultural, what?' A Yorkshireman in a nearby seat greeted the sally with disdain. 'Yes, but bloomin' fertile,' he replied.

A.A. Thomson in his book, *Cricket My Happiness,* told the charming story of Wardle in another match at Lord's. A dull day's cricket was drifting drowsily to a close when Wardle emerged from the pavilion. 'At his first six-hit the crowd roared with delight; at his second they stood on their seats and cheered; at his third many were collapsing in half-joyous, half-hysterical laughter. We were told at school that Shakespeare introduced a comedy scene to relieve the tension of his tragedies. If that was so, Johnny Wardle that evening played a scene equalling the combined efforts of Hamlet's gravediggers and the porter in Macbeth. By the force of his blows he might have awakened Duncan with his knocking.'

'Smiling broadly, he made 22 off, I think, seven balls, and a few minutes later I found myself walking down St John's Wood Road along with 20,000 people, all laughing as if they had been witnessing the greatest joke in the world. But I imagine that Johnny, in the players' dressing-room, was laughing loudest of all.'

The bowling alliance of Wardle and Appleyard was one of the most feared in the land. They were intensely proud Yorkshiremen. 'We didn't like to lose,' says Appleyard. 'It was unforgivable for Yorkshiremen. The first time I was on the losing side I thought the world had come to an end.' Wardle reinforced the point in one of our conversations. 'You either got the buggers out or stopped them scoring. It used to break our hearts if they scored a run off us. It was bloody cut-throat in those days. The runs were hard to come by off Bob and me.'

Norman Yardley said that Appleyard's chief asset was his direction. 'On the "stickies" he often bowled with just two fieldsmen on the offside at extra cover and mid-off. His line was so good that we didn't need a man behind for the ball slipping outside the off-stump.' Wardle also laid emphasis on the accuracy of his partner. 'In his first year he was a medium-pacer, with a very good quicker ball.

Bob was dead on line – leg stump or middle and leg – and straight over the top. He had the ability to vary his pace without the batsman being aware of it until it was too late. He sometimes bowled like Alec Bedser and sometimes like Jim Laker and you scarcely realised the difference until you were out.'

Bob Appleyard had privileged access to 'fountains of knowledge' during his swift learning curve with Yorkshire. As chauffeur to his mentors, Emmott Robinson and the county coach, Arthur Mitchell, on their journeys to and from cricket, he had earnestly questioned them on tactical topics. His sojourn in Australia did, though, call for a reappraisal of his bowling. It was yet another beginning and test of his skills.

The acclimatisation to alien conditions was a long haul and was not fully completed until his sterling endeavours at Adelaide. 'I had to develop a different form of attack. Spin was sparingly achieved so I had to rely on changes of pace and flight unlike in England where the wickets had provided much of the help. By the time of the Adelaide Test I felt that I had adjusted my bowling methods and done my homework on the Australian batsmen.' There was also the not inconsiderable factor of retaining focus in bowling eight ball overs. 'The extra two balls in that heat make a huge difference. A bowler must concentrate all the harder.'

Crawford White in the *News Chronicle,* praised Appleyard's newly wrought deceptions. 'They demand a refinement of bowling craft which only a few achieve. Appleyard had it in England when he took 200 wickets before he fell ill. He rediscovered it when he returned. And in Australia he fought to adjust his technique in entirely different circumstances to find it yet again.'

Frank Tyson has said that Appleyard was unlucky to bowl in a fast bowler's series in Australia. 'Bob swung and cut the ball and achieved a disconcerting bounce.' Tyson believes that with the supporting cast of Trevor Bailey, Appleyard and Wardle at Len Hutton's disposal England might easily have produced results comparable to those actually achieved. The proposition does not find favour with Bailey who contends that the pressure – psychological as well as physical – would have been lessened.

By his own account Appleyard regrets that his bowling workload was restricted in Australia. Back home in county cricket he revelled in his industry. 'If you didn't bowl a minimum of 20 overs – 28 was the average – in an innings you hadn't had your money's-worth. It was a poor day.' An equivalent share was denied him under Hutton's command. 'Len was, though, a great captain and his tactics were right. He was able to control affairs with his bowling. In a low-scoring series he couldn't afford to give runs away. He always had the quickies on against a new batsman.'

Ray Robinson, the Australian writer, pointedly disagreed with those who said that England's spoils were entirely due to Tyson and Statham. He maintained that the support given to the fast bowlers was much more than a fill-in nature. 'Both Appleyard and Bailey had an influence in taking good wickets at important times.' Robinson singled out Appleyard in his appreciative study. 'As a newcomer to Australian wickets, he found difficulty in making his off-spin turn at medium pace. But his craftsmanship was evident in his subtle changes of pace, his ability to make the ball drop and pop and his outward drift.'

Trevor Bailey, with his key all-round gifts, was a reassuring presence in Australia. He rarely opened with the new ball but few sides have had in reserve such an experienced bowler. His speed, as Arthur Morris, one Australian opponent noted, was below Statham's and directly paralleled the gap in pace between the latter and Tyson. Bailey was also a superb close fieldsman and his agility in this area was coupled with the limpet qualities as the anchor in England's middle order.

Bailey, on the second of his three tours of Australia, was especially effective against the left-handers and did much to restrain the aggression of Neil Harvey, Australia's greatest batsman. Neville Cardus, in his description of Bailey as a bowler, said that when he released the ball it was as strenuous and determined as the leap of a man at a bus that is nearly leaving him behind. The fluency of his cover-driving that he displayed with Essex contrasted with his patience in defensive vigils on Test duty. His Australian rivals testified to the frustrations they endured against a bat as completely locked as the door of a safe deposit.

The sobriquet of 'Barnacle' was in keeping with a player who positively thrived in adversity. It was never better demonstrated than in his rearguard action against Australia at Lord's in 1953. England looked doomed to defeat until his fifth wicket partnership of 163 runs with Willie Watson. It extended over four hours on a nerve-racking final day. The resolute pair kept Australia at bay and held the nation in suspense as the minutes and hours ticked by before the game was saved. Salvaging a draw at Lord's could be considered one of the turning points in the series. There was, though, another hurdle to overcome before England moved to a famous sporting climax.

Bailey was at his most influential in stemming a threatening advance by Australia at Leeds. First, when the expenditure of time was imperative, he resisted for over four hours in England's second innings. Then, his intervention as a bowler was crucial. Australia had been set a target of 177 in three minutes under two hours. Despite the loss of Hassett, who played on to Lock and Morris stumped off Laker, it was quickly apparent that they had taken up the chase. In a golden half hour Harvey and Hole scored 57 runs. The whirling scoreboard promised a win for Australia with time to spare.

Len Hutton, as captain, had spared Bailey because of his earlier batting exertions. Versions differ but it is said that Bailey seized the ball and belatedly entered the fray to halt the gallop. His con-centrated attack on the leg stump was sufficient to lower the tempo. 'Until the end the young Australians made strokes and took all they could from them,' reported Jim Swanton. 'Bailey's six overs had cost only nine runs and it was his excellent support of the unflagging Bedser that had tipped the scales.'

England in some disorder survived the ordeal. Bailey's leg-theory had won a reprieve and the opportunity to adhere to the winning script in regaining the Ashes at the Oval. A coveted victory was an event to remain in the hearts and minds of all that witnessed it. One observer expressed his delight in a moving phrase. He said: 'We are given memories so we can have roses in December.'

Richard Whitington was one Australian who responded to the die-hard spirit. 'If there was one adversary who got our goat in 1953 it was Bailey.' His contribution to the recovery of the Ashes, he wrote, ranked only after those of Hutton and Bedser. Bailey's stock in England was so high that he headed a popularity poll conducted by the *Daily Express*.

England – and Len Hutton – owed much to Bailey at this and other times. His record amply confirms his status as an all-rounder in the 1950s. In a span of ten years, covering tours to Australia, the West Indies, New Zealand and South Africa, he completed the rare feat of making 2,000 runs and taking 100 wickets in Tests. Bailey also achieved the double of 1,000 runs and 100 wickets on eight occasions, a record only exceeded by Wilfred Rhodes, George Hirst, Ewart Astill and Vallance Jupp. In 1959 he scored 2,000 runs and took 100 wickets, the first to achieve that feat since the second world war.

Bailey's penchant for slow scoring sometimes went beyond respectable bounds. At Brisbane in 1958 he spent nearly six hours – and faced 350 balls – in scoring 68. It is still the slowest fifty recorded in first-class cricket. The laborious effort, suggested Richie Benaud, the Australian captain in the series, must have brought about some clearing of the spectators' throats. Such trickles of runs – and the dead bat approach – have tended to overshadow his true stature as a team man. Bailey was a cricketer who believed that for a game to be played it must always first have a win as the principal objective. There were no half-measures whether he was looking for victory or trying to battle for an honourable draw.

Frank Tyson also applauds Bailey for his selflessness and his willingness to place the team before his own interests and to bat in whatever position the captain wanted him. In Australia in 1954–55 Len Hutton called upon Bailey to desert his normal middle order anchor role and open the innings in an attempt to resolve a persistent dilemma.

*

Bailey found a kindred spirit in Hutton, a like-minded man, circumspect and cautious in judgement and slow to praise or criticise. Their association, with the Essex man as vice-captain, prospered in the West Indies in the winter of 1953–54. This was a tour marred by menacing crowds and ill-temper. Alex Bannister considered it a 'sheer miracle that with so many distractions and worries off the field, Hutton was able to stand head and shoulders above any batsman on either side and to maintain his consistency and concentration.' Hutton headed the England batting averages with 677 runs, including a superb double century to help level the series in Jamaica.

At Sabina Park, Bailey was in inspired mood as a bowler. He took seven wickets for 34 runs in 16 overs. The figures were a record for England against the West Indies. They were also Bailey's best in Test cricket. 'Madness,' shrieked the *Jamaica Gleaner*. 'This can be the only reason for the West Indies batting side, accepted as the best in the world, scoring only 139 on a perfect wicket.' The *Wisden* correspondent was also perplexed by an unexpected downfall. 'In the circumstances, the utter collapse of the West Indians was incredible.' As Bailey himself admitted, he would have been pleased with figures only half as good in a county match played in similar conditions.

Bailey was buoyed by his sequence of successes. It began with the dismissal of Holt, superbly caught by Lock at short leg. The deadly thrusts continued as he swung the ball each way off a precise length. Occasionally he cut the ball sharply off the seam. One such ball claimed the prized wicket of Everton Weekes. It whipped back to bowl the West Indian champion. Fred Trueman then intervened to dismiss Worrell, another feared member of the powerful batting line-up. Worrell stabbed apprehensively at a fast short ball and was caught in the leg trap by Wardle.

The West Indies had lost four wickets for 13 runs in the opening 40 minutes. Bailey took three of them, including Stollmeyer, the home captain, at a personal cost of five runs. Clyde Walcott, the lynchpin of the West Indian batting in the series, almost alone saved his team from complete humiliation. He scored fifty in a fifth wicket recovery stand with Atkinson; and then hit 116, his third century of the series, in the second innings.

After his epic bowling feat Bailey still had work to do as he padded up to open England's innings with Hutton. But it was his bowling that had set the stage for the subsequent victory by nine wickets. One of the ironies of Bailey's triumph was that had Statham not been absent injured he might have been restricted to just a few overs. The West Indians, skittled by England's 'second-string' bowler, could not have fared worse against Statham.

In his sporting infancy Trevor Bailey had moved lightly on the stepping stones to a distinguished career. He was prolific as a schoolboy cricketer at Dulwich College. He would become revered for his wisdom among his fellow players, the greatest accolade of all. It was alleged that only a controversial newspaper article published under his name prevented his tactical acumen being translated into the England captaincy. Perhaps the truth is that he did not really covet the responsibility. His intelligence was always to be tapped by those appointed above him.

Bailey, himself a loyal lieutenant, confirms that Len Hutton inspired the same emotion in his team in Australia. 'Len was tactically excellent and didn't make many mistakes. He was very shrewd, having been raised in cricket among very tough competitors in Yorkshire.' Hutton's captaincy eschewed undue manipulation of his bowlers. 'Provided they were able, he would let them set their own fields, and only seek to bolster them with occasional suggestions,' adds Bailey.

Above all, in Australia, the fitness of the team was paramount. That it remained constant was due in no small measure to the decision of the MCC to appoint their own masseur, Harold Dalton, for the first time on an overseas tour. The secret of the staying powers, explains Bailey, was that 'we weren't over-trained.' The veteran does not hide his disdain at marathon preparations that dissipate energies required for cricket. 'The great thing is to bowl a good spell in the morning, another in the afternoon, and again in the

Australia bound: The *SS Orsova* which carried the MCC tourists to Australia, autographed by all of the party except Denis Compton, who went by air and Harold Dalton, masseur. Trevor Bailey signed twice.

The party: Back row, left to right: George Duckworth (baggage master & scorer), Keith Andrew, Peter Loader, Tom Graveney, Frank Tyson, Harold Dalton (masseur).
Middle row: Johnny Wardle, Reg Simpson, Vic Wilson, Bob Appleyard, Jim McConnon, Brian Statham, Colin Cowdrey, Geoffrey Howard (manager).
Front row: Trevor Bailey, Bill Edrich, Peter May, Len Hutton (captain), Denis Compton, Alec Bedser, Godfrey Evans.

A good luck sprig of white heather for Len Hutton. Colin Cowdrey, Harold Dalton and Alec Bedser share the spirit of optimism.

The England captain in relaxed mood during the stopover in Colombo.

A porter at Northampton's Castle railway station gives Frank Tyson a low-key send off before the tour.

WICKET KEEPER   20 YDS.   22

Tyson's run – 72 yards to the wicket-keeper.

Two bowling executioners together. Tyson with Harold Larwood at his Sydney home. (Frank Tyson)

Inspecting the wicket before a match against a local eleven in Colombo: Hutton, Appleyard, Loader, Wilson and Bedser.

Tyson (seated far left with his mentor Dennis Brookes and Raman Subba Row alongside him) in a Northamptonshire team group, 1959. (Sport & General.)

Len Hutton, the peerless champion in his apprentice days with Yorkshire. (Topical Times.) Fleet-footed on the attack with a resplendent off-drive. (MCC.)

Len Hutton leads out the England team against India at Headingley in 1952. Also pictured left to right: Alec Bedser, Peter May, Denis Compton, Reg Simpson, Allan Watkins, Jim Laker, Godfrey Evans, Tom Graveney. Obscured are Roley Jenkins and Fred Trueman. (Mick Pope.)

Hutton with his vice-captain Peter May at Melbourne in 1954.

Godfrey Evans demonstrates his wicket-keeping acrobatics as he gathers a return to sweep off the bails.
(Mary Willis-Evans/The Cricketers Club.)

The agility of Evans was best demonstrated in this astounding catch in the third Test at Melbourne. Neil Harvey was the prized victim and his dismissal effectively won the game for England. Frank Tyson was the bowler.

On the final morning Tyson took six wickets for 16 runs as Australia collapsed to 111 all out. Richie Benaud was another of the hapless batsmen, pictured here dragging the ball onto his wicket.

The majesty of Keith Miller, the unpredictable genius who caused tremors of anxiety in his opening spells at Melbourne and Adelaide. At Melbourne he reduced England to 41 for four, conceding only five runs in nine overs.

Trevor Bailey – England's premier allrounder in the 1950s. (Trevor Bailey.)

An aerial view of the Adelaide Oval where England clinched the Ashes.

Spectators at the turnstiles, counting their shillings and pence then the currency for admission. (Bernard Whimpress/Adelaide Advertiser.)

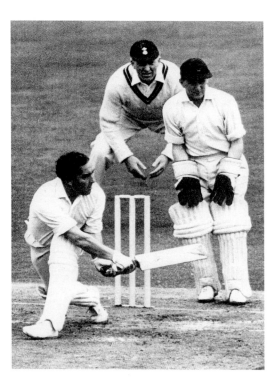

The Middlesex twins Compton and Edrich in characteristic action studies. The 1954-55 Ashes series was their farewell tour of Australia. At Adelaide, as in the Coronation year at the Oval, Compton once more stepped into the breach to resist Australia.

Tom Graveney (centre) whose century in the fifth Test at Sydney earned him belated recognition is pictured with Peter May (left) and Peter Loader. (Daily News.)

A morning run on the sands at the Adelaide resort of Glenelg for Frank Tyson, Johnny Wardle, Bill Edrich and Vic Wilson.

evening, a total of 28 overs in the day.' Faced with such challenges, it is, he contends an unnecessary imposition to be subjected to a pre-match fitness regime. 'You don't want to have bowled the equivalent of another eight overs before the game has started.'

Harry Altham, the chairman of the selectors, ascribed a well-being other than fitness in his assessment of England's recovery in Australia. He reflected on the moral stamina of the team, which had enabled them to close ranks when the seams might have burst open after the early reverse in Brisbane. One incident after that devastating defeat seemed to communicate his own low state. 'The day after the news reached us of the loss in Brisbane, I was leaving my house in London carrying a small bag. One bystander, clearly aware of the dire sports bulletin, jokingly tried to rally him. A painter perched on a ladder at a first floor window looked down on the disconsolate Altham and said: 'Fleeing the country, I see, sir!'

The depression of the cricket chairman would be lifted in the ensuing months by more encouraging news of events in Australia. He did not have to raise a rueful smile at the smug posters that festoon the boundary walls at Adelaide. 'In the city of churches England does not have a prayer,' is how Australians greet visiting supporters on Ashes days. Bob Appleyard remembers a time when the parochial local partisans did not have cause to gloat in their devotions. 'They were sympathetic at first in our plight but this became less so as the series progressed.'

Appleyard was the bowler waiting to seize his opportunity in the decisive fourth Test at Adelaide. The bells ringing out at nearby St Peter's Cathedral seemed to herald his coming success. By a cruel irony, in these idyllic surroundings, he was deprived of a handsome haul of wickets on a wearing pitch.

10

Trouncing the Doubters
at Adelaide

'England held the psychological advantage after Melbourne but they were only marginal favourites, if that, to win the Ashes.'

John Woodcock, former *Times* cricket correspondent.

England's cricketers would have been excused a rueful smile as they took the field in the fourth Test at Adelaide. Australia had won the toss and had elected to bat to the surprise of nobody. The wicket was perfect – the best in the series so far – and the Australian camp was in buoyant mood in anticipation of a good performance and a levelling of the series. On this broiling January day the temperature was rising inexorably into the upper nineties. Stretching out on the skyline were the thickly wooded slopes of the Mount Lofties burnt dappled shades of brown by the summer heat.

The task confronting England appeared to be in contradiction of the confident forecasts in London where odds of three to one had been laid against Australia. Jim Swanton voiced disagreement when he said that for those on the spot a level bet more accurately gauged the situation.

Percy Beames in the *Melbourne Age* also went along with the pre-match theories. He believed that Australia, given first use of a docile wicket, could bounce back and produce a victory similar to that obtained at Brisbane. 'Friendly allies to our batsmen will be the easy-paced Adelaide wicket and the enervating heat.' Bill O'Reilly, while accepting that England were favourites, thought that their attack would falter as it wrestled with the irritating demands of a featherbed pitch.

Stifling the menace of Tyson and Statham was by now a familiar rallying call from all Australia's commentators. Could they be revealed as lambs in wolves' clothing on these gentle pastures? The fervent hope was that the opening batsmen, McDonald and Morris would emerge unharmed. O'Reilly's views for home consumption carried a note of wishful thinking. As a former spinner, he might have been inclined to consider more closely the threat posed to Australia by England's spin attack Instead he assured his readers in the *Sydney Morning Herald* that he did not expect either Wardle or Appleyard, to worry the Australian batsmen.

Appleyard, 'this shrewd, determined cricket character', as Crawford White described him, confounded the prophecy. The Yorkshireman took the wickets of McDonald, Miller and Benaud, the latter two in the space of three overs, and on the morning of the second day Australia had lost eight wickets for 229 runs. Appleyard was the prime cause of unease among the home batsmen as he acclimatised to Australian conditions. Richard Whitington offered a glimpse of the ensuing events in his eulogy: 'The probing Appleyard was the kangaroo tamer, unwaveringly he held the whip in his hand. It was a whip made of perfect length, occasional spin and subtle variations in pace and lift.'

The much cooler weather on the second day seemed to invigorate Australia's ninth wicket pair, Ian Johnson and Len Maddocks. Denzil Batchelor, in his watching brief, wrote: 'The five palms and towering gum trees ringing the ground stirred as a pleasant breeze rose in the morning and behind the foliage, at the river end, a fountain shimmered like a plume of smoke. In the evening, flocks of gulls soared above the pitch and floated to settle like some miraculous snowfall inside the boundary. Eleven tram conductors sat posed, like a school group, on the top of a tramcar on the edge of the ground.'

The disinterested onlookers were resting before the exodus of spectators began. Talk on the trams would be all about Australia's remarkable recovery. Johnson and Maddocks, who was again preferred as wicket-keeper ahead of his South Australian rival, Gil Langley, added 92 runs in as many minutes. 'With enterprise and daring, they completely wrecked the normal England field placing and tamed an unrelenting attack that had shamed the best Australian batting for a day and a half,' wrote Percy Beames.

Maddocks, top scorer with 69, was hailed as the saviour of the hour. It was his best innings for Australia and his straight drives were applauded by Denzil Batchelor. 'Twice in an over he hit rising balls from Tyson off his ear lobe, once to the boundary and another thereabouts.' Maddocks though, did survive two chances, both difficult, before opening his account. After the dismissal of Davidson, and when batting with the Australian captain Ian Johnson, he was restored in heart and confidence.

Beames enthused about the influence of Johnson in helping to retrieve the situation. 'His batting was a resounding answer to those critics who claim he has served no useful purpose in the team.' The aggression displayed in his innings of 41 was reflected in the fact that half of the runs came in boundaries. 'If the same adventurous spirit is infused into the fielding of his team and driven into the bowlers his captaincy will leave nothing for criticism,' added the *Melbourne Age* correspondent.

Bill O'Reilly maintained that Maddocks had fully merited his much criticised selection. Until he ran himself out he had become the newly-enthroned hero of the Adelaide public. 'The ovation given to him,' said O'Reilly, 'was one of the most spontaneously friendly that I can remember. Maddocks's innings could be held up as a shining example of the intelligent application of fundamental batting principles.' Australia were finally dismissed for 323, a total beyond expectations before the rousing partnership. It had begun in the utmost extremity and defiantly changed the whole complexion of the game.

It was a plucky if fortuitous catch by Alan Davidson that deprived Len Hutton of a deserved century in England's reply. One Yorkshire journalist clearly expressed his allegiance when he said: 'They never catch Denis Compton like that!' It was a departure from neutrality of the press. The debonair Compton was known as the 'Brylcreem Boy' because he advertised a glowing hair cream then in vogue. In Yorkshire this only served to increase the rivalry between him and their own favourite son. Hutton was dismissed for 80, his best innings of the series, after adding 99 runs for the third wicket with Colin Cowdrey. 'It had been,' said Alan Ross, 'a monastic innings, for which Hutton had prepared himself mentally through the same kind of contemplative discipline as a Cistercian exercises towards the refining of his soul.'

Hutton chose Australia Day for his own celebration and revival in form. For four and a half hours he kept his opponents at bay. In his vigil against a consistently dangerous and unflagging attack, he provided an exemplary display of his skills. It was an innings, said one Australian observer, to communicate joy as well as an education for friend and foe alike. 'Not even Bradman has used more of the ground between his stumps and the popping crease than did Hutton with such decisive and geometrical precision.'

Denzil Batchelor wrote that the long afternoon was a golden day-dream for England. 'Hutton had become again the Hutton of auld lang syne: firm in defence, coldly accurate in keeping the spinners out of the wicket, even if he had to bend backwards over it to preserve his life. And once in a while greatness flowered from his bat, like a miraculous thorn in a mid-winter garden. When Benaud bowled at him into the wind he hit him through the covers as if the place was Taunton and the time a relaxing hour after the tea interval on the third day.'

Wisden reported that the pitch was already favouring spin, a fact duly noted by Ian Johnson in his bowling plan. His off-spin was deployed in tandem with Benaud's leg-breaks. Between them they delivered 73 overs of the 140 sent down during England's innings of 341. At tea on the third day Johnson's analysis was a remarkable 30–17–27–1. His accuracy gave substance to the merits of Hutton and Cowdrey. The copybook defence of the junior partner was also attuned to the exigencies of the situation. He was the epitome of correctness and ordered judgement.

A cultured partnership, with Cowdrey as impenetrable as his captain, was severed by the sharp reflexes of Davidson, one of the finest close fieldsmen in the game. He risked decapitation as Hutton unerringly hooked a long hop from Johnston. Davidson, only a few yards from the bat at forward short-leg, put up his hands to protect himself. It resulted in a spectacular catch as he doubled up and extracted the ball from his middle. Davidson recalls: 'I don't think Len expected me to see it. He was very upset. I caught him off a full-blooded pull. It was one of my better catches.'

England, once again bolstered by late order contributions, led by 18 runs on the first innings. The tempo was increased in a flurry of hitting, notably by Evans. He was disdainful in his treatment of Miller and Davidson and hooked the former twice to the boundary in one over. The stage was now set for Bob Appleyard, as Frank Tyson recalls. 'Brian (Statham) and I did not make much of an impression when Australia batted for the second time just after the tea interval. So Len brought Bob on at the Cathedral End. This is where it all started to happen. Bob bowled like a dream. He was an awkward bugger, making the ball bounce and turn. The press was in no doubt that he would win the Test for England on the following day.'

Hutton, in fact, gave only two overs to Statham before introducing Appleyard. The move was hailed as a touch of genius. Appleyard exploited the worn patches caused by the bowlers' footmarks. He also opened up a mental chasm as deep as a mountain gorge. Deft spin accounted for Morris, Burke and Harvey – the latter from a ball, which pitched on leg and knocked out the off stump. The seductive weapon was flight, the secret of which, in the bright atmosphere of Australia, Appleyard had worked so hard to discover. It first undermined Morris who gave a return catch. Harvey was then deceived so badly that he was halfway round to square leg in attempting a hook when the ball rattled his stumps.

There was one distressing factor, which may have contributed to the dismissal of Morris. It was an accident to Cowdrey, fielding very close in the gully. It occurred in the fourth ball of an over delivered by Appleyard. Morris struck it hard and the ball came steeply off the ground and fractured Cowdrey's nose. Richard Whitington wrote:

'For minutes Cowdrey lay prone on his back, not a sign of life in his body and blood streaming down his face.' 'I thought I had killed him,' said Morris afterwards. 'Of all the cricketers I'd least like to hurt, Colin is number one.' Two balls later Morris, his concentration broken by the interruption, played too soon and Appleyard happily accepted the return catch.

During this phase, Appleyard's control caught the attention of one Australian observer. 'It spoke volumes for his accuracy that May and Compton could stand, quite safely, in a two-man leg trap, fore and aft of square, and almost as close as Vic Richardson and Jack Fingleton ever stood for that master of control, Bill O'Reilly.' In his first six overs Appleyard recorded figures of three wickets for six runs. Australia, at the close, were 69 for three, with McDonald and Miller at the crease.

Crawford White, in the *News Chronicle*, reflected on what had been for Australia a demoralising spell. Appleyard's brilliant bowling in the closing stages of the fourth day, he wrote, had done as much as anything to bring about the exceptional events of the fifth. Appleyard had swept aside the backbone of Australia's batting. With three key opponents safely snared – and the remaining batsmen undoubtedly worried – the torch had been ignited to plunge Australia into the flames.

'Curtains' was a favourite Australian expression for last orders and it was bleakly voiced that night by the partisans making their way under the paths by the elms and plane trees that lead from the cricket Oval to North Terrace in the city. Even the most fervent of patriots in the crowds could not escape the general pessimism.

'Oh! For an Appleyard Sigh the Aussies' crowed the headline in the *Daily Express* on the following morning. Hutton however had no further use for his bowling despite a wicket especially suited to his off-breaks. Appleyard had engineered the breakthrough and his job was now done. Len Hutton had been haunted by the consequences of losing the toss but he maintained his belief that the fury of Tyson and Statham would not be curbed by Adelaide's gentle wicket. On the last morning he turned once again to his young pacemen.

Frank Tyson recalled: 'On that morning Brian Statham and I had returned from a run along the Glenelg beach. I lay on my bed, eating breakfast and reading the papers. Every one, down to the last drop of ink, confidently stated that Appleyard was the danger man to Australia's hopes and that he would be the player to watch.'

Eyebrows were raised at Hutton's decision but Sidney Barnes, the former Australian Test batsmen, wrote that the pair bowled as if they were rivals in a speed test. 'They took over from where Appleyard left off and mowed Australia down as though they were bursting soap bubbles.'

The zest of Statham was not impaired by an injury to his big toe which had festered after a nail had been removed. He wore a specially adapted boot. *Wisden* reported: 'Statham, freed from pain by having a hole cut in his left boot, which allowed his injured toe to move freely, staggered Australia.' It was yet another episode of shattering pace. Statham began the rout with his third ball of the day, a fast yorker that made a whirligig of McDonald's middle stump. The total had moved on by just seven runs when Miller was back in the pavilion. He sought to aim a blow at Statham and, in keeping with the Lancastrian's philosophy, the batsman missed and the bowler hit, the ball trimming Miller's stumps.

Denzil Batchelor reported: 'Then Benaud came and went. He moved like a sleepwalker in front of the wicket to a buzzing beauty from Tyson. Next it was Maddocks' turn. The champion of the lost cause in the first innings was a cowed prisoner of circumstance in the second. He padded across to cover his stumps like a victim of hypnosis.'

Batchelor continued: 'Statham's speed and accuracy had set their hallmark on the day, but Tyson was bowling with flamboyant brilliance, too. It was his turn next, when Archer, with a torn thigh muscle, arrived at the wicket. He played in a dazed fashion for seventeen minutes before he swung with villainous abandon at a ball scurrying away from the off-stump, to be caught by Evans, almost genteelly.' Australia, at lunch, were 103 for nine, having lost six wickets for 34 runs.

Tyson and Statham bowled unchanged for 90 minutes, sharing the wickets and together conceding only 29 runs. Davidson, who had alone baulked England, was dismissed by spin after the interval. In a neat finale it would have been fitting for Appleyard to claim the last wicket, but it was Wardle, his Yorkshire partner, who trapped Davidson leg before. Australia's total of 111 was the lowest at Adelaide for over sixty years. It was also, oddly enough, the same score as in their second innings in the previous Test at Melbourne.

Frank Tyson recalled another boiling hot morning and how after an hour's bowling Hutton had given no indication that he and Statham were to be rested. 'It was a paradoxical piece of captaincy that a skipper who had given his fast bowlers only a taste of the new ball on a turning wicket, should persevere with them when the ball was old and the wicket still turning.'

Hutton was aware of the psychological advantage presented to him by Tyson and Statham. He drove them almost to breaking point on that dramatic morning. In temperatures that never fell below 90 degrees even to walk about was a drain on energy. For the bowlers the last 15 minutes before lunch dragged interminably. 'Somewhere along the way,' said Tyson, 'I had strained my groin. Towards the end of the morning I felt I could continue no longer.'

Tyson communicated his exhausted state to Statham who was fielding at mid-off. 'Come on,' urged Brian. 'Just another few overs. We've only one wicket to go.' The morning came to a merciful end for the bowlers. Tyson said that it was fortunate that Wardle took the final wicket. 'Had it been left to me, I doubt whether I could have summoned up energy to have even appealed.'

England needed 94 to win, a gentle stroll in most circumstances, except that this was another occasion when Keith Miller decided that it was a far from easy task. The unpredictable genius was stirred into mighty action. 'Who is going to win?' was the apparently banal question posed by one bystander as the Australians took the field. Miller, with an evil grin, replied: 'I've got a feeling that somebody is in for a nasty half hour.'

The cricketer he had in mind was his old adversary, Len Hutton.

He was shocked by his own swift dismissal and even more aggrieved when Miller also took the wickets of Edrich and Cowdrey for 10 runs in 20 balls. 'Miller's magnificent effort came after Australia's cocktail-party batting had left her hopes of regaining the Ashes right in the bottom of the ashcan,' commented Richard Whitington. 'Three perfect length and perfectly directed out-cutters worked this miracle.'

The rout started when Edrich was bowled for a duck by one late moving and unplayable ball in the first over. Five minutes later Miller repeated the delivery to Hutton and Davidson blandly took a low catch at second slip. Eight runs were added in 15 tense minutes before Cowdrey edged another lethal outswinger and was athletically caught by Archer.

Alan Davidson recalls the counter-attack by Miller. He says that unlike in England's first innings his second catch to take Hutton's wicket was in the more orthodox category. 'Len nicked one and I dived and caught it with my left hand virtually off Ron Archer's boots at first slip.' Davidson recalls the dismay of Hutton at the tumble of wickets. 'The buggers have done us,' was his forlorn cry. It was not quite as dire as that but it was a jolt to plunge an anxious man into gloom again. He carried a weight of responsibility and his own dismissal was a personal blow because of his belief that he could bat individually through to an ardently desired conclusion. Davidson says: 'It was one of those games where a modest score became quite a challenge.'

England's total now stood at 18 for three but calm appeared to have been restored when Miller, exhausted by his supreme effort, was withdrawn from the attack. May now carried the fight to Australia with a bold onslaught. 'No praise could be too high for May,' commented Jim Swanton. 'He met the Australian challenge with a series of fine forceful strokes and yet never verged on rashness.'

The innings came to an abrupt end through a controversial catch off Johnston. Miller hurtled to the ground to clutch the ball from a powerful drive to extra cover. It was one of those marginal instances where doubt could be cast on whether the ball had carried to the fieldsman. Denis Compton, at the other end, thought it was not a clean catch and signalled frantically for May to remain at the wicket.

Frank Tyson recalls the incident: 'Peter drove a low skimmer into the covers. Miller dived to his right and picked the ball up. Peter asked: "Did you catch that, Keith?" Miller replied: "Yes" and Peter walked off.' It was an important if dubious breakthrough with the target still 45 runs away. Tyson does not directly charge Miller with unfairness except to say that in the pressure of the situation the Australian might have slipped below his normal gallantry.

It was the old hands, Compton and Bailey, who at last steered England home. The inconsolable Hutton had been cheered by Compton's response to his downfall. 'Denis was livid,' said Frank Tyson. 'He grabbed his bat and marched out of the pavilion, mouthing his defiance: "I'll show you who has beaten us."' Here was no swashbuckling playboy but a craftsman, well versed in a crisis, using all the canons of correctness in England's cause.

Jim Swanton wrote: 'Compton has had much ill luck to fight in these last few years. It was good indeed to see him playing so masterfully in the crisis and taking out his bat at the finish as he had done at the Oval in 1953.'

The England veterans 'slowly and carefully handled Australia's panoply of bowling like beekeepers safe from sting until Bailey faltered on the threshold of victory,' wrote Frank Rostron. Bailey, with four runs needed, attempted a spectacular flourish to end the game and was lbw to Johnston. Godfrey Evans, capering like a vaudevillian, came in to lift the final boundary over the head of square leg to seal the issue.

It was Swanton again, in the *Daily Telegraph*, who provided a wondering postscript on the transformation in England's fortunes. 'Nine weeks ago this evening Australia inflicted upon Len Hutton's team one of the most conclusive defeats in Test history by an innings and 154 runs. If anyone on that depressing day at Brisbane had expressed the belief that England would have won the series by the end of the Adelaide Test, he would have been supposed an insane optimist.'

A revealing sidelight on England's supremacy was shown just a few months later. Australia escaped the chains of their destroyers on their first tour of the West Indies, which immediately followed the Ashes series. A virtually unchanged Australian team, admittedly in propitious batting conditions and against modest bowling, scored massively and fully rehabilitated themselves. It was a commanding statement to help reduce the shame of the performance against England. They achieved a feat that had eluded all previous touring teams to the Caribbean. The margin of victory was 3–0, with two matches drawn. In twenty years before this reverse the West Indies had never been beaten at home. Neil Harvey headed the Australian comeback with 650 runs in the rubber and the old firm of Lindwall and Miller shared 40 wickets.

England's victory in Australia did not exceed the expectations of a bravely resilient group of cricketers. Before the euphoria of the Ashes triumph Bill Edrich and Godfrey Evans – and the rest of the MCC party – demonstrated their faith in a successful outcome to the series. The post-match odds after the overwhelming defeat at Brisbane were eight to one in Australia's favour. The response seemed to be the wildest of wagers. 'All the boys clubbed together to put £100 into the kitty for the bet,' said Evans. When victory was finally sealed Godfrey and Bill were deputed to go along to Tattersalls to collect the winnings, amounting to £800.

They entered the seedy premises in a state of some apprehension. In the darkened office they encountered a group of steely-eyed and roughly attired bookmakers. It is perhaps not overstating the matter to say that in these quarters they seemed likely to assaulted. All the men displayed an obvious reluctance to part with the money. Bill said: 'We've got to be careful here, Godders.' Godfrey whispered words of encouragement.

The prospect of a battle, extending to fisticuffs, appeared certain. The cricketers stood their ground but it was a moment of disquiet. Edrich said: 'Let's get the money and move out quickly.' They grimly asked for the bet to be honoured. At length the wager was acknowledged and the winnings released, but it was a close call. Bill and Godfrey thankfully sought the safety of the street.

Edrich never did waver in a crisis, nor did he ever give way to pain. A competitive soccer interlude in Australia provided one example. At the age of thirty-eight, he played in a match between the MCC and the press on Christmas Day. It was played on the beach at Glenelg, the seaside suburb of Adelaide, just outside the team's headquarters at the Pier Hotel. Frank Tyson recalled: 'Bill received the ball and made his way towards the opposition goal, slowly sinking lower and lower as he yielded to the earlier festive spirits and the taxing demands of sand under foot.

'Eventually he sprawled full-length in the shingle, skinning the whole of one side of his face. It was an awful mess. But he got up immediately, shook and wiped the blood away and carried on playing.' Tyson added: 'I don't know what the spectators thought when they saw "Scarface" going jauntily out to bat on the following day at the Adelaide Oval.'

Edrich belied his advancing years in another outrageous escapade. It was a daring and exuberant display of his own joy, as England celebrated the winning of the Ashes at the Pier Hotel. His stunning late night party trick was to swarm twenty feet to the pinnacle of a glistening marble pillar in the foyer of the hotel. He stayed there, like a puckish Nelson, grinning hugely and refused to come down. His team-mates, in a nervous huddle below, could not help but laugh and rejoice with him.

A glorious triumph was celebrated more soberly back home in England. Harry Altham was listening in his pyjamas to the broadcast of the last overs at Adelaide. He was staying with Billy Griffith, the MCC Assistant Secretary. One of the first duties of England's cricket chairman after breakfast was to ask his host to send a cable to Hutton's men in Australia. 'Well done,' announced the wire, 'Magnificent performance. Flags hoisted at Lord's.'

Herbert Sutcliffe, a member of England's last winning team in Australia in 1932–33, sent his congratulations from Yorkshire. He expressed his pleasure at an unexpected achievement. 'I hardly expected our team to win the Ashes. I feel that a touring side has to be 20 per cent better than their opponents to win a series in Australia.' Sutcliffe especially praised the team for overcoming conditions entirely different from those experienced in England. 'We are delighted that Hutton has been able to make use of his great knowledge of the game which has been such an important part in turning the tables on Australia.'

Harry Altham also applauded the endurance of the England captain amid the strain of his responsibilities, and constant, sometimes crippling, back pains. So intense had been Hutton's involvement even before the Adelaide Test that a case full of congratulations on England's recovery remained unanswered. Geoffrey Howard, the MCC manager, was alerted to his captain's lapse. He was anxious not to offend the well-wishers and organised stereotyped replies and asked Hutton to 'top and tail' the messages.

As a dutiful and absent father, Hutton would surely not have failed to acknowledge one family greeting. His sons, Richard and John, along with their fellow pupils at Wood Hall School, Wetherby, were given the afternoon off by their headmaster, John Catlow. The boys had listened on a portable radio in the matron's room to the news from Adelaide. Mr Catlow paid for a telegram of congratulations to be sent to their father. It read: 'Hooray! Love, Richard and John.'

The happy ending laid the seal on a tale of good companions in Australia. Their relations would be formalised in the setting up of a little social club on another tour down under four years later. Three veterans of the glory days – Trevor Bailey, Godfrey Evans and Frank Tyson -were joined by a newcomer, Raman Subba Row, the Surrey and Northamptonshire batsman. Their initials – B-E-S-T – had an appealing ring to them. At the head of the table was the last named. The 'Typhoon' had not forgotten the pleasures of his mastery. Glasses were raised at his direction. 'Drink up,' he said, 'remember we are the best.'

11

Silver Lining for a Cavalier

'Graveney's batting was a revelation in opening tactics. No one could say that he was anything but Test match material in temperament, poise and technique today.'

Bill O'Reilly.

Exceptional storms, the worst in New South Wales for fifty years, delayed the start of the fifth Test in Sydney until two o'clock on the fourth day. The rains relented just in time for Tom Graveney to deliver a batting masterpiece. The composure of his maiden Test century against Australia silenced his critics, who could not but marvel at this overdue demonstration of a flawless technique and intense concentration. The innings was judged in many quarters as the finest exhibition of complete batsmanship seen during the whole tour.

Graveney's century came in exactly 150 minutes, including fourteen fours that made it one of the fastest hundreds by an English player against Australia. He plundered the Australian attack in the way that Matthew Hayden and Adam Gilchrist, of today's Australians usually treat opposing bowlers.

Graveney was a late replacement as opening batsman for Bill Edrich and recalls: 'I didn't know I was playing. Len went out and lost the toss and Ian Johnson put us in. As he walked back to the pavilion, Len called out: "Tom, put your pads on and come in with me"' Their association did not last long as Hutton was out in the first over of the match, the result of some clever tactics by Lindwall.

Graveney remembers that Peter Burge, one of Lindwall's colleagues in Queensland, was playing in his first Test. 'Keep your eyes open for me,' was Lindwall's exhortation to the new recruit. Hutton leg-glanced the first ball for four; off the fourth he looked to repeat the stroke. As the ball swung in and away outside leg stump, Hutton followed it as if mesmerised. Burge, fielding 10 yards away at leg slip, juggled the catch then took it at the second attempt. Graveney adds: 'Lindwall was a magnificent bowler, the best I've ever played against. He had actually nominated how Len would be out before he went on to the field.'

Then followed a partnership between Graveney and Peter May which yielded 182 runs in two hours and 40 minutes and included Graveney's own classic innings. Bill O'Reilly reported: 'Graveney's batting was a revelation in opening tactics. Enthusiastic and well-timed front of the wicket play is not generally associated with batting against the new ball. Such methods are commonly regarded as highly dangerous. But Graveney drove gracefully and powerfully, and much too frequently for the peace of mind of the Australian captain and his attack.'

'I have never seen a greater Graveney,' enthused Denzil Batchelor. 'He wasn't saucy – he was superior. He picked Lindwall off his toes to propel him through the sluggish outfield. He square-cut Miller lavishly for three. He swung Johnson to the legside boundary for the four that gave him his half century in an hour and a quarter, and immediately afterwards stroked him past fine leg, as one imagines Ranji might have done, for another boundary.'

Richard Whitington commented that Graveney resembled a master cricket coach giving the Australians a much-needed batting lesson. Peter May also joined in the revelry, making deep incisions in the field. One onlooker remarked that he turned a 'respectable dance into ragtime' as he bombarded the picket fence.

Graveney moved like a king to his coronation as he advanced to his first hundred against Australia. With his score at 84, he struck four boundaries in succession to reach his goal.

Keith Miller, the bowler under assault at Sydney, was a good and valued friend. 'Keith was bowling around the wicket really just to keep things quiet,' remembers Graveney. 'I hit the first boundary wide of cover and the second wide of mid-on. Four balls later I cracked one straight past him for another four.'

There were now two balls remaining in Miller's over. 'Keith bowled the slowest long hop you've ever seen down the legside and I missed it. Then he did it again so I could get my hundred.' Graveney says that this was a typical example of Miller's generosity. 'He knew that I'd had a rough time on the tour. That's the sort of bloke he was.'

Bill Bowes, in the *Yorkshire Evening News*, enthused about the stand between Graveney and May. Eleven runs after reaching his century Graveney was out. A brilliant display ended when he 'hit the ball like a kicking horse straight back, knee high, at Johnson, who caught it.' Bowes said that Graveney was cheered ecstatically all the way back to the pavilion. 'Even the Australian fieldsmen ran to congratulate him. With Peter May, at the other end also taking full toll, the Australian bowling suffered punishment not seen since that other Gloucestershire batsman, Charles Barnett scored 98 before lunch at Nottingham in 1938.'

Len Hutton was reported to have said that he regretted not giving Graveney more opportunities as an opening batsman in the series. The apologia elicited a waggish response from one Australian humorist. 'Who is going to open with Graveney in New Zealand?' he asked.

An exhilarating innings prompted Bill O'Reilly to say that England had discovered a batsman for the opening vacancy. Graveney was aware of the expectations but he adds a rueful footnote. 'It did mean that I was retained as opening batsman for three Tests for England against South Africa in the following summer. My reward was to face their fast bowlers, Heine and Adcock, no easy task.'

There was one other statistic to place alongside his century and produce a beam of pleasure. Graveney took his only Test wicket at Sydney when he dismissed McDonald – caught by Evans – in Australia's second innings.

The label of 'fair weather' cricketer borne by Graveney during the series carried derisive overtones. It was, according to Geoffrey

Howard, the MCC manager, at least in part due to the fact that Len Hutton was prejudiced against his Gloucestershire colleague. 'I'm sure Tom should have played in more than the two Tests allocated to him, on both occasions at Sydney,' said Howard. 'He was not one of Len's favourites and not the sort of character to attract his admiration. Tom could be a little flippant, perhaps because he was aware of Len's view of him.'

Hutton, observed one writer, rationed his brilliance because day in day out, year in, year out, cricket was his life and livelihood. Bob Appleyard portrays the differing attitudes. 'Len had had to work for his success and he suspected those like Tom who did not make the most of their abilities.'

If, as was suggested, Graveney lacked discipline in his early years, it was because he could make glorious waves and then succumb ingloriously. An analogy has been made with another fine stroke-maker, David Gower. Graveney would later tell Patrick Murphy: 'He went through the same wall of criticism as I faced. If he played a lovely shot, he won all the praise but if a stump was uprooted, they'd say: "what a terrible shot." You simply have to play the way it suits you as a batsman.'

Graveney insists that for him cricket was just a game which probably gave cause for offence to those who invested it with a loftier significance. Conversely, he was strict in his preparations – an avid practiser in the nets – and he was just as hurt as anyone if he erred in judgement as a batsman. In Australia an attack of influenza kept him out of the first Test at Brisbane. It paved the way for the entry of the gifted newcomer, Colin Cowdrey. Graveney was selected for the next Test at Sydney in place of the injured Denis Compton.

'I batted quite well in the first innings when the wicket was doing a bit,' says Graveney. His downfall in the second innings was, he says, the time when 'Len gave up on me.' He was considered a liability by Hutton and did not feature in his battle plan. 'Big Bill (Johnston) bowled his first ball across me and I let it go. I thought the next one was a half volley and went for the drive.' It took the edge and he was out – c Langley b Johnston, 0.

This was one of those indiscreet ventures and Graveney admits his guilt. 'I enjoyed every minute of my time in cricket except when I did silly things like that.'

Assertions by Australians that Graveney would never have been omitted from one of their Test sides were cynically regarded in some English quarters as a kind of double bluff, an instance of their sharp practice. Richie Benaud, a future Australian captain, was one admiring competitor. 'We never sung Tom's praises unless we were asked and then we said he should be in the England team.' Benaud strongly believed that a prejudice existed against Graveney's style of batting.'

The latent genius of Graveney inevitably drew him into an illustrious assembly of Gloucestershire cricketers. Before him W.G. Grace, Gilbert Jessop, Charles Barnett and Wally Hammond had held centre stage at Bristol. For one West Country spokesman, writing in the *Cricketer* in 1957, the debate had to concentrate on the merits of Grace, Hammond and Graveney. Dr. E.M Grace, a nephew of 'W.G.', had told him: 'He [Grace]was more dominating than Hammond. He could be ruthless on the field, but kind and appreciative afterwards. His word was law.'

In 1948 when Sir Pelham Warner spoke at the unveiling of plaques during the Grace Centenary at Bristol, Gloucestershire were playing Derbyshire. Two young professionals from the Peak county inspected the plaques. 'Why did he cock his left foot like that?' asked one. 'That – me lad', said a senior player, 'was to trap the yorker.'

Charles Barnett testified to Hammond's dominance in his heyday between the two world wars. 'It was an education to bat with him,' he recalled. 'But you were lucky to get two balls in an over if he was in the mood to plunder the bowling. With the lightest of strides, he could make a good length ball into an overpitched one.'

So how did Graveney fit into the roll call of Gloucestershire personalities? The *Cricketer* correspondent regarded him as the greatest enigma of the time. 'It is impossible to write him off merely as a brilliant county batsman, for he treats Test bowlers – *outside Tests* –with contempt. Dr. Grace, he said, had probably summed up the situation best when he maintained that 'W.G' was ruthless on the field. Hammond had possessed the same trait, but Graveney has it only to a minor degree.

Graveney expressed himself as a batsman in a different manner from Hammond. Even in the heat of the battle he could enjoy a joke with the opposition. 'The present Gloucestershire star occasionally talks to fielders and the bowlers,' continued the correspondent. 'He thoroughly enjoys his cricket – a D'Artagnan of a player who entertains first and treats record breaking as a by-product. In contrast Hammond's taciturnity was intensified by his terrific powers of concentration.'

The expectation that Graveney would assume the mantle of Hammond was an unfair imposition. But by his own lights Graveney shone as one of the most brilliant stroke-playing batsmen in the country in the 1950s. The writer in the *Cricketer* brushed aside the doubting critics. 'Twenty minutes of Graveney was worth two hours of a back-to-the-wall innings by any other Test batsman.'

The paean of praise by a West Countryman was a counter to the indictment of Graveney as a player who self-destructed under pressure. 'Had he continued to play the same type of cricket he showed with Gloucestershire when he first played for England we might have been privileged to watch some of the finest stroke-play ever seen in Test matches.' Jim Laker was steadfast in his judgement. 'They said Tom wasn't as good as Hammond. He'd only averaged 40 to Hammond's 60 – then they'd go and pick someone who averaged 25! It didn't make sense. Tom was class.'

Geoffrey Howard, as the MCC manager in India and Pakistan in 1951–52, held up to the mirror a buoyant impression of Graveney on his first overseas tour. It was an encouraging overture for the 24-year-old in the enervating conditions of the sub-continent. Graveney paraded a commendable reliability in heading the tour averages with 1,393 runs, 200 ahead of his nearest contender. It included six centuries. *Wisden* commented: 'He looked a definite England prospect and gave promise of developing into a real personality.'

At Karachi Graveney hit 123, his second century in successive matches. It was played on a coir mat, on which the ball rose viciously, and against a Pakistan attack, which included the leg-cutters of Fazal Mahmood and the formidable pace of Khan Mohammad. Pakistan won by four wickets, convincingly in the end, thanks to the poise of another exciting newcomer, the 16-year-old Hanif. The perversity of the umpiring did, however, incense the visitors. 'The MCC were very surprised at some of the decisions in the match, not one of over 30 appeals being granted in their favour,' blandly reported *Wisden*.

Graveney maintained his fine form at Lahore. He scored 109 and shared an unbroken second wicket partnership of 259 with Spooner. He was complimented on his 'study in concentration' against India at Bombay. The innings of 175 occupied eight and a quarter hours. The timescale indicated the graft involved in an unusually subdued performance, which was studded with compact stroke-play.

Arthur Milton, the former Gloucestershire and England batsman, has referred to the taxing conditions at his home ground at Bristol. Rarely did a batsman dominate the proceedings on the wickets there, notorious for their turn. Milton believes that Graveney discovered his true métier when, at the age of thirty-five, he moved from the West Country to the smoother pastures of New Road, Worcester. It was made clear to him by his new county that his responsibility, as the best player in the side, was to play major innings. 'Tom *had* to score runs there,' remarks Trevor Bailey dryly. There was an added incentive in that Worcestershire were genuine championship contenders. As Patrick Murphy related, Graveney desperately wanted the seal of honours after the years of dilettante enjoyment.

Graveney was said in his apprentice years to be susceptible to outright pace. He disproved this theory in his maturity. At the age of thirty-nine in 1966 he was again recalled to the England colours against the West Indies at Lord's. His 96 against the fearsome bowling combination of Wes Hall and Charlie Griffith is recalled as an innings of the highest valour. It was the beginning of a late flowering of his undoubted talents. Graveney surpassed his achievement at Lord's in this series with centuries at Nottingham and the Oval. In 19 Tests against vaunted opponents from the Caribbean he scored 1,532 runs at an average of 58.92.

Hubert Doggart, another England contemporary, provided a recollection of the admiration Graveney enjoyed in the West Indies. They were both recruited for a private cricket tour of Barbados and Trinidad, arranged by Jim Swanton. At the Marine Hotel in Barbados, Doggart shared a room with J.J. Warr, the Middlesex bowler. (The attendant was coincidentally named Martindale but not related to the renowned West Indian cricketer of the 1930s.) 'One morning he brought in our shaving water and "J.J.", who had gone in the previous evening as night watchman, asked him for advice on how to pursue his innings when play began. "Play a few licks," was the reply, "and then make way for Mister Tom."' Martindale had clearly revelled in Graveney's batting on the 1953–54 tour by England. He did not wish to wait long for a reprise of the entertainment given by his favourite player.

Doggart was also engaged as a correspondent for the London *Times* on this tour. In one of his messages he whimsically reported on the 'prince of on-side players'. It was inspired by Graveney's response to the packed off-side field in one match. 'He moved well over to the off and played the bowling elegantly to fine leg! ' It was a departure from the normal approach of a predominantly off-side driver with his rousing full swing of the bat. Doggart added: 'Tom was also a fine cutter and player off the back foot, who would at the same time, when the occasion arose, score effectively on the on-side.' The latter facility served Graveney well when the angle of attack changed in that direction in the 1950s.

A cheerful cavalier remains self-effacingly in thrall to contemporaries such as Peter May and Colin Cowdrey despite the fact that he scored more runs than anyone did in this time. The statistics record the fact that only Geoffrey Boycott and latterly Graham Gooch and Graeme Hick, exceeded his sum of 122 centuries among players who began their careers after the second world war. His Test average was 44 and his first-class aggregate of 47,793 runs compiled over 22 seasons was the second highest in post-war cricket.

England were probably fortunate that Australia were without the combined firepower of Ray Lindwall and Keith Miller in two Tests in the series, the second at Sydney and the fourth at Adelaide. In the fifth Test, also at Sydney, Lindwall's tactical acumen resulted in Hutton's early dismissal in England's first innings. Others who faced the great Australian bowler endorsed Lindwall's skills although, in this series, he had been outshone by England's own pace bowlers.

Lindwall took his 100th wicket against England in the Test. It was a hesitant progress to the milestone as chance after chance was spilled. Lindwall's luck seemed to be right out when Ian Johnson squandered a catch at mid-on and he seemed destined to remain on 99 when Davidson fumbled a lofted drive off Wardle. A declaration by England was imminent. Before that happened Trevor Bailey in a 'frivolous moment' ended the suspense by surrendering his wicket to an old rival. As Lindwall began his run-up to deliver his last ball, Bailey made it obvious to him that a straight one only was required.

'He stood a foot back from his leg stump, and, as unostentatiously as he could, seemed to indicate to Lindwall that his stumps were his to be hit,' wrote Richard Whitington. 'Then as the ball swerved in a gentle parabola in towards the wicket, Bailey walked right across to the offside, and went through the motions of a hook which had little relation to the course of the ball. This collided with his left pad and ricocheted into the stumps.'

Bailey's score was 72 and his sacrifice in allowing Lindwall to bowl him had the effect of lowering his series average. It would have been 42.29 instead of 37 for the 296 runs he scored. Bill O'Reilly said the incident reinforced Bailey's reputation as a generous cricketer. 'He made himself many friends who will be slow to forget the gesture.' It did not, it must be said, prevent Lindwall from responding less generously. He inflicted upon Bailey the indignity of a pair in his last Test at Melbourne four years later.

Lindwall, at Sydney, became the seventh Australian bowler to take 100 wickets against England. He would go on to increase his tally in Tests to 228, eight short of what was then the world record held by Alec Bedser. Lindwall's figures place him seventh behind his Australian compatriots, Shane Warne, Glen McGrath, Dennis Lillee, Craig McDermott, Richie Benaud and Graham McKenzie. His peak years during Australia's post-war supremacy were on the tours of England in 1948 and 1953. He twice headed the Test averages recording 27 wickets at 19.62 runs each and 26 wickets at an average of 18.84. Collectively on both tours in all first-class matches he took 171 wickets each at a cost of about 16 runs. He claimed five wickets or more in Tests on twelve occasions.

The menace of Lindwall has rarely been equalled. Watching him bowl in a Test generated an excitement which reached fever pitch. John Warr remembered the acceleration to the crease and how Lindwall's feet presented an impression of him being 'pulled along on wheels by a hidden wire.'

Peter Loader, another English rival, describes Lindwall as the most tigerish of all in his category as a bowler. 'He had a low arm action and his bouncer, instead of rearing up, would skim off the turf and rise chest high. You had a split second to choose whether to fend off the ball and risk a catch or take the punishment.'

Lindwall was in his 39th year when he retired in March 1960. He had set a record for endurance as the most resilient of cricketers. It was calculated that he bowled more than 40,000 balls. Ray Robinson, in an appreciation in the *Cricketer*, referred to Lindwall's fitness preparations in the close season. 'Besides running alone on cold dark nights, he would carry out stretching exercises to toughen his groin against the jarring strain of hurling the ball along at almost 90 miles an hour.'

Before a match started, if Australia had lost the toss, Lindwall would loosen his muscles in the dressing room, jogging on the spot and touching his toes. On the field he would continue his exercises before beginning his run of 13 strides, the model of smooth acceleration which others of his time sought to emulate. The muscular strength that he had built up was shown on one occasion when he and two others, Keith Miller and Bill Johnston, sightseeing in Naples, found themselves locked in the opera house. Lindwall grasped the door handle and with one tremendous wrench broke the lock.

Lindwall rated Hutton and Compton as the best of the English opposition but he considered the West Indian, Everton Weekes as the most devastating of his rivals. 'Others punished my poor balls,' he said, 'but Weekes, when in top form, could hit my good balls, too.' Ray Robinson considered that in sheer velocity Lindwall was outdone by Frank Tyson at his quickest, but no fast bowler of his time had rivalled the bewildering mixture of speed and subtlety. 'His controlled outswingers and inswingers confronted batsmen with more curves than Marilyn Monroe possessed.'

Len Hutton, with a grim memory of a second ball duck in one Test at Headingley, ranked Lindwall ahead of all the fast bowlers he had encountered. But Hutton was already plotting revenge for this and other indignities. After one hectic duel with the Australian, he turned to him and said: 'Remember, lad, one day we'll have a fast bowler' – and, with a sigh, 'I hope that day is not far off.' Frank Tyson and Brian Statham were the young avengers who would soon assert their domination and fulfil Hutton's promise.

The retention of the Ashes at Adelaide in the fourth Test cleared the stage for Johnny Wardle to spring into back-handed action in the final Test at Sydney. Release from his 'change bowler' duties enabled him to harass and bewilder the Australians with his beguiling mixture of bowling allsorts.

It was a belated concession by Len Hutton to his fellow Yorkshireman. The expression, 'I know you're dyin' to . . .' does not relate to an imminent decease, but is a Yorkshire way of recognising an urge of somebody to do something. Hutton did not grant Wardle his wish without prior knowledge of his adeptness as a wrist-spinner. He once recalled his confusion against the aspiring young bowler during a Yorkshire net practice following the 1946–47 tour of Australia.

Hutton wrote: 'Wardle joined two other young bowlers who were bowling to me in the nets. He bowled orthodox left-arm spinners to me for quite some time and then without a word of warning produced a chinaman to be followed a few balls later by a googly, both pitched on a perfect length. The chinaman turned considerably and the googly enough to beat the bat. "That surprised you", called Johnny from down the net. Not only was I surprised, I was elated and my thoughts turned to the outstanding talent of this young cricketer. I was so impressed by his natural cricketing ability.'

Wardle, the master of bowling varieties, would later remember with justifiable pride how he foxed his renowned Yorkshire senior. 'I don't want to sound immodest, but I have never made such a great player seem so much at sea.' Hutton's puzzlement should have ensured a greater use of Wardle's diverse talents. Had his artistry been allowed to develop at an earlier stage, it would perhaps have made him unassailable as England's left-arm spinner.

Geoffrey Howard recalled a magnificent bowling performance by Wardle at Sydney. There had been serious flooding all over the state and the cricket ground was under water for days. Howard said the indecision of the Australian batsmen could not be put down to the wicket. It had been protected by flat tarpaulin covers, and when the waters at last subsided it was found to be as dry as a biscuit.

Australia ended the match 32 runs short of England's total of 371. They had only four wickets left and narrowly avoided an innings defeat in less than three days. Wardle took five wickets in the first innings and three more when Australia batted again. The hapless batsmen were drawn into a web as tight and unyielding as that of a devouring spider. He made his chinaman and googly spin prodigiously. Benaud, in the first innings, was confounded by an off-break that spun grotesquely. Maddocks was also placed in the dock of confusion. Godfrey Evans, behind the wicket, expressed his own disbelief when four times in one over the ball missed the stumps. 'The Australian batting failed miserably against Wardle, who turned his off-breaks a considerable distance. He has found his true métier on Australian pitches,' commented Ian Peebles.

Percy Beames, in the *Melbourne Age*, reported that the last remnants of Australia's cricket prestige was torn to shreds. The clock alone had deprived England of another victory. 'There was a time,' lamented Beames, 'when Australian batsmen were noted for their daring footwork and aggressive approach against slow spinners. Yet, against Wardle, almost without exception the batsmen stayed home and fiddled about as though every ball was dynamite.'

The one saving grace for Australia was the resistance of Colin

McDonald, the Victorian opening batsman. He scored 72 in the first innings and 37 in the second innings. His surprising conqueror then was the very occasional bowler, Tom Graveney. As McDonald notes, it was the failures against Tyson and Statham that enabled him first to regain his position in the team at Adelaide. 'In a strange way my good friends, Frank and Brian, did me a favour.' He had been highly displeased when Les Favell had 'pinched' his position in the opening Tests. Admiringly, he watched Graveney's remarkable innings at Sydney. It took him, as he says, two innings to get within two runs of his rival's 111.

The stigma of near defeat for Australia was more keenly felt because England believed they could bowl them out again in less than two hours. The looming crisis had, as a precedent, the bizarre happenings at Old Trafford in 1953. Wardle was again the tormentor on that occasion, taking four wickets for seven runs in five overs in the last hour of the Test. Australia finished the game in an unseemly muddle and lost eight wickets for 35 runs.

At the end of that game, Len Hutton rejected the apologia of some of the Australians. They feebly protested: 'Don't take any notice of our innings. We knew we couldn't lose, so we didn't try.' Hutton replied: 'It wouldn't have made any difference either way. Thirty-five runs was as many as you would have made in any case.'

John Arlott commented that at least three Australians all went making strokes that could not be described as 'business'. 'Several of the players, too, scrambled out of their town clothes to bat – with a delay which the crowd bore with little patience. No batsman likes to be shot out in this manner and I am sure these wickets were not deliberately thrown away.'

The situation at Sydney was not quite as humiliating as the events at Manchester three years earlier. Australia were thrown into disarray after losing seven wickets for just 157 runs in their first innings. Maddocks and Davidson lifted the score to 202 but the position worsened when Maddocks tried to sweep Wardle and was caught by Appleyard at mid-wicket. Five runs were needed to save the follow-on when Australia suffered another reverse. Davidson, jumping out to drive Wardle, was caught at the wicket by Evans. Three more runs were added to reduce the target for safety to one run. Then Lindwall drove fiercely at a half volley and the ball spun away across to Compton behind cover. Johnson raced up the wicket for what should have been a comfortable single but his partner refused it. His captain was run out by Compton's swift return throw.

Ian Johnson did, in fact, miscalculate the deficit at the end of the innings. The scores were level on his dismissal. 'Len,' says Frank Tyson, 'had the great delight in telling his rival skipper that 150 was not 149 and would he therefore please follow-on.' There were only a couple of hours left for play but Hutton had scored another telling blow. The series had come full circle. England had followed on at Brisbane and now Australia, for the first time since 1938 at the Oval, were asked to bat again. For Hutton, the record collector of 364 runs beneath the gasholders, the moment was just as precious as his youthful marathon.

The final stages of a momentous series were relaxed and filled with merriment. Fourteen Australian wickets had fallen in the day and Johnny Wardle had taken seven of them in 29 overs. He was in the happiest of humours, clowning away and bowling his last over almost on his knees to signify his exhaustion. Hutton's last act on Australian soil was to turn back the years and reintroduce his leg-spin to deceive and bowl Richie Benaud.

12

All Time Low at Auckland

'It seems to me that England and Australia arrange a world fair and if there is a spare corner New Zealand walks nervously in and puts up a tent.'

Arthur Mailey.

The inferiority complex affecting New Zealand's cricketers was never more starkly illustrated than in their meek surrender at Eden Park, Auckland in March 1955. The side was bowled out for 26, which remains the lowest score in Test history.

'Inquest on a painful subject' was the doleful headline on the editorial in the *New Zealand Herald*. It referred to a long-standing tradition of fatal lapses and the reversion again to the role of cricket paupers. 'At lunch yesterday the New Zealand team had every reason to be pleased with its showing against England. Within a few hours calamity had struck, complete and unrelieved by any redeeming feature.'

An afternoon of torment was another study in subservience. For twenty-five years since their entry on the Test scene in January 1930 New Zealand had languished in the shadow of their sporting compatriots – the mighty warriors of rugby, the All-Blacks. Writing in the *Weekly News*, Lindsay Weir said that the most disappointing feature was that the downward trend of recent seasons showed no signs of being arrested.

Weir exempted the New Zealand bowling and fielding from criticism and considered the former was now of a standard 'worthy of Test cricket.' The batting, though, had continued to deteriorate. 'It is not only colourless but it is frequently unsound. For some reason, beyond the appreciation of many,

New Zealand has tried to develop a batting style that eschews attack.

'Most of our batsmen play back far too much and allow themselves to be pinned down on the defensive because they are unable to play scoring shots in front of the wicket. Very few of them use their feet to slow or medium-pace bowling, and their lack of aggression leaves them vulnerable when faced with good spin bowling of the quality of England's Appleyard and Wardle.

The gulf in ability had lessened by the time that Glenn Turner, the hero from Dunedin, emerged to delight his countrymen. Turner, writing in 1990, ruefully acknowledged the weaknesses of the past. 'For many years the New Zealanders were acutely aware of being the underdogs and this made the players a little too self-effacing and over-anxious to prove that they were truly worthy of full international status. Both the players and the administrators behaved as if they were inferior and, as a consequence, were patronised.'

There were, in mitigation, limited first-class opportunities in a country with a population less than half that of London. Basically amateurs, playing weekend cricket, the players had not been subjected to the lessons of hard experience. Geoff Howarth, one of a later breed of successful New Zealand captains, explained that in the existing regime the selectors could only call upon about 70 players from provincial cricket. 'In real terms,' he said, 'there were only around 20 with the calibre, both in ability and mentality, to select from and to compete on the international scene.'

The paucity of talent did, in turn, place an immense burden on New Zealand's star players in the immediate post-war era. The dependence on such celebrities as Bert Sutcliffe, Martin Donnelly and John Reid meant that if they failed, the 'rot would set in and the rest would fall like a row of dominoes.' The dominant central characters were reduced to vain heroics, like leading actors in a play when others repeatedly forgot their lines. Sutcliffe and Reid were the ill-supported standard bearers against a rampant England in 1955. Illustrating the reliance on the pair was the fact that they scored more than half the runs – 270 out of a total of 483 in the two Tests at Dunedin and Auckland. At Auckland Reid (73) and Sutcliffe (49) added 63 for the third wicket and contributed 122 out of the first innings total of 200. At Dunedin, Reid was the bowling mainstay. He took the wickets of Hutton, Cowdrey, Bailey and Evans and in all bowled 27 overs at a cost of 36 runs.

The negative policy pursued by Geoff Rabone, the New Zealand captain, played into England's hands. It could be reasonably argued that he had no option but to adopt defensive tactics. But it was his batting that set the tone for the series. In the first official Test to be played at Dunedin he batted three hours for 18 as New Zealand were bowled out for 125 in their first innings. At Auckland he prevailed for two and a half hours in scoring 29 out of a stand of 78 with Reid. He was stubborn if uninspiring and it was dismal fare for the home supporters.

New Zealand were irresolute against spin, especially at Auckland, when all the signs pointed to a slaughter by pace exceeding that which had so recently devoured the Australians. Walter Hadlee, the former New Zealand captain, remembers the qualms of his compatriots as they prepared to face Tyson and Statham, both fresh from their triumphs in Australia. At Wellington the proud young pacemen underwent speed trials at the Aeronautical College. The scientific checks were part of an investigation in measuring the relatively high speeds of small objects travelling over short distances.

Hitherto high-speed photography had been used but it was considered that a sonic beam would be a more accurate measuring medium. It was decided to make initial tests on the velocity of a cricket ball. The scientists checked Tyson at a shade over 87 mph and Statham at just over 85 mph. Bowling conditions, said one observer, were not ideal and it was obvious that the two bowlers were not at full stretch.

Tyson says that the validity of the trial was diminished by their preparations. 'We bowled on a saturated pitch, wearing two sweaters and without bothering to change into cricket gear, just slipping on our cricket boots.' The results, however inexact, did inspire an amusing cartoon in the *New Zealand Herald*. It depicted two uncertain batsmen emerging from the pavilion. One carried aloft, in a gesture of distress, a traffic sign bearing a plea for reduced speed. 'I think you'll find that is not allowed,' remarked his companion.

A pact of non-aggression also seemed to be the wish of the ultra-defensive New Zealand batsmen in what became a dispiriting series for them. Among the spectators witnessing the rout at Eden Park, Auckland was Arthur Gilligan who had led England against the South Africans at Edgbaston in 1924. Gilligan and Maurice Tate were the Sussex combination who took all 10 wickets as South Africa were bowled out for 30 (eleven of them extras) in 75 balls. The innings lasted for just 48 minutes. In six overs Tate took four wickets for 12 runs. Gilligan's performance was the most memorable of his career. He returned figures of six wickets for seven runs in 6.3 overs, including four maidens. Before the turn of the century England had humbled South Africa for the same score at Port Elizabeth. Surrey's George Lohmann, with eight wickets for seven runs, including the hat-trick, was the successful bowler in the 1895–96 series.

The plummeting fortunes of New Zealand were judged as due to their failure to take the initiative. 'They had the moral advantage of having tied up the top English batsmen and they were batting on a wicket that was anything but treacherous,' reported the *Herald* correspondent. Walter Hadlee recalls his pleasure in watching the fightback of his fellow Kiwis. 'I felt that our bowlers had done well and we were still in the game. England would have to bat last. We were in with a chance.'

At Auckland Len Hutton set a record for the English Test captaincy when he skippered the team for the twenty-second time. He demoted himself down the order and contributed a polished half-century. Despite this effort England led by only 40 runs on the first innings. For that small advantage they were indebted to Frank Tyson unbeaten on 27. He shared a last wicket stand of 28 with Statham. The tally amounted to two runs more than New Zealand would muster in a forlorn second innings.

Hutton was heard to voice an incredible thought: 'We've got just enough runs to win by an innings.' He was to be proved right. The debacle on a glorious summer afternoon lasted 162 balls, bowled in one and threequarter hours. New Zealand collapsed unbelievably to 26 all out. There was one boundary in the innings, struck by Harry Cave, the third top scorer. One batsman, Bert Sutcliffe, reached double figures and five others failed to score. The last five wickets fell for four runs and the fall of wickets: 1–6, 2–8, 3–9, 4–14, 5–14, 6–22, 7–22, 8–22, 9–26, 10–26, starkly portrayed the New Zealanders' misery.

The match ended shortly after tea, with more than two days to spare. The only consolation for New Zealand was that they had bowled well to keep England's batsmen on a tight leash. Their own batting humiliation, when the match was evenly poised, added to the deep sense of failure.

Spin propelled by Otago bowler, Alec Moir, with his best Test figures of five for 62, had helped to sustain his team and contain England. Bob Appleyard responded with his own brand of guile after Tyson and Statham had wrenched open the door of the innings. In six overs Appleyard, with his sharp cut and bounce, took four wickets for seven runs, three of them in four balls. A packed legside cordon, hovering almost at the end of the bat, assisted in the submission. One of them was Tom Graveney, who recalls: 'I caught two blinders off Bob at short leg.' The catch with which he dismissed Colquhoun was taken after he had dived with his left-hand outstretched to hold the ball inches from the ground.

Bert Sutcliffe was New Zealand's top scorer with 11 before being deceived and bowled by Wardle's chinaman. It was his only wicket of the innings but in the Yorkshire manner he kept one end tight and did not concede a run in his five overs.

England's fast bowlers for once had taken a secondary role in the dramatic proceedings. Hutton relented at last to give his match-winners one final thrust. Only one over from Statham was needed to complete victory. Rabone, who had batted stubbornly for seven runs, was lbw off the fourth delivery after a vain appeal against the failing light. Statham then ensured the unenviable total by shattering Hayes's stumps. Frank Tyson, while praising Appleyard's success at

Auckland, expresses a flicker of regret that he could not be allied with his trusty partner to end the tour on the right note. He wryly adds: 'And after all – only taking two wickets for 10 runs meant that I was positively expensive!'

The interlude in New Zealand was a time of family and cricket reunions. Len Hutton and his wife, Dorothy, who had joined him in Australia, met her brother, Frank Dennis in Christchurch. Dennis, the former Yorkshire fast bowler and then a Canterbury selector, was also able to reminisce with a former county colleague, Bill Bowes, a member of the English press corps. Bill Edrich was reunited with another exile, his elder brother, Eric, a South Canterbury farmer. The strains of an exacting tour of Australia were dispelled among other welcoming hosts. Hutton, at one of the many receptions, expressed his pleasure at the change to 'lush green fields and the quieter atmosphere.'

The England captain, like others in the MCC party, was able to indulge in nostalgia after the months away from home. In contrast to the hard and fast wickets of Australia they now enjoyed familiar conditions. 'We see the ball moving in the air just like it does at home.' Hutton reflected on the glee of his bowlers. 'We see them rubbing the ball on their trousers and shirts more often than in Australia. They would like more pace in the pitches but I've never known bowlers to be really happy unless they are turning the ball both ways and also moving it off the seam.' He revealed one personal recollection of New Zealand cricket, embarrassing to him at the time. This was when Jack Cowie dismissed him for a duck on his Test debut at Lord's in 1937.

Tom Graveney also revelled in his newly discovered freedom. The batting revival begun in the final Test at Sydney continued in New Zealand. In six innings he scored 323 runs at an average of 80. At Christchurch against Canterbury, Graveney, again cast as an opener with Hutton, stole the show with the most handsome of centuries. 'In one of the best innings it would be possible to see,' reported the *New Zealand Herald*, 'Graveney's delightful and quick footwork and lovely wristy shots enabled him to score boundaries with ease.' There were 17 boundaries and a six in an innings lasting just over an hour and a half.

Graveney's dismissal – bowled by MacGibbon – was just the tonic needed by Canterbury's bowlers. In two hours the MCC lost five wickets for 35 runs to the pace of John Hayes and the spin of the veteran, Tom Burtt, making his final appearance in first-class cricket. Nine wickets had fallen for 227 before Frank Tyson embarked on the salvage operation. His batting abilities, respected by knowledgeable judges back home in Northampton, were well above those of the easily discharged tailender. The menace of his bowling was exchanged for a tremendous display of big hitting.

Tyson was unbeaten on 62 which included two sixes, one hoisted into the far reaches of the main stand and another scattering a contingent of soldiers on the other side of the ground. 'Canterbury under-rated the potential danger of a batsman who had nothing to lose', wrote Arthur Mailey in the *New Zealand Herald.* 'He clouted his runs in even time to swing the game towards the tourists.' Tyson was allied with Statham in a stand of 75 for the last wicket. Tom Burtt, in New Zealand's reply, also struck mighty blows, hitting Wardle for 24 in one over. The boisterous flurry of runs represented a gallant finale to his career, but the MCC in the end needed only 45 runs for victory.

Tom Graveney continued on his winning ways at the Basin Reserve at Wellington. He hit another century, his third in four consecutive matches, against the Plunket Shield champions. It was recorded out of the MCC total of 207 and the next highest scorer was Peter May with 22. Arthur Mailey observed: 'England's batting has had its ups and downs and consequently provides food for thought among the selectors. Graveney was a Test suspect throughout Australia but he is now the most reliable and demoralising batsman in the party.'

Accelerating the victory by 187 runs at Wellington was the bowling of Wardle and Appleyard, who shared 18 wickets in the match. Wellington lost their last nine wickets for 57 runs. Appleyard's return in the morning gallop was five wickets for 10 runs.

Mailey, in another report in the *Auckland Star*, shunned the widespread criticism that greeted New Zealand's cricketers after the first Test. He observed that New Zealand, beaten by eight wickets, had no reason to feel ashamed. 'England was already a well-regulated and experienced machine, while the selection of the New Zealand team seemed to be based on past experience and potential.'

Another sorry episode at Dunedin did have the redeeming feature of an innings of character by Bert Sutcliffe. While others were overwhelmed by sheer pace, Sutcliffe was staunch in his resistance on a lively wicket. He was last out after a stay of four and a half hours. His innings of 74 (out of 125) was sprinkled with sixes off Bailey, Appleyard and Wardle. As he doggedly took root, Hutton was compelled to station five men on boundary patrol to curb his aggression. Arthur Mailey was prompted to describe Sutcliffe as the world's best left-hand batsman after the performance at Dunedin. 'I prefer him to Arthur Morris and Neil Harvey at the moment because he was never troubled by England's attack, whereas the two Australians appeared jittery and out of touch.'

It was Walter Hadlee, the former New Zealand and Otago captain who ushered the 'good looking, golden-haired' Sutcliffe into the ranks of the great opening batsmen. In his native Auckland, where he made his first-class debut in 1946, Sutcliffe batted at number 5. His move to Otago coincided with his selection to play against the MCC later in the summer. Hadlee remembered that Sutcliffe arrived at the Carisbrook ground a little later than was usual for the game. He mildly remonstrated when his captain told him that he was to open the innings. Hadlee was adamant and Sutcliffe, possibly stung by the rebuke, thereupon became the first cricketer to hit two separate hundreds on his first appearance against a first-class touring side. With 197 in the first innings for Otago and 128 in the second innings, the 23-year-old announced himself as a candidate for the highest honours in the game.

There was genuine regret, even among her rivals, at the decline of New Zealand in the calamitous weeks in March 1955. Ron Roberts, in the *Daily Telegraph*, was one sympathetic observer. 'The batting in this Dominion does not at present bear a healthy comparison with the sunny days of 1949, but, whichever way you look at it, this was another fine win for Hutton's team.'

It was a reverse in fortunes sufficient to arouse the dismay of T.P. McLean in *Barclay's World of Cricket.* He lamented 'the total disaster of the afternoon at Eden Park when Statham, Tyson and Appleyard reduced New Zealand to one of the saddest jokes in cricket – a second innings of 26.' McLean described it as 'an afternoon when terror stalked abroad – a terror in the hearts of administrators and cricket-lovers, too, for this sort of performance turning a noble pastime into a caricature, could in repetition do the game irreparable harm.'

Six years before the stunning reverse at Auckland Walter Hadlee's tourists had forged a happier image of New Zealand cricket. Richard Streeton, the former *Times* correspondent, was one young follower engaged by the efficiency and flair of the visitors. 'They actually scored more runs than the 1948 Australians; their only loss came at Oxford on a wet pitch; and as far as the layman was concerned, they remained chivalrous and friendly right to the end of an arduous itinerary.' Despite a lack of penetrative bowling, the team was thought to be one of the best to represent their country.

The New Zealanders of 1949 were unbeaten against England, admittedly in four Tests of only three days' duration, and in a summer of blissful sunshine fashioned for tall scores. Streeton, writing in 1986, believed that the merits of this combination had not received true recognition. 'Sutcliffe and Donnelly were the nonpareils because they made scoring 2,000 runs look so easy but there were other heroes on that tour. Hadlee's own batting had a well ordered stateliness; Wallace had his own brand of belligerence; and young Reid's cricket had an appealing lustiness about it even at that early stage in his career. It was Tom Burtt, though, plumpish but a model of classical left-arm spin and flight, who was the mainstay of the bowling. He finished the tour with 128 wickets at 22.88 each and bowled 1,245 overs, with scarcely a long hop from May to September.'

Older supporters remembered the distinctive style of Stewart Dempster, who captained Leicestershire in the 1930s, but it was Sutcliffe, Donnelly and Reid who almost alone upheld the cricket status of their country in the immediate post-war years. It was said of Sutcliffe that had he been an Australian he would have been second only to Don Bradman. The adventure and artistry of his play reached its zenith in England in 1949. He recorded an aggregate of 2,627 runs, including seven centuries, on the tour.

There was also the yield of 423 Test runs that summer at an average of 60.42. Few make triple centuries in their careers yet Sutcliffe scored two with a top figure of 385, still New Zealand's highest individual score, with Otago. His tally also included six double centuries in a total of 44 innings of three figures. Sutcliffe was in his 42nd year when he hit the last of his five Test centuries against India at Calcutta in 1965. The reverence and affection in which he was held, latterly as president of the Auckland Cricket Society, was shown after his death in April 2001. The Oval at the Lincoln High Performance Centre in Christchurch now bears his name as a lasting memorial.

Sutcliffe is linked with another Auckland man in New Zealand's hall of cricket fame. John Reid was unquestionably his country's greatest allrounder until the arrival of Richard Hadlee. One observer wrote of him: 'Reid in any guise on the cricket field ensured the most cynical supporter full reward for the price of admission.' As captain in 34 Tests, Reid led New Zealand to their first three victories in Auckland, Cape Town and Port Elizabeth. In South Africa in 1953–54 he became the first player to score 1,000 runs and take 50 wickets. Eight years later, also in South Africa, he broke every record as a batsman, including Denis Compton's aggregate of 1,781 runs in the 1948–49 series.

Reid was, by nature, an aggressive batsman. Fielders carefully withdrew a little deeper when the hardest of hitters was in full flight. It was calculated that he made a century every fourth game. He was at his most trenchant in striking 15 sixes in an innings of 296 in one game at Wellington.

Optimism was the keynote of the leader writer in the *New Zealand Herald* after the annihilation at Auckland in March 1955. 'It is not beyond the bounds of possibility that some day a well-balanced team will emerge to confound the Jeremiahs.' Building such a team would require faith and boldness, not a retreat from international cricket. 'So long as our players get an opportunity to play in a big match only at long intervals, so long will they be liable to psychological failures at key moments.' He urged the vigorous promotion of contests with other countries to expand experience. A more frequent interchange of visits with Australia ought to be pressed with all possible resolution.

From the turn of the twentieth century a fledgling cricket nation had been bolstered by the support of English coaches. The exceptional warmth afforded them in New Zealand expressed the pride of kinship between the two countries. Jim Laker was one of a notable assembly at Auckland. Four of his predecessors, three of them Test cricketers, came from Sussex. They included the Edwardian allrounder, Albert Relf, and Ted Bowley, whose renowned back-foot play was mirrored in a generation of Auckland batsmen. Another was the England slow left-arm bowler, Jim Langridge, who suffered from tuberculosis as a boy and, after a renewal of the illness, went out to recuperate as well as coach in New Zealand. A more vigorous Sussex personality was Bert Wensley. His hosts recalled Wensley 'with broad shoulders and massive arm, toiling away through a scorching Auckland day, slaving to get some response out of a heartbreaking Eden Park wicket.'

All made major contributions in nurturing the growth of cricket in New Zealand. It stuttered for identity over the years and the setback against England in 1955 was yet another misfortune. The revival, to considerable disbelief, was swifter than expected. Within a year, on March 13, 1956, the West Indies were beaten by 190 runs at Eden Park. Tony MacGibbon and Harry Cave, two of the defeated eleven against England, and Don Beard dismissed the West Indies for 145 and 77. After twenty-six years of Test cricket New Zealand had registered their first victory.

It was the equivalent, in cricket terms, of Roger Bannister's sub-four-minute mile. Stan Cowman related: 'It was a case of "nadir to apogee" in 50 weeks. I have heard recounted the tales of strong men with tears in their eyes as they took in the magnitude of the triumph.'

By an extraordinary coincidence it was again on March 13, eighteen years later, that a win over Australia was finally achieved. Glenn Turner scored two centuries in the match at Christchurch. Then, in another inspirational moment in February, 1978, England were bowled out for 64 at Wellington. Richard Hadlee was hailed as a national hero. He took 10 wickets in the match and six for 26 in the rout in the second innings. New Zealand, after forty-eight years and in the 48th Test between the two countries, had beaten England for the first time.

It was somehow appropriate that the avenger who dispelled the shivers of history should be the son of Walter Hadlee, the zealous campaigner of so many years before. The famous victory over England would help to foster a self-belief and signal the coming of age for New Zealand cricket.

13

The Single Aim of the Solitary Man

'England won the series because she was operating under a Wellington-like leader who kept the pressure on the opposition until it broke to pieces under it.'

Richard Whitington, former South Australian cricketer and writer.

The 1954–55 tour of Australia and New Zealand was an expedition which, Len Hutton well knew, would either crown his career or sully it. On his frail shoulders he bore the responsibility of a huge undertaking. By the end of the tour he was shattered in health but had become the first English professional of the century to win two consecutive series against Australia. Eric Stanger in the *Yorkshire Post*, delivered his verdict on the trials of a dedicated and conscientious man. 'Hutton succeeded in his job not because he was a born leader but because he planned down to the last detail. He has lived and dreamed cricket and now the toll has been taken.'

The uniqueness of Hutton's pioneering quest has to be placed in the context of the prevailing attitudes of cricket's Establishment. The challenges of the game for the professional were not confined to exceptional playing talent. However implausible it may seem today, they had to include the niceties of etiquette. Herbert Sutcliffe, his mentor, had told the aspiring Hutton that his conduct must be irreproachable. 'If you were an amateur you could please yourself,' said Sutcliffe. 'But as a Yorkshire professional you have to do everything better than the amateur. Your manners must be better and, if possible, you must speak and dress better, too.'

Hutton, then a mature campaigner, had to measure up to these tenets when he was elevated to the England captaincy against India in 1952. He was quite clearly still on probation on the tour of the West Indies in the winter of 1953–54. It was an unenviable assignment in a volatile region where emotions can run high among partisan spectators.

Hutton was always quiet and withdrawn as a man. Any form of horseplay was distasteful to him. Among his charges was the raw, inexperienced and quick-tempered Fred Trueman. Gerald Howat, Hutton's biographer, believed that one of the problems was that Trueman found it difficult to distinguish between the man he played with in Yorkshire and the man who was now his captain. Hutton took a discretionary view of the situation. His remedy was to 'nurse Trueman by not being over-strict and allowing him his high spirits.'

One press correspondent suggested that Hutton gave the 'volcanic Fred Trueman far too much liberty with his gestures of annoyance' while recognising that the principal dilemma – and not just for Trueman – resided in the stories being circulated from island to island and magnified to unbelievable proportions. Hutton would later say that the West Indies made heavy demands on young players and 'were not the ideal place to send immature English cricketers.'

It was remarkable, in the circumstances, that Hutton was able to maintain his own high batting standards in the Caribbean. He had been handed the equivalent of a poisoned chalice. The tour was marred by political disturbances, riots at grounds, and contentious umpiring decisions. Yet he did manage to rise above the climate of dissension. Two superb innings of 165 and 205 by him helped England to recover and draw the series.

Jim Kilburn, the Yorkshire historian and a close friend, was aware of the pressures borne by Hutton as he sought to reconcile himself to the class distinctions. 'He was persistently anxious not to tread on corns.' Hutton also knew that any inability to discharge the diplomatic or disciplinary side of his duties would be taken as confirming the inadequacy of a paid player for the post.

Any review of Hutton's captaincy has to take into account that he did carry the main burden of the batting. His form rarely faltered despite recurring bouts of illness, including severe fibrositis. He showed an uncommon resilience in overcoming many setbacks. Chief among these was a wartime injury, which threatened to end his career. One day, in March 1941, while on an army physical training course at York, Hutton fell in attempting a 'flyspring' in the gymnasium when the mat slipped from under him. The x-ray showed a fracture of his left arm and the dislocation of the ulna at the base of his wrist.

The serious nature of the injury was not immediately apparent. But there was a rapid change in medical opinion when it was realised that an operation was necessary to make a bone graft from his right leg to his left arm. The grafting was not successful and, towards the end of 1941, he underwent another operation, this time with a bone graft from his left leg. It was estimated that twelve plaster casts were made in the course of the treatment.

It was a long road to recovery and Hutton confessed to feelings of despair through weeks of complete immobility. Anyone who saw the wan, tired-looking man umpiring in a charity match at Roundhay Park, Leeds in the convalescent aftermath would have pronounced his cricket future uncertain. Happily, these doubts were laid to rest when his Leeds surgeon, Reginald Broomhead, relayed better news. It enabled Sir Stanley Jackson, the club president, to tell the Yorkshire members at the annual general meeting early in 1942 that there was every hope that Hutton would make a good recovery. The gratitude of the county for restoring an illustrious cricketer to fitness was shown when they made Broomhead a life member of the club.

The summer brought Hutton's discharge from the army and, after weeks of massage and therapy, came the realisation that, when he played cricket again, he would need to readjust his batting technique. His left arm was now almost two inches shorter than his right arm. It meant that he had reduced power in his grip and he was forced to eliminate the hook shot, previously a productive source of runs. As one writer said, a right-hand batsman with a left hand that does not function satisfactorily is at a disadvantage.

Hutton once confided that his best days were in the few short years leading up the second world war. He now had to rein in the flair he had displayed during that time. Caution, except on rare occasions, was the keynote of his cricket. He carried an immense responsibility as England's opening anchor in the immediate post-war period.

The supreme tactician overcame his handicap to withstand the assaults of the Australians, Lindwall and Miller. Hutton had to use the lightest possible bat to counteract his disability and he also had to negotiate the imposition, in 1948, of regulations allowing one new ball every 55 overs. As a testimony to his adjustment of technique, Hutton four times scored 50 against Don Bradman's 'invincibles'. At the Oval England were bowled out for 52 and the sorry story would have been worse but for Hutton. A forlorn innings included thirty from his bat.

The precision of Hutton's batting – the adroit placements into unguarded areas as he delayed his shots until the last possible moment – was revealed in one story related by Roley Jenkins, the Worcestershire and England allrounder. Jenkins was regarded as a brilliant cover point yet he was unable to curb Hutton's unerring ability to find the gaps. In one match at Sheffield, Jenkins was busily occupied in watching Hutton's footwork. 'I was trying to work out where Len was going to play his off drive. I managed to stop a magnificent drive on my right side but to the next half-volley, he played a little inside out and it screamed past my left hand. So I moved a shade towards my left and next time, it went whistling past my right hand. He used his left arm to manipulate the ball away from me.'

One innings on a spinners' wicket at the Oval in the early 1950s was a majestic exercise in Hutton's skills. He made 79 out of the Yorkshire total of 130. Raymond Illingworth was among those who marvelled at the innings. 'At the moment of contact with the ball he was so relaxed. He picked the length of the ball up remarkably quickly. Without him we would have been pushed to make thirty that day.'

Johnny Wardle was also among the admiring throng. 'I defy anyone to have ever played better. He was playing Lock's quicker ones off his chest, yet somehow keeping the ball away from the leg trap.' Jim Laker, another of the harassed bowlers, described it as the greatest bad wicket innings he had seen. 'Len just toyed with Tony Lock, just hitting him that little bit squarer on the offside, just out of reach of the fielder. And he placed my off-breaks with uncanny precision.'

Great generals, it is said, require the seclusion of their tents to draw up their battle plans without distractions. Hutton, in his finest hours in Australia, was frequently absorbed in contemplation of his tactical manoeuvres. Geoffrey Howard, the MCC manager, recalled: 'Off the field, while the series was in progress, Len spent a lot of time, sitting alone and deep in thought.' There was ultimately a recognition that Hutton needed to conserve his energies in the taxing circumstances. Howard and Peter May, England's vice-captain, allowed the necessary respite and took on all the tasks required off the field.

Jim Swanton remembered a man who possessed an instinctive dignity but who was by nature inclined to be shy, withdrawn and introspective. Colin Cowdrey, one of the inspired choices for the tour, also dwelt upon the wariness of his captain. 'Len could be ill at ease with strangers and was slow to trust them, but his striking blue eyes and open smile were evidence of a warm Yorkshire heart.'

Cowdrey thought that Hutton's streak of isolationism might have contributed to his greatness as a captain. There was, for example, one episode in which Hutton appeared to have lapsed almost into a coma. The England captain did not play in the match against Queensland immediately preceding the first Test at Brisbane. But he was still very much on duty. Cowdrey recalled: 'He took a chair out to the front of the pavilion and watched every ball bowled in the game without uttering a word. They even brought drinks out to him, left them by the chair and departed without daring to interrupt his concentration. Len was absorbing every factor, planning every move in the battle for which we had come across the world.'

The contradictions in Hutton's personality led to him being labelled an enigma. There was a jester at play in the trailing *non sequitors*. His jousts with the press corps often saw him in roguish mood. Alan Ross wrote: 'Hutton is not by nature explicit: he inhabits a world of hints, allusions and obscure ironies.' Faced with an especially earnest questioner, he would slip into a companionable mode. As if talking to an old friend, he would inquire: 'Have you booked your holiday yet?' The riposte was precisely intended to divert attention from an intrusive subject.

Hubert Doggart, an England contemporary, provided one anecdote to illustrate Hutton's quizzical manner. It concerned Robin Marlar, the former Cambridge and Sussex captain. In 1951 at Fenners, Marlar bowled Hutton for 22 in the morning session. Afterwards they were seated together at lunch. 'I suppose,' confided Hutton, 'you'll be thinking you might get your blue now you've got me out.'

Joe Hardstaff, who was at the wicket when Hutton broke Bradman's record at the Oval in 1938, recounted another gem. Hardstaff said a moment of reflection occurred after Hutton had passed the milestone of 300. He came down the wicket to his partner and said: 'Joe, I'm having trouble with this fellow O'Reilly. He's a bit difficult.' Hardstaff glanced at the imposing scoreboard and commented dryly: 'It's taken you a so-and-so long while to reach that conclusion.'

Roy Tattersall, another Test colleague, afforded a glimpse of Hutton, then the England captain, at his most enigmatic. It occurred during one swiftly concluded spell in which the Lancastrian had failed to take a wicket. He was summoned by Hutton at the end of one over and asked: 'What's the matter. Are you tired?' It was often difficult to know whether Hutton was in earnest or in impish mood. Tattersall resolved to match one jest with another. 'I thought I would play him at his own mocking game. "I think you're right, Len; I do feel buggered."' Hutton offered a quiet, perplexed smile at the response, perhaps a little abashed at his own severity.

Frank Tyson remembered the puzzlement of his Northampton-shire colleague and friend, Keith Andrew when he approached the England captain for permission to play golf during a MCC match. 'Eh, lad,' said Hutton, 'when I was your age, I used to eat, drink and sleep cricket.' Andrew produced a sly, impertinent rejoinder. 'Well, if you'd spent all that time watching cricket, how did your handicap reach eight?' Hutton smilingly acknowledged this smart piece of repartee and told Andrew to go off and improve his own handicap.

Alan Ross remembered Hutton as a master of strategy but a 'strange compound of personal charm and great diffidence. If he lacked an imposing presence, he possessed a curious magnetism of his own. His smile, emerging from lips and eyes with the freshness of sun dispersing the clouds, is worth a fortune.'

Those who entered the sanctum of his friendship would learn that that smile placed them in his special regard. It was a means of overcoming his sparse gifts as a communicator. A shy man was betrayed by his inhibitions, even to the extent of avoiding close contact with those in the Yorkshire dressing room. Hutton was idolised by his young colleagues and it is a matter for regret that he felt unable to impose his authority as a senior player during the troubled 1950s. Raymond Illingworth was among the hero-worshippers; he lived within a stone's throw of the great man at Pudsey; and yet, as he says: 'I never really got to know Len'.

Geoffrey Howard remembered the barrier which often deterred others looking for Hutton's guidance in Australia. 'Leonard's attitude to the players was if they wanted his help they could have it, so long as they came along and asked him.'

Frank Tyson was one who did profit from Hutton's counsel in his surge to glory in Australia. Yet he remembers a 'perverse and enigmatic sort of fellow.' Socialising was a trial for Hutton and Tyson believes that he would have been far happier working on his batting. The waspish humour could be disconcerting to those unaccustomed to the laconic Yorkshire flavour. Extravagant conceit is a defect in character in the broad acres. 'Getting above yourself' is an attitude which offends the instinct to reward modesty. Few, if any, concessions would have been made to Hutton's prodigious talents in his apprentice years. He, in turn, would not have encouraged swollen heads among the juniors under his command in Australia.

Hutton once confessed that there was a little of the actor in his make-up. So it might be suspected that the enigmatic manner was a pose. Frank Tyson does not believe that his old captain was feigning on one Test occasion at Perth in the 1970s. Hutton was then employed in a public relations capacity with Fenners, the power transmission engineers. Tyson was engaged as a broadcaster. 'For six hours Len sat in a VIP box 10 metres away from me and never said a word.' On the following morning Tyson received a telephone call from Hutton. 'He invited me for a coffee before the game and I visited him at his hotel for a chat.' There was no mention of their close proximity at the WACA. 'He just had not seen me at the ground on the previous day. I never saw him again.'

Bob Appleyard says that Hutton, however inscrutable in manner, enjoyed the admiration and respect of those such as Denis Compton and Bill Edrich who were his keenest rivals back home in England. 'There was no animosity in the party, as would have been prevalent in matches between Yorkshire and Surrey, Middlesex and Lancashire. We were all pulling in the same direction.' Appleyard remembers the effect upon Hutton caused by the demands of a tense and tight series. 'Len was struggling physically and I think there were times when he felt he ought to let someone else in. But we all wanted Len out there even if he wasn't 100 per cent fit.'

The steel of Hutton's unwavering command was never better demonstrated than after the debacle at Brisbane. He regrouped at Sydney and placed his faith in Tyson and Statham, and regretfully, amid much censure, left out Alec Bedser. Amazingly, so soon after being overwhelmed in the first Test, England marshalled their forces to stage a comeback. Australia, whose confidence should have been sky-high, could not capitalise on their ascendancy.

It was, though, the closest possible call at Sydney. Jim Swanton reported: 'Tyson and Statham, with a superb effort of skill and fortitude, pulled England's chestnuts out of the fire in the Test and thereafter never looked back. But had it not been for the partnership between May and Cowdrey which held up the Australian bowlers at the last ditch when the position looked practically hopeless, England would have been as good as beaten in three days. The Ashes challenge would have gone up in smoke and Hutton's captaincy written off as a failure.'

The torrid duels with Lindwall and Miller in earlier depressive days provided the key to Hutton's blueprint in Australia. His obsession with speed raged to erase the wounds of the past. The ammunition, lethal and threatening, was now in younger hands than those of the Australian aggressors. Even so, it remains a matter for debate whether the tables would have been turned had Australia not been regularly denied the services of their experienced twin spearheads.

Lindwall and Miller were available in only two of the four Tests that decided the series. Miller missed the second Test at Sydney because of a swollen knee and Lindwall the fourth at Adelaide because of a calf injury. Ray Robinson, the Australian writer, reflected on the absences and said that it was impossible to calculate the difference this had made in the fortunes of his compatriots.

At all events it was clear by the time that England edged ahead at Melbourne that Australia had no counter to the bowling of Tyson and Statham. Robinson, in *The Cricketer*, reported: 'Tyson, with his purposeful stride and obvious shoulder power, and Statham, with his rhythmic run and flexible arm, made an unforgettable sight which never failed to stir me. They desolated Australia's batting in a way not seen since Larwood and his fellow bowlers ravaged it in the bodyline Tests twenty-two years earlier.'

Frank Tyson, as one of these destroyers, remembers the merciless approach of his captain, which was stirred to the pitch of tyranny. 'Len did not miss a trick; he was a great psychological leader; and he knew when we established our supremacy at Sydney that he had the quicker attack and he used Brian and me in that context.'

Hutton, acutely conscious of the need to preserve his assets, rationed the workload of his bowlers. Tyson says: 'Len only used me in short spells of five or six overs as a shock bowler. It was only when we were closing in for the kill – as in the second innings at Melbourne and in Australia's second knock at Adelaide – that he relaxed that rule.'

The astute tactical master, observes Tyson, could pinpoint exactly a critical moment in the match. Then, having accurately assessed the situation, he could be consumed with mental doubt and stress. There was a sudden alarm that he just might have erred in judgement. The ruthless side of Hutton's character was seen when he dragged out the torture of his opponents. Tyson remembers how his captain would walk up from his position at first slip with apparently some urgent instruction preying on his mind. At the crease and out of earshot of the batsman, he uttered the soothing words: 'Are you all right, lad?'

It was all part of the psychological warfare waged against Australia. Colin Cowdrey said that he was conscious throughout the crucial second Test at Sydney that Hutton was manipulating a campaign as though playing a tight game of chess. One adroit ploy involved Richie Benaud. Johnny Wardle was just about to bowl to Benaud. The over was halted as Hutton moved within conversational distance of the batsman. Seconds passed while he deliberated on some devious scheme. 'What's going on?' asked the perplexed Wardle. 'Put your sweater on,' said Hutton. He then briskly clapped his hands, looking over towards Tyson, fielding in the deep. 'Come on, Frank, have a bowl. Richie's in.'

Another world and more leisurely times beckoned the MCC tourists in 1954–55. Geoffrey Howard, in those days of flying infancy, described his party as adventurers in Australia. For the first time they made the journey from Perth to Adelaide by air. It telescoped the days and nights spent by train in travel across the vast Nullabor plain that separates the isolated splendour of the Western Australian capital from the eastern states.

Twenty-two years earlier Hedley Verity, the Yorkshire and

England bowler on his first tour of Australia, had penned his impressions of the mode of transport and primitive rolling stock. 'There are two trains per week on this 2,000 mile run from Perth (the journey to Adelaide involved three nights on the trans-Australian express). The train goes jolting and rolling along, so much so that one is apt to get jumped out of bed in the night. Hour after hour it is the same landscape, sandy and dry, barren and sun-parched. You cannot imagine the extent of it. All ideas of distance must be revised.'

As on Verity's tour, the 'approach' games gave another generation precious interludes of relaxation between more serious contests. Glimpses of the rural interior gave insights into the Australian lifestyle. At Bunbury in Western Australia, which had never before staged a major fixture, there was the opportunity to take reins in pony trotting. Vic Wilson, the farmer from the Yorkshire Wolds, went to a five thousand-acre farm near Rockhampton in Queensland. He was able to admire the nine hundred head of Hereford cattle and learn that in this climate you could keep your herd out all winter without fear or worry.

Then there was the visit paid by Johnny Wardle, Keith Andrew and Jim McConnon to an aboriginal settlement in Queensland. They had been warned against making this formidable trip, but started at 7.00am, drove 120 miles each way, chiefly over bush roads, and returned laden with boomerangs and other souvenirs. At stages in their journey they viewed kangaroos resting in the bush.

Mount Gambier in South Australia, then celebrating its elevation to city status, was another centre playing host to the cricket pilgrims. Yallourn, the opencast mining town in Victoria, carries the memory of a tormenting myriad of flies for Tom Graveney. The temperature on the day at Yallourn was about 100 degrees and the humidity was in the seventies. One of their lunch companions was a local police sergeant. He sported a three-inch gash on his face to which eleven flies were glued like pigs at a trough. The flies were so bad on the pitch that Peter Loader swallowed one and was instantly sick. The worst of Yallourn, said one tourist, was the coal dust. After a day on the picturesque tree-ringed ground you could come home apparently clean only to find your legs from toes to thighs deep in grime.

Geoffrey Howard said that his tour was leavened by the cheery presence of George Duckworth as scorer and baggage master. He remembered the former Lancashire and England wicket-keeper as a 'very remarkable man and a great raconteur.' When he needed counsel in maintaining discipline within the party he turned to Duckworth. 'Duckie' did not permit any lapses in behaviour. 'He would march straight into the dressing-room at the close of play and unhesitatingly tell the team, if it were necessary, exactly what he thought of them.' Howard remembered his accord with Duckworth and presented a fine tribute: 'Basically with George, it was his love of the game and his loyalty to it.'

There was one uneasy episode for Howard at the start of the tour. At Perth he went into the office of the appointed bank to confirm monetary arrangements. By some mischance the MCC had omitted to convey the necessary travel credit permissions. There was no money to pay the hotel bills. Howard had to negotiate a personal overdraft of £10,000, which lasted from early October until the New Year before it was paid off.

Denzil Batchelor related that one of the manager's ambitions was to play for the MCC team on the tour. Howard did have some pedigree as a London club cricketer; he had also played three games for Middlesex in 1930. The veteran achieved his goal in a Victorian country match. As luck would have it, he injured a knee while fielding on the first day. He was able to bat just before lunch on the second day. In the process, perhaps because of his lameness, he ran out one of his own side. Howard did not score but he was undefeated when Len Hutton declared at the interval. As he limped off the field, the England captain banteringly said: 'If he hadn't been the manager, he'd have been given out lbw already.'

Howard was on happier ground as the arbiter in keeping official entertainment within bounds. His rigour in reducing attendances at the often nerve-racking receptions was especially appreciated by the players. These were cut down, at his insistence, to one per city when a combined civic, political and cricketing function was accorded the team, with the Lord Mayor, Premier and President of the Cricket Association sharing the honours as hosts.

The MCC players received tour fees of around £1,000 and were able to draw five Australian pounds for weekly expenses. 'They can walk it on that sum,' said one observer. 'They seldom have to put their hands in their pockets. Moreover, they get their cigarettes given to them.' There were also occasional small perquisites. During the Adelaide Test there were earnings for Hutton and other members of the team from photographs of them enjoying a certain soft drink after nets.

Godfrey Evans was the star squash enthusiast. 'I played him at Perth,' said Geoffrey Howard. 'And I thought I was going to die. After a while I hoped I was.' Frank Tyson endorses the ordeal of his manager. 'Many times I faced Godfrey at squash or deck tennis, only to be run off my feet by a man nearly ten years my senior. Everything he touched seemed to be charged with a dynamic force.'

A happy team unit was constantly entertained by the antics of Johnny Wardle. Tyson recalls the special brand of humour which was always intended to astonish rather than cause uproarious laughter. One golfing escapade at the Glenelg Club at Adelaide was of the staggering variety.

Wardle was a member of the last MCC foursomes into the clubhouse, the lounge of which was on a hill overlooking the eighteenth green. 'Johnny', said Tyson, 'hooked his approach shot to the green and it landed with a clatter on the concave corrugated iron roof of the building. The "19th" hole was crowded and all its occupants were amazed when Johnny appeared in front of the large lounge windows with a ladder which he propped against the roof and gravely mounted with a nine-iron in his hand.

'He climbed the ladder and disappeared from view. Moments later there was the noise of a club head striking the roof and the ball lobbed on to the green to finish inches from the pin. The shot was greeted with loud applause. We did not find out until later that Johnny had hit the roof with the club and thrown the ball on to the green!'

Len Hutton expressed another kind of disbelief in Australia when he was accused of presiding over what his critics considered to be dilatory over-rates. For someone apprenticed to the tough but fair trade in championship tactics in Yorkshire in the 1930s it was a wounding indictment. Hutton once wistfully looked back on the attitude of his elders and said: 'They got on with the job of playing cricket and did it in the right and proper way. There was no sharp practice; they were winning, but they were winning without a smell.'

Richie Benaud was among the Australian spokesmen who led the fusillade of criticism in the 1954–55 series. Hutton was said to have perpetrated an act of extreme gamesmanship. Benaud contended that the England captain over-ran the bounds of cricket etiquette. 'Unfortunately, Len was the one who started the business of slow over-rates.' Ray Robinson, a respected Australian writer, also referred to the irritation of spectators during Hutton's frequent talks with his bowlers. These briefings reduced play to below 60 eight-ball overs in a day. During the series, reported Robinson, 58 overs were bowled in Brisbane and Adelaide and 54 in Melbourne. At Adelaide the allocation had been divided in nineteen separate spells.

On the Saturday of the Melbourne Test Tyson and Statham delivered all except two of the 27 overs bowled from the higher end. 'The batsmen,' said Robinson, 'were allowed little respite from fast bowling, though Hutton contrived to give each bowler half hour rests between turns of three or four overs.' The emphasis on slow over-rates, maintained Richie Benaud, was a deliberate ploy to 'frustrate our batsmen and make them wait for ball after ball.'

Alan Davidson, another Australian rival, is also critical of Hutton's strategy. 'England only bowled around 65 overs a day, so it was pretty tough stuff with their fast bowlers. You would get three runs an over and the most you could score was 200 in a day. It gave England an enormous batting advantage. On the other hand, we were bowling around 90 eight-ball overs in a day. So England could score 300 against our 200. The only exception was at Brisbane where Len put us in and we totalled over 600. We never really had an opportunity to wrest the initiative from them afterwards. We were batting uphill all the way.'

Frank Tyson, as the English advocate, expresses his disdain at the charges. He strongly resents the implication that England's over-rates devalued their victory in the series. In his view, the proposition put by Davidson is misguided in equating the substantial scoring with the opportunity to score. Surveying the series, he says that England only twice exceeded 300, at Adelaide and again at Sydney when the outcome of the Ashes was decided. The sequence of low scores by both sides cancelled out any supposed tactical advantage in England's favour.

Tyson believes that a proper analysis is to be found in the *effective* bowling of each team, as reflected in the comparative strike rates. His own researches reveal that Australia bowled 200 overs more than England with the percentages of each of the team's fast bowlers not dissimilar. The key variation was in the strike rates of the respective pacemen. England's bowlers took 57 wickets at a rate of 7.2 and an average of 25.77. The Australians registered a tally of 59 wickets at a rate of 8.96 and an average of 25.11. The division of work pointed to cheaper averages by the home bowlers but at a markedly worse strike rate.

Tyson also believes that England's slow bowlers played a much greater role in their team's victory than has previously been recognised. The batting of Wardle and Appleyard had been crucial at Sydney. As bowlers, their combined average of 21.57 was less than the fast men. Between them the spinners completed 149 overs against the 294 by Tyson, Statham and Bailey. They had also outbowled their Australian counterparts, Ian Johnson and Benaud, taking key wickets at nearly two balls fewer per wicket. Their victims at the top of the order included Harvey, Favell, Morris and Miller. Finally, even more telling than any statistic was the tempo of play. The first four Tests all ended with more than a day to spare.

Len Hutton later strongly denied that he had set out, with cold-blooded deliberation, to restrain over-rates as a tactical policy. 'It is a fact that fast bowlers must take time to bowl their overs and, as far as my memory goes back, that has been accepted in the game.' There was a further obligation as captain; he considered it his duty to assist two relative newcomers to Test cricket in every possible way.' The talks during play with Tyson and Statham were, he thought a legitimate device. 'I had learned this from watching Don Bradman. They formed part of his strategy regime.'

Writing in 1984, Hutton concluded: 'The matches were far too tense and dramatic for serious complaints of tempo to be entertained. It is unfair to link my series in Australia with the deliberate slowing down tactics employed in later years.'

Hutton, in his retirement, might have had cause to ponder on the deterioration of over-rates. It is estimated that the rates in Australia in 1954–55, taking account of the shorter playing hours, would not be different from the current ICC minimum. This is 15 overs an hour less reductions for interruptions and changes of innings. It would also be better than the over-rates prevalent in Test cricket before the ICC systems of minimum overs and fines were instigated. A general judgement is that Hutton's tactics in Australia might have been slow by contemporary standards, but not in present-day terms.

Modern cricket tactics, as Les Ames, the former Kent and England player once said, would have debarred Don Bradman from ever again scoring 300 in a day. Ames, as a stylish and fleet-footed batsman, always laid the accent on attack. He was saddened by the cowardice of prolonged bowling containment. 'Come on, come on, slow the buggers down,' was the refrain beginning to be voiced on the county circuit at the end of Ames's career. Colin Cowdrey expressed his own thoughts after his return from a tour of the West Indies. The steepling, short-pitched deliveries he had encountered there meant that he could score off – or simply hit – a maximum of three balls an over. His plight epitomised the mounting frustrations. They would be shown to be far worse than those that vexed Len Hutton's Australian rivals and become a deterrent to batting endeavours.

14

Reflections on the Young Guard

'Peter had come through the fire of great Test matches and he was even hungrier for runs than he had been before.'

David Sheppard.

The stars in their courses shone on the ferocious conqueror. Peter May confirmed his credentials as a premier batsman among the daring young men in Australia. He had, as one observer put it, 'crammed himself into the mould of Hutton'. The grooming by the master was now completed; the baton could be passed on to his faithful disciple; he was the successor who would bridge the amateur-professional divide.

At twenty-five, May became the youngest player, apart from David Sheppard in a caretaker capacity in 1954, to captain England for thirty years. Percy Chapman, a fellow Reading townsman, was the same age as May when he famously won his first laurels in the Ashes triumph of 1926. England, with May at the helm, did not lose a Test series for eight years. He led his country in a then record 41 Tests (35 in an unbroken sequence) until 1961 and he was victorious in 21 Tests, another record.

By May's side as he built upon the legacy bequeathed to him were six of Hutton's victorious team, two of whom – Cowdrey and Graveney – would prove to be long stayers in the demanding fields of Test cricket. Cowdrey would go on to make, in all, six tours of Australia, to equal the record of Johnny Briggs, the Lancashire slow bowler in the years between 1884 and 1898.

Cowdrey was nearing his forty-second birthday when he was summoned in an emergency for his last Australian assignment in the 1974–75 series. Twenty years had elapsed since his memorable exploits as a youth under Len Hutton. It was in character that he should be prepared to risk his reputation in a hostile environment. Back in England he had watched on television the embattled English batsmen, as they collapsed against the bowling of Dennis Lillee and Jeff Thomson at Brisbane. Alec Bedser, the chairman of the selectors, said: 'The best batsmen in the world would have been sorely troubled by these superb bowlers.'

Only four days after his arrival in Australia Cowdrey was called up at Perth to offer solace amid the carnage in scoring 41 with grace and courage. Cowdrey recalled the avuncular care of Bedser for his beleaguered players. 'He so wanted me to do well. And he was terribly anxious that I didn't get hurt.'

The curses of this anxious time were long distant in the untroubled 1950s. England followed their success in Australia in 1954–55 with another victory in a closely contested series with Jack Cheetham's South Africans in the following summer. The encores of celebrities returning to Test cricket against Australia in 1956 were rarities in conception and enterprise. This was the year of Jim Laker; at Old Trafford he took 19 wickets in the match; and England achieved their third consecutive win over Australia in retaining the Ashes.

The summer of inspired selections included the recalls of David Sheppard (a century-maker at Old Trafford) and the 41-year-old Cyril Washbrook at Leeds. Entering the fray for the last time in England was Denis Compton. The scene was appropriately the Oval where he had combined with Bill Edrich to hit the winning runs against Australia on a glorious day in 1953.

Three years on Australia once again had to bow to his mastery. After England had lost three wickets for 66, Compton scored 94 out of a partnership of 156 with Peter May. *Wisden* commented: 'He unfolded all the familiar strokes of his golden days. The special leg sweeps of his own brand and the most delicate of late cuts as well as the peerless cover-drives took him and England to prosperity.'

The invincible march in the 1950s also included a memorable stand at Edgbaston in 1957. The conundrums of Sonny Ramadhin, the wily West Indian spinner, were unravelled by May and Cowdrey. They added 411 for the fourth wicket in a record England partnership. May's 285 was his highest in first-class cricket and the biggest post-war innings. Ramadhin, in a marathon and unavailing performance, bowled 774 balls, the most delivered in a Test. After his ordeal the West Indian said: 'I was terribly tired. I had a hot bath and, when I got to bed, I was aching all over. I couldn't sleep.'

Prospering alongside the young guard in these years were Trevor Bailey and Godfrey Evans, two of the stalwarts in Hutton's campaign in Australia. Their departures at the end of the decade had been preceded by the break-up of the spinning combination of Johnny Wardle and Bob Appleyard. Appleyard, handicapped by a persistent shoulder injury, which would end his career, played in only two more Tests, both at Nottingham, in 1955 and 1956.

The exit of Wardle was a self-inflicted calamity. Aged thirty-five, he was a premier bowler at the peak of his career and esteemed for his intelligence. It was a spectacular march into exile and one which careered from a domestic squabble in Yorkshire into a national furore. The downfall of a cricketing giant stemmed from a contro-versial series of articles in a Fleet Street newspaper which dwelt upon what he considered was a lamentable decision to appoint Ronnie Burnet as Yorkshire captain. The subsequent withdrawal by the MCC of Wardle's invitation to tour Australia in 1958–59 must rank as one of the most drastic actions ever taken against an established Test cricketer.

Wardle's talents as a wrist-spinner had flowered gloriously in his international swan song in South Africa in 1956–57. He took 26 wickets in four Tests in the series at a cost of 13.80 runs each and headed the tour averages with 90 wickets at 12.26 runs apiece. At Cape Town, at the beginning of the New Year, he obtained seven wickets for 36 runs in the rout of South Africa for 72.

Charles Fortune, the broadcaster, wrote: 'Had the Wardle who bowled South Africa out at Newlands been on English television screens during his great hours he would have introduced millions to a type of bowling few have so much as seen. Wardle bowled it with rare accuracy and uncanny skill.'

The magnificent pairing of Brian Statham and Frank Tyson, which had gorged freely on other frailties in Australia in 1954–55, was destined to be a brief liaison. Of the two Lancastrians, Statham would prove to be the more enduring bowler; he forged a new and exciting partnership with Fred Trueman; and went on to play in 43 more Tests for England. In 19 first-class seasons Statham took 2,260 wickets at an astonishing average of 16.37 runs each. Among the bowlers in his category the achievement has not been surpassed.

Colin Cowdrey paid tribute to 'one of the nicest cricketers I have been privileged to know' when Statham was rewarded with the Lancashire presidency in his 70th year. 'His strength lay in his accuracy, aiming to pitch the ball just outside the off stump and flick the off bail. He varied his pace cleverly, throwing in a nasty yorker. One other speciality was a very fast break back off-cutter bowled from wide of the crease.'

Cowdrey recalled that the first glimpse of the deceiving ball led to a belief that it would go harmlessly wide of the wicket. 'Then, as it pitched, the yellow light went up to shout to you to move; but so often it would be too late – the ball would nip back to take the off stump.'

Frank Tyson was associated with Statham on only three occasions after their triumphs in Australia. They came together against South Africa at Nottingham in 1955; then against Australia at the Oval in 1956; and finally on the tour of South Africa in 1956–57. By his own admission, Tyson's pace was muted in English conditions and he was undoubtedly disadvantaged in having to bowl at Northampton, a noted 'graveyard' for fast bowlers. Raman Subba Row, one county colleague, remembers the 'slow, turning wicket. It helped George Tribe who could spin the ball a mile. They took a lot of grass off it and Frank suffered as a result.'

Len Hutton had struck a note of warning soon after the return from Australia. He had told Tyson that if he stayed at Northampton his Test career would be in jeopardy. Dennis Brookes, his county captain, recalled the directive of the club chairman. 'He wanted to win some matches and so he ordered the groundsman to under-prepare the wicket. Consequently I used to give Frank four or five overs to get the shine off and then bowl the spinners, which was a travesty.'

Tyson himself reflected on the fact that his success in Australia was not just the peak but the climax of his career. 'Slowly, ever so slowly, the desire, the incentive and will to bowl fast evaporated, and with it went the real and precious gift of being able to do so. Fast bowling was hard work, and what was once a pleasure was now a job.'

There was also a persistent heel injury, which had first hampered him in New Zealand, to impede further progress. It surfaced again in the match against Kent at Tunbridge Wells in 1955 and kept him out of a number of games in that season. He explains that the problem – a blood vessel in his left heel – was incurable at the time. 'The way I put my foot down and twisted on it created a bruise. Every time they let the blood out to relieve the pressure it produced an open wound. I couldn't bowl until it healed.'

Towards the end of his career the Shoes and Allied Research Trade Association at Kettering discovered a heel glove. 'When it was placed on my heel it cut out all the bruising. It wasn't the actual impact of my foot coming down that was the trouble. It was the twisting of my heel as I delivered the ball.' It had taken two years to locate the remedy for Tyson's injury.

The huge ferocious pace for a brief time could still induce awe among opponents and spectators. Gasping for breath against his expresses were the South Africans in 1955. Tyson was at his domineering best at Nottingham in June. England won by an innings and five runs, with a day to spare. South Africa, at one stage, 73 without loss, were bowled out for 148 in their second innings. Tyson took six wickets for 28 runs in 21.3 overs. The feat brought up a total of 52 wickets in his first 10 months in Test cricket.

The recipe once again was sheer speed and, reported *Wisden,* 'the astute use of the odd bouncer coupled with the more valuable yorker.' In a final furious flurry Tyson took five wickets, three of them bowled, for five runs in seven overs.

Away from Northampton, in confirmation of Len Hutton's

advice, Tyson demonstrated that he was not entirely a spent force on the county scene. One anecdote reveals that he was still to be feared in the right conditions. A local reporter arrived at an Essex ground to find Trevor Bailey helping the ground staff move the sightscreens so that the game could be played on a slower pitch. It had just been established that Tyson was playing. Keith Andrew's response was to threaten to 'tell my friend, Frank' if anyone dropped one short at him.

Northamptonshire, under the captaincy of Dennis Brookes, enjoyed the most successful season in their history in 1957. They finished second in the championship behind Surrey, the honour being slightly flawed by the difference of 94 points. Tyson for the first time in his career exceeded 100 wickets; and, as an expression of his assurance, took 13 wickets for 112 runs in the victory by 72 runs at the Oval. It was Northamptonshire's fourth successive victory over Surrey,

Three England bowlers dominated affairs at the Oval. They were Alec Bedser, Peter Loader and Tyson. Bedser took 10 wickets in the match and he and Loader dismissed Northamptonshire for 113 in their first innings. Tyson was even more formidable on a helpful pitch. His first innings figures of eight for 60 were the best of his career. 'He was a difficult proposition and nearly half the runs off him came off the edge,' commented *Wisden*. For those watching a venomous conquest it was a reminder of the form which had made Tyson the toast of English cricket.

The testimonies to the meteoric rise of Frank Tyson festoon him with undiminished praise. Alan Ross remembered the 'phenomenal endurance' in Australia. 'He put on weight, got the sun on his back and caught an unprepared generation of Australians with their bats horizontal.' now aged eighty-nine, Dennis Brookes looks back over seventy years, playing and watching cricket. 'I never saw anyone faster than Frank. He didn't do a great deal with the ball apart from running it a little off the seam. But he didn't have to at his speed.'

Brookes, as a young cricketer, played against Harold Larwood shortly after the bodyline tour in 1932–33. 'Harold was not as quick as Frank but he moved the ball about – in and out.' Larwood reined in his aggression against the tyro Brookes. 'He wouldn't bounce one at me.' The converse was true of Bill Voce, Larwood's Notts and England partner. Voce was a malevolent force; he did not take any prisoners as a bowler; and he was less respectful of youth.

Laurie Lee summoned up an evocative image of cricket on the village green in his book, *Cider with Rosie*. The memory of his Uncle Sid carries a touch of the vibrant menace of Frank Tyson on more exalted fields. 'His murderous bowling reduced heroes to panic; they just waved goodbye and ran.' Witnesses of Tyson attested to the same brutal power. Those who watched him in Australia judged him faster than Australian Jeff Thomson who came under their scrutiny twenty years later.

Trevor Bailey says no bowler in the period under review approached the speed of Tyson. 'He was really quick for four years – and the fastest in the world in making a comparison with those bowlers in action for twenty years after the resumption of first-class cricket in 1946.'

Neville Cardus lyrically wrote about a 'whirlwind force of destructive energy.' For those on the receiving end like Arthur Morris the pace that Tyson mustered went beyond normal bounds. 'All fast bowlers are fast enough,' ruefully observed the Australian batsman. 'But Frank had that extra yard, and you'd hardly time to pick your bat up.'

Hubert Doggart remembered one titanic encounter between Tyson and the great West Indian, Clyde Walcott on the tour of the West Indies under the aegis of Jim Swanton in 1956. 'At a time when Frank was not bowling the cry would go up from stand to stand and tree to tree, 'Typhoon, Typhoon. We want Typhoon.' Doggart said that Tyson from his shorter run generated immense power from a far from classical action. 'Clyde was then one of the world's most powerful batsmen, but in his first two innings Frank dismissed him through sheer accuracy and speed.' Walcott did get his revenge in the second innings of the second match with a stunning century. 'That innings was a joy to watch – though distinctly painful on the covers' hands – but so was Frank's bowling throughout the tour.'

Raman Subba Row, a later Northamptonshire captain, remembers the lack of angry gestures as an accompaniment to bowling, so common today. 'Frank was never malicious and always played in a civilised manner.' That is not to say that there was any lessening of competitive fervour. Ted Dexter remembers one instance when views were being expressed of a decline in Tyson's powers. Tyson chose a match at the Scarborough Festival to refute his critics.

'His first ball, says Dexter, 'sent Godfrey Evans rocking back on his heels.' It was enough to persuade the wicket-keeper and the slip cordon to make a respectful retreat to a safer distance. Then, with another vigorous swing of his arm, a rocket of a ball burst through the hands of third slip to thump against the boundary boards in a quite startling manner.

Ralph Barker wrote that for English supporters Frank Tyson was something of a mystery. They longed for him to repeat his great days in Australia and suffered and endured his frustrations as their own. The introduction of guile into his armoury, which he was obliged to attempt on the wickets at Northampton, did not suit his style or temperament, and injuries reduced his opportunities for England. Demoralising speed was Tyson's major asset and, with its disappearance, his efficiency inevitably declined.

After the 1954–55 series Tyson played in nine more Tests and took 76 wickets in all, two less than his predecessor, Harold Larwood in four fewer matches at a cheaper cost – 18.56 against 28.35. Larwood's inferior average was largely at the dictation of Don Bradman, who wrecked the statistics of all bowlers in his golden years from 1930 to 1948.

Tyson's average of 4.5 wickets per Test had seldom been bettered. An even more telling statistic is his strike rate of 45.72 compared with Larwood's 63.70. His average was lower than that of any Test bowler of any country to reach 75 wickets since Sydney Barnes, before the first world war. When he retired after the 1960 season he had taken 767 first-class wickets at an average of 20.89.

Scholastic commitments claimed him; he had perhaps always considered playing cricket as an interlude, however precious in the memory. He married an Australian girl, followed his great predecessor, Harold Larwood and joined two other England contemporaries – Peter Loader and Tony Lock – in settling in a beautiful and hospitable land. His cricket expertise was not neglected in the years ahead. He won further renown as a much-respected coach in Melbourne.

Len Hutton, in his blissful time, had rejoiced in the discovery of an avenging bowler. Out of the darkened pavilions would emerge, in turn, the tremulous batsmen, blinking in the bright Australian sunlight. He knew then that it was time to urge his matchwinner in another blistering assault. Frank Tyson would rub his hands with glee, alertly poised to obey the command.

Epilogue

The End of an Exhausting Journey

'He must surely look back with the greatest pride on the fact that in the 23 matches he captained England he lost only four and never lost a rubber.'

Harry Altham, former chairman of the Test selectors.

Len Hutton's appointment as captain for the home series against South Africa in 1955 must have carried a special satisfaction for him. His tenacity as the Ashes winner was a persuasive statement to the hitherto wary selectors. It had all been so different in the previous summer when he had narrowly escaped demotion. The weight of argument was then slanted towards the fitness of Hutton and whether he would be physically able to cope with the pressures awaiting him in Australia.

A strong lobby supported David Sheppard, the Sussex amateur and Establishment favourite, as England captain. One of the most intriguing discoveries during that debate was that Sheppard had actually been pencilled in as England captain as early as 1952. Before Hutton's own appointment was confirmed, he had met privately with Sheppard at Cambridge during the match against Yorkshire. 'Len came round to my room one evening and said that he expected me to be offered the captaincy.' Sheppard believed that, later in 1954, after his arduous tour of the West Indies, Hutton would have been glad not to carry the burden of captaincy as well as that of England's premier batsman.

But the tide turned in Hutton's favour. Sheppard, when caretaker captain against Pakistan, supported the view that his senior had been unfairly criticised as captain in the West Indies. Hutton expressed his relief at the decision to renew his appointment for the tour of Australia and New Zealand. 'I am very pleased that the MCC have thought I'm the right chap to take an England team to Australia. Physically, I know I can stand up to it.'

The stewardship of Hutton in Australia was a vindication of his overlooked merits. There was now a sense of shame, or at least regret, by the selectors that he had been misjudged. A hurried decision was taken to make amends for that at a special general meeting at Lord's. The MCC changed its rules to enable Hutton to be elected a member of the club. He was the first professional cricketer to be accorded that honour while still playing first-class cricket.

After the tour to Australia, Hutton was desperately in need of a rest. The Yorkshire county club gave him a chance to recuperate on a leisurely voyage home by sea. When he arrived back in England in early May, he was met by Billy Griffith, the MCC secretary, who presented Hutton with the famous red and yellow tie of MCC, a gift from the club.

The recollections of Jim Kilburn, the Yorkshire historian and a confidante for many years, were intriguing for the light they shed on Hutton's time as England captain. Until he received the invitation Hutton had never publicly stated that he wanted the job. He had, though, made plain his belief in private that he ought to be given the responsibility. In the circumstances of the time, it was clear that no one was better qualified. 'He was a senior cricketer and a thoughtful cricketer,' observed Kilburn. 'He could remember, he could illustrate and design.'

In the event, Hutton fully measured up to these descriptions and his appointment meant more to him than any of his other achievements. He proved to be one of the most successful captains in England's history. He was the first professional to be appointed since Arthur Shrewsbury, of Nottinghamshire, in 1886. Over three gruelling years and in five series Hutton led England back to a commanding place in world cricket. Kilburn added: 'He never gave an opportunity for the captaincy to be taken away from him. He relinquished it at his own request without ever having lost a Test match rubber.'

Neville Cardus also commented on the special qualities of a resolute cricketer. 'Hutton showed that a professional can wear the robes of leadership in the field of play with dignity. At first, no doubt, he appeared at the head of his troops not wearing anything like a Caesarian toga, but rather the uniform of a sergeant major. But he moved up in rank and prestige until he became worthy of his command. He defeated Australia twice in successive rubbers, wresting one from the enemy at the pinch and then looting the other, after a series of Tests, which were the Australians' Austerlitz.'

The record of Hutton's MCC tourists in Australia and New Zealand surpassed that of Johnny Douglas's team in the 1911–12 series. Victory in the second Test at Auckland gave a total of 12 first-class wins, one better than the number achieved by Douglas.

The record against Australia, of three wins, one defeat and one draw, was the best by any England side at home or in Australia since Douglas Jardine's 4–1 triumph in the bodyline series in 1932–33. England had earlier secured the Ashes by the same margin under Percy Chapman's captaincy in 1928–29 and also in 1911–12.

By the end of the 1954–55 tour, Hutton had led England in a record 23 Test matches and beaten Archie McLaren's total of 22 Tests, set between 1897 and 1909.

Yet, as Alan Ross observed, the bare statistics of Hutton's team conveyed little of the dramatic revolution that had taken place within the English party over five months in Australia. Hutton had presided over the replacement of maturity by youth.

He was the wise counsellor who guided his young adventurers from the bleakness of defeat at Brisbane to euphoric success in Sydney, Melbourne and Adelaide. While many of England's experienced batsmen went into decline, Peter May and Colin Cowdrey firmly established themselves as international cricketers of the highest class.

Alan Ross enthused about May's match-winning efforts at Sydney and Melbourne. 'He destroyed the legend of Lindwall and dominated him to such an extent that he no longer dared to bowl his deadly ball – the fast swinging half-volley. May put his left leg down the wicket and thrashed them to the sightscreen.'

Cowdrey, if less punishing than May, fulfilled a key role in largely taking on Hutton's mantle as the batting anchor. 'His defensive technique was of unassailable soundness,' said Ross. 'He placed and drove the ball to the on with a distribution of balance that would have delighted Michelangelo. It was Cowdrey who rendered the Australian bowling human: May domesticated it and taught it tricks.'

Len Hutton, now a member in his own right, captained the MCC against the South Africans at Lord's in late May 1955. He was given a rousing reception when he went out to bat on the Saturday evening. It was a fleeting appearance. By Monday morning he was so stricken with lumbago that he could not continue his innings. His reluctant decision to retire from international cricket was communicated to the chairman of the selectors, Gubby Allen. Peter May, at twenty-five years of age, was suddenly and unexpectedly called in as his replacement. That he had been presented with an onerous task was recognised by May. 'Len's retirement was a melancholy event because it seemed so abrupt and premature. Yet I had realised that he was no longer enjoying his cricket.'

As vice-captain in Australia, May had been chosen ahead of seasoned players, Trevor Bailey and Denis Compton. He was aware of Hutton's high regard for his ability. It had long been clear that he was being groomed to succeed the Yorkshireman. The message of tough leadership bequeathed to him by Hutton would become the keynote of May's own captaincy.

The *esprit* of the team naturally nourished by success, said Jim Swanton, had been greatly helped by May's conception of his role as vice-captain in Australia. The harmony of his partnership with Hutton was especially reflected in the understanding that his captain should be spared, as far as possible, the chores off the field. It was a commendable act of courtesy, and a sign that May was addressing the responsibilities which were all too soon to be thrust upon him.

For Len Hutton, his announcement at Lord's was the signal that he was moving towards the end of his playing career. As Jim Kilburn would later write, the timing of his retirement was not entirely free, but it was in character. 'He would have resented any decline towards obscurity, any descent from the highest estate.'

Hutton, in an interview with Ronald Crowther in the *Yorkshire Evening News,* expressed his sadness at having to withdraw from the series against South Africa. He was realistic about the dwindling prospects of a recovery in health. 'The lumbago is bad enough but the main source of trouble is my left arm which I damaged in an accident in the war.'

Unknown to cricket supporters even in Yorkshire, the severely damaged arm had become an increasing source of worry and anxiety to Hutton over the previous five years. He was particularly prone to pains caused by rheumatism which affected his left arm and shoulder. They were exacerbated by the damp and chill climate at home. Overseas, in the West Indies and Australia, the warm sunshine gave relief from the English weather and its consequences.

Hutton was then approaching his 40th birthday. He had feared for a long time as he got nearer this mark that his playing days would be numbered. 'The nuisance of it all is the constant nag,' said Hutton. 'When a day of cricket is over it continues through the night. I have a heat lamp at home and I use it to get relief, but after another day of wind and rain the trouble breaks out again.'

Hutton's admirers would be treated to one final glimpse of his artistry. It was preceded by his last appearance at the Oval where Surrey and Yorkshire were once more locked in championship combat. The match had its own unique quality in that the old and new England captains – Hutton and May – each played under their respective county captains, Norman Yardley and Stuart Surridge.

At the end of June, Hutton flourished in a farewell innings of 194 against Nottinghamshire at Trent Bridge. The sun was shining on him as he unfurled his repertoire of classical strokes. For five hours he excited the crowd, as he masterfully recreated the glories of his early career. He struck three sixes and 24 fours and his final 94 runs were scored in just over an hour as Yorkshire chased victory. It was his last century in first-class cricket and he took his last catch – from Vic Wilson's occasional bowling – to dismiss another veteran, Joe

Hardstaff, one of his allies during his batting marathon at the Oval in 1938.

Three weeks later it was truly goodbye when Hutton was stricken by another bout of lumbago during the match against Hampshire at Dean Park, Bournemouth. He did not play again for Yorkshire in that season and in the following January, after consultations with a specialist, he announced his retirement. It was relayed to a saddened public on BBC News and followed by a tribute from Harry Altham, who had been the chairman of the selectors in 1954.

Altham observed that a great chapter in the history of cricket was closed. Hutton as a batsman had represented in person, 'the complete development of modern techniques, confronting the problems posed by bowlers and the field dispositions which supported them.' The yield of this excellence was 6,971 runs, including 19 centuries, at an average of 56.67 in 79 Tests for England. Only two others – Hammond and Bradman, Hutton's models in his cricket infancy – could then claim superior records.

The accolade of a knighthood was conferred in the Queen's Birthday Honours in June 1956. Sir Leonard was the second English professional to receive the honour after Sir Jack Hobbs. It is entirely appropriate that memorials to both great cricketers have been erected at Kennington Oval. A merger of two illustrious eras is forged by the Hobbs Gates and within a few short steps, the magnificent sculpture depicting Hutton's record Test score of 364, an achievement that propelled him into cricket folklore.

Jim Kilburn said that the outstanding feature of Hutton's captaincy was his shrewdness. 'He did not expect his players to enjoy their Test matches until the scoreboard showed victory. He could not countenance a light-hearted approach to any cricket match when the result of that match had a meaning. Even in success he was prudent, avoiding extravagance as rainy days would inevitably follow. He never attacked his opponents with a flourish of displayed confidence and he never dismissed the conquered with lordly superiority. He knew the unreliability of fortune and he looked a long way ahead.'

Frivolities on major cricket occasions did, as Kilburn suggested, arouse Hutton's anger. Anyone eavesdropping on one brisk tutorial would have been aware of the intensity of his purpose as a cricketer. He once batted with a young player acknowledged as stylish but prone to indiscretions. 'What are you thinking about?' Hutton asked him at the start of the innings. There was a non-committal reply. Hutton thereupon proceeded to expand on his own train of thought. 'Well, let me tell you what I'm thinking. I'm thinking about how the wicket's going to play, which bowler will have the breeze, what shots I should not try in the first hour, which fielders aren't too quick on their feet, and I'm wondering about the sightscreens.'

The earnest recital did not cease until they reached the wicket. Hutton then summed it all up as they parted to their respective positions. 'You've got to think it through, lad.' The address was the trademark of a cricketer who had plotted and toiled to direct his young guard as they thrillingly came of age in Australia.

Appendix

Miscellany

Colin Cowdrey scored 102 out of 160 in 227 minutes in England's first innings at Melbourne. He equalled Bradman's record of achieving three figures in the lowest total (191) in Anglo-Australian Tests to contain a century. He was also the youngest Englishman, at twenty-two, to make a Test hundred in Australia since J.W. Hearne on the same ground in the 1911–12 series.

Frank Tyson took 10 wickets (4 for 65 and 6 for 85) in the second Test at Sydney. He joined an elite group of English fast bowlers in the match. In the entire twentieth century only two others – Tate and Larwood – had taken 10 wickets on this ground against Australia. George Lohmann (twice and Tom Richardson achieved the feat in the nineteenth century. Andrew Caddick also took 10 wickets in England's victory at Sydney in 2003. Neither Lindwall nor Miller for all their great exploits, could boast the distinction.

In Australia's second innings at Melbourne, Tyson claimed seven wickets for 27 runs, taking six wickets for 16 runs in 51 balls on the final morning. This is one of the best spells of bowling ever recorded by a genuine fast bowler in Test cricket.

The batting of England's lower order played a crucial part in the series. Johnny Wardle (4–2–2–4–4–0–1) and Brian Statham (2) scored 19 runs off an eight-ball over from Bill Johnston in the second Test at Sydney. Wardle also scored 30 runs off two consecutive overs in the third Test at Melbourne: 16 (0–0–4–4–4–0–4) off Johnston and 14 (4–0–2–0–4–4–0–0) off Ian Johnson.

*

Keith Miller bowled unchanged before lunch on the first day of the third Test at Melbourne. He conceded only five runs – all in his fourth over – in nine overs, eight of them maidens, for the wickets of Hutton, Edrich and Compton. It ranked with the exploit of S.F. Barnes on the same ground in December 1911. Barnes took five wickets for one run in five overs and his opening spell of 11 overs yielded figures of five wickets for six runs.

Peter May held four catches in the first Australian innings at Adelaide, equalling the record by an English fieldsman. Only one player (Victor Richardson for Australia v South Africa at Durban in 1935–36) had held five catches in a Test innings.

Three England batsmen – Peter May (Sydney, second Test), Colin Cowdrey (Melbourne) and Tom Graveney (Sydney, fifth Test) recorded their maiden centuries against Australia. Neil Harvey's century at Brisbane was his third against England and 12th in all Test cricket. Arthur Morris's century in the same match was his eighth against England, his 11th in Tests and his first since he scored 206 against England at Adelaide in 1950–51.

Ray Lindwall claimed his 100th Test wicket against England when he bowled Trevor Bailey in the fifth Test at Sydney.

New Zealand were bowled out for 26, which is still the world's lowest Test innings, at Auckland in March 1955. The innings lasted one and threequarter hours and 162 balls. The last five wickets fell for four runs. Only one batsman, Bert Sutcliffe, with 11, reached double figures, and five others failed to score. The previous lowest score of 30, twice against England, was recorded by South Africa in 1924 and 1895–96.

England's Bob Appleyard took four wickets for seven runs, three of them in four balls, in the rout at Auckland.

Bert Sutcliffe and John Reid were the ill-supported standard bearers in the series. They scored more than half the runs scored by New Zealand – 270 out of 483 in the two Tests at Dunedin and Auckland.

At Auckland Reid (73) and Sutcliffe (49) added 63 for the third wicket and contributed 122 out of the first innings total of 200. At Dunedin Reid dismissed Hutton, Cowdrey, Bailey and Evans in taking four wickets for 36 runs in 27 overs.

Sutcliffe, last out after batting for four and a half hours, hit 74 out of a total of 125 at Dunedin.

At Auckland Len Hutton set a record for the English Test captaincy when he led the team for the twenty-second time.

Tom Graveney continued his batting revival following his maiden century against Australia in the final Test at Sydney. In seven innings in New Zealand he scored 336 runs at an average of 67. His century against Wellington, the Plunket Shield champions, was his third in four consecutive matches.

Appendix

Statistics

MCC tour of Australia and New Zealand, 1954–55

Touring party

L Hutton (captain), Yorkshire (38)
P B H May (vice-captain), Surrey (24)
R Appleyard, Yorkshire (30)
T E Bailey, Essex (30)
D C S Compton, Middlesex (36)
M C Cowdrey, Kent (21)
W J Edrich, Middlesex (38)
T G Evans, Kent (33)
T W Graveney, Gloucestershire (27)
P J Loader, Surrey (24)
J E McConnon, Glamorgan (31)
R T Simpson, Nottinghamshire (34)
J B Statham, Lancashire (24)
F H Tyson, Northamptonshire (24)
J V Wilson, Yorkshire (33)
C G Howard, Lancashire (manager)
G Duckworth, Lancashire (scorer and baggage master)
H W Dalton, Essex (masseur)

Summary of the Tour

All matches – Played 28, Won 17, Lost 2, Drawn 9
First-class matches – Played 21, Won 12, Lost 2, Drawn 7
Test matches – Played 7, Won 5, Lost 1, Drawn 1

England versus Australia
Test Match Averages

England

Batting	Matches	Innings	Not out	Runs	Highest Score	Average
T W Graveney	2	3	0	132	111	44.00
P B H May	5	9	0	351	104	39.00
D C S Compton	4	7	2	191	84	38.20
T E Bailey	5	9	1	296	88	37.00
M C Cowdrey	5	9	0	319	102	35.44
L Hutton	5	9	0	220	80	24.44
W J Edrich	4	8	0	180	88	22.50
R Appleyard	4	5	3	44	*19	22.00
J H Wardle	4	6	1	109	38	21.80
T G Evans	4	7	1	102	37	17.00
J B Statham	5	7	1	67	25	11.17
F H Tyson	5	7	1	66	*37	11.00
R T Simpson	1	2	0	11	9	5.50
K V Andrew	1	2	0	11	6	5.50
A V Bedser	1	2	0	10	5	5.00

Bowling	Overs	Maidens	Runs	Wickets	Average
R Appleyard	79.0	22	224	11	20.36
F H Tyson	151.0	16	583	28	20.82
J H Wardle	70.6	15	229	10	22.90
J B Statham	143.3	16	499	18	27.72
T E Bailey	73.4	8	306	10	30.60

Also bowled

	Overs	Maidens	Runs	Wickets	
A V Bedser	37.0	4	131	1	
W J Edrich	3.0	0	28	0	
T W Graveney	6.0	0	34	1	
L Hutton	0.6	0	2	1	

Australia

Batting	Matches	Innings	Not out	Runs	Highest Score	Average
I W Johnson	4	6	4	116	–	58.00
C C McDonald	2	4	0	186		46.50
R N Harvey	5	9	1	354		44.25
P Burge	1	2	1	35		35.00
A R Morris	4	7	0	223		31.86
L Maddocks	3	5	0	150		30.00
R R Lindwall	4	6	2	106		26.50
K R Miller	4	7	0	167		23.86
J Burke	2	4	0	81		20.25
L Favell	4	7	0	130		18.57
G B Hole	3	5	0	85		17.00
R G Archer	4	7	0	117		16.71
R Benaud	5	9	0	148		16.44
A K Davidson	3	5	0	71		14.20
W Watson	1	2	0	21		10.50
G R Langley	2	3	0	21		7.00
W A Johnston	4	6	2	25		6.25

Bowling	Overs	Maidens	Runs	Wickets	Average
R G Archer	97.6	32	215	13	16.54
I W Johnson	111.0	37	243	12	20.25
W A Johnston	141.4	37	423	19	22.26
K R Miller	88.4	28	243	10	24.30
R R Lindwall	130.6	28	381	14	27.21
A K Davidson	71.0	16	220	3	73.33

Also bowled

J. Burke	2.0	0	7	0	

ENGLAND v. AUSTRALIA
First Test Match
Brisbane, November 26, 27, 29, 30, December 1
Australia won by an innings and 154 runs

AUSTRALIA v. ENGLAND AT BRISBANE

1ST INNINGS OF AUSTRALIA

	BATSMEN		HOW OUT	BOWLER	TOTAL
1	L. FAVELL	1112111144 1114 /	c COWDREY	STATHAM	23
2	A.R. MORRIS	3144146113144 12112 1111111212 11414114124111 141412112 4 41144361441411111141131131 /	c COWDREY	BAILEY	153
3	K.R. MILLER	21111226211111424 1143 11114 /	BOWLED	BAILEY	49
4	R.N. HARVEY	132111141121121152144112112143 14412141211141111121111 3 1112241142 11114 1141221441141411241 3114441 /	c BAILEY	BEDSER	162
5	G.B. HOLE	11111311341311121114211411141 4 21312121121 /	RUN	OUT	57
6	R. BENAUD	2111114 1111122121112611 /	c MAY	TYSON	34
7	R.G. ARCHER	0 /	c BEDSER	STATHAM	0
8	R.R. LINDWALL	1144114411144114 114241111114424114	NOT	OUT	64
9	G.R. LANGLEY	41122411 /	BOWLED	BAILEY	16
10	I.W. JOHNSON	1121416242	NOT	OUT	24
11	W.A. JOHNSTON	Did not bat.			

WIDES							
BYES	14 14 111						
LEG BYES	1111 1111			TOTAL	11	TOTAL EXTRAS	19
NO BALLS	1				7	TOTAL	601

FALL OF WICKETS	1	51	2	123	3	325	4	456	5	443	6	464	7	545	8	572	9		8 WKTS
BATSMAN	FAVELL		MILLER		MORRIS		HOLE		HARVEY		ARCHER		BENAUD		LANGLEY				Dec.

BOWLERS	RUNS EACH OVER																				OVRS	MDNS	RUNS	WKTS
	1	2	3	4	5	6	7	8	9	10	11	12	13	14	15	16	17	18	19	20				
BEDSER																								
–11–																					37	4	131	1
STATHAM																								
–11–																					34	2	123	2
TYSON																								
–4–																					29	1	160	1
BAILEY																								
–4–																					26	1	140	3
EDRICH																					3	0	28	0

AUSTRALIA   v.   ENGLAND   at   BRISBANE

1st innings of ENGLAND

	BATSMEN	HOW OUT	BOWLER	TOTAL
1	L. HUTTON	c. LANGLEY	LINDWALL	4
2	R.T. SIMPSON	BOWLED	MILLER	2
3	W.J. EDRICH	c. LANGLEY	ARCHER	15
4	P.B.H. MAY	BOWLED	LINDWALL	1
5	M.C. COWDREY	c. HOLE	JOHNSTON	40
6	T.E. BAILEY	BOWLED	JOHNSTON	88
7	F.H. TYSON	BOWLED	JOHNSON	7
8	A.V. BEDSER	BOWLED	JOHNSON	5
9	K.V. ANDREW	BOWLED	LINDWALL	6
10	J.B. STATHAM	BOWLED	JOHNSON	11
11	D.C.S. COMPTON	NOT OUT		2

WIDES
BYES 2
LEG BYES 1
NO BALLS

TOTAL EXTRAS 9

TOTAL 190

FALL OF WICKETS	1	2	3	4	5	6	7	8	9	10
	4	10	11	25	107	132	141	156	181	190
BATSMAN	HUTTON	SIMPSON	MAY	EDRICH	COWDREY	TYSON	BEDSER	ANDREW	STATHAM	BAILEY

BOWLERS	OVRS	MDNS	RUNS	WKTS
LINDWALL	14	4	27	3
MILLER	11	5	19	1
ARCHER	4	1	14	1
JOHNSON	19	5	46	3
BENAUD	12	5	25	0
JOHNSTON	16.1	5	47	2

AUSTRALIA v. ENGLAND AT BRISBANE

2nd innings of ENGLAND

	BATSMEN	RUNS	HOW OUT	BOWLER	TOTAL
1	L. HUTTON	41422 /	LBW	MILLER	13
2	R.T. SIMPSON	212211 /	RUN	OUT	9
3	W.J. EDRICH	11444412414261242444111431412411223 /	BOWLED	JOHNSTON	88
4	P.B.H. MAY	321424441111431214441 /	LBW	LINDWALL	44
5	M.C. COWDREY	424 /	BOWLED	BENAUD	10
6	T.E. BAILEY	114424844 /	c LANGLEY	LINDWALL	23
7	F.H. TYSON	41113112422111112211221	NOT	OUT	37
8	A.V. BEDSER	113 /	c ARCHER	JOHNSON	5
9	K.V. ANDREW	14 /	BOWLED	JOHNSON	5
10	D.C.S. COMPTON	0 /	c LANGLEY	BENAUD	0
11	J.B. STATHAM	414221 /	c HARVEY	BENAUD	14

			EXTRAS	
WIDES				
BYES	21211		TOTAL EXTRAS	9
LEG BYES	11		7	
NO BALLS			2 TOTAL	257

FALL OF WICKETS	1	2	3	4	5	6	7	8	9	10
	22	23	147	163	181	220	231	242	243	257
BATSMAN	SIMPSON	HUTTON	MAY	EDRICH	COWDREY	BAILEY	BEDSER	ANDREW	COMPTON	STATHAM

BOWLERS	OVRS	MDNS	RUNS	WKTS
LINDWALL	17	3	50	2
MILLER	12	2	30	1
ARCHER	15	4	28	0
JOHNSTON	21	8	59	1
—″—				
JOHNSON	17	5	38	2
BENAUD	8.1	1	43	3

ENGLAND v. AUSTRALIA
Second Test Match
Sydney, December 17, 18, 20, 21, 22
England won by 38 runs

AUSTRALIA v. ENGLAND at SYDNEY

1st INNINGS OF ENGLAND

	BATSMEN		HOW OUT	BOWLER	TOTAL
1	L. HUTTON	2 44 112 4 111111 3 111 /	c DAVIDSON	JOHNSTON	30
2	T. E. BAILEY	0 /	BOWLED	LINDWALL	0
3	P. B. H. MAY	113 /	c JOHNSTON	ARCHER	5
4	T. W. GRAVENEY	113112114411121 /	c FAVELL	JOHNSTON	21
5	M. C. COWDREY	2232241223 /	c LANGLEY	DAVIDSON	23
6	W. J. EDRICH	2124 /	c BENAUD	ARCHER	10
7	F. H. TYSON	0 /	BOWLED	LINDWALL	0
8	T. G. EVANS	3 /	c LANGLEY	ARCHER	3
9	J. H. WARDLE	4 111 4 3244 114 2112 /	c BURKE	JOHNSTON	35
10	R. APPLEYARD	21131 /	c HOLE	DAVIDSON	8
11	J. B. STATHAM	142121131	NOT	OUT	14

WIDES		
BYES		
LEG BYES	1211	
NO BALLS		5

TOTAL EXTRAS 5
TOTAL 154

FALL OF WICKETS	1	2	3	4	5	6	7	8	9	10
	14	19	58	63	84	85	88	99	111	154
BATSMAN	BAILEY	MAY	HUTTON	GRAVENEY	EDRICH	TYSON	EVANS	COWDREY	APPLEYARD	WARDLE

BOWLERS	RUNS EACH OVER	OVRS	MDNS	RUNS	WKTS
LINDWALL		17	3	47	2
ARCHER		12	7	12	3
DAVIDSON		12	3	34	2
JOHNSTON		13.3	1	56	3

AUSTRALIA v. ENGLAND AT SYDNEY

1st INNINGS OF AUSTRALIA

#	BATSMEN	Runs	HOW OUT	BOWLER	TOTAL
1	L. FAVELL	42222143231/	c GRAVENEY	BAILEY	26
2	A.R. MORRIS	2424/	c HUTTON	BAILEY	12
3	J.W. BURKE	323221212 4311211212121111211	c GRAVENEY	BAILEY	44
4	R.N. HARVEY	44112131/	c COWDREY	TYSON	12
5	G.B. HOLE	1314111/	BOWLED	TYSON	12
6	R. BENAUD	3411214211/	L.B.W.	STATHAM	20
7	R.G. ARCHER	1214111446111141411114421/	c HUTTON	TYSON	49
8	A.K. DAVIDSON	11411113142/	BOWLED	STATHAM	20
9	R.R. LINDWALL	141213241/	c EVANS	TYSON	19
10	G.R. LANGLEY	14/	BOWLED	BAILEY	5
11	W.A. JOHNSTON		NOT	OUT	0

WIDES		
BYES	1211	
LEG BYES	11	
NO BALLS	11 (BOTH BY TYSON)	

TOTAL EXTRAS 9

TOTAL 228

FALL OF WICKETS	1	2	3	4	5	6	7	8	9	10
	18	65	100	104	122	141	193	213	224	228
BATSMAN	MORRIS	FAVELL	BURKE	HARVEY	HOLE	BENAUD	DAVIDSON	ARCHER	LINDWALL	LANGLEY

BOWLERS	OVRS	MDNS	RUNS	WKTS
STATHAM	18	1	83	2
BAILEY	8.4	3	59	4
TYSON	13	2	45	4
APPLEYARD	7	1	32	0

AUSTRALIA v. ENGLAND at SYDNEY

2ND INNINGS OF ENGLAND

	BATSMEN		HOW OUT	BOWLER	TOTAL
1	L. HUTTON	114·114·1·3·4·4·113/	c. BENAUD	JOHNSTON	28
2	T.E. BAILEY	1·4·1/	c. LANGLEY	ARCHER	6
3	P.B.H. MAY	3·4·4·3·11·11·1·3·1·2·4·4·14·4·1·1·2·111·2·14·3·23·23·1·1·333·14·11·21111/	BOWLED	LINDWALL	104
4	T.W. GRAVENEY	0/	c. LANGLEY	JOHNSTON	0
5	M.C. COWDREY	3·2·11·3·11·3·1·4·4·12·14·11·111·2·113·4·4·11/	c. ARCHER	BENAUD	54
6	W.J. EDRICH	4·4·4·2·1·2·14·11·131/	BOWLED	ARCHER	29
7	F.H. TYSON	1·111·4·1/	BOWLED	LINDWALL	9
8	T.G. EVANS	1·111/	c. LINDWALL	ARCHER	4
9	J.H. WARDLE	1·133/	LBW	LINDWALL	8
10	R. APPLEYARD	11·2·3·4·1·2·113	NOT	OUT	19
11	J.B. STATHAM	4·2·4·4·1·2·14·4·/	c. LANGLEY	JOHNSTON	25

WIDES			TOTAL EXTRAS	10
BYES				
LEG BYES	1·111·2	6		
NO BALLS	4 (BY JOHNSTON)	4	TOTAL	296

FALL OF WICKETS	1	18	2	55	3	55	4	191	5	222	6	232	7	239	8	249	9	250	10	296
BATSMAN	BAILEY		HUTTON		GRAVENEY		COWDREY		MAY		EDRICH		EVANS		WARDLE		TYSON		STATHAM	

BOWLERS	RUNS EACH OVER	OVRS	MDNS	RUNS	WKTS
LINDWALL					
—		31	10	69	3
ARCHER					
—		22	9	53	3
JOHNSTON		19·3	2	70	3
DAVIDSON		13	2	52	0
BENAUD		19	3	42	1

AUSTRALIA v. ENGLAND AT SYDNEY

2nd INNINGS OF AUSTRALIA

BATSMEN		HOW OUT	BOWLER	TOTAL
1 L.FAVELL	1+2+13/	c EDRICH	TYSON	16
2 A.R.MORRIS	324/	LBW	STATHAM	10
3 J.W.BURKE	33+1111/	BOWLED	TYSON	14
4 R.N.HARVEY	3+2+1+2221++4321+1+1331+22+11+1+131+2+2+1+221+11++4	NOT	OUT	92
5 G.B.HOLE	0/	BOWLED	TYSON	0
6 R.BENAUD	42+11+23/	c TYSON	APPLEYARD	12
7 R.G.ARCHER	4+2+1/	BOWLED	TYSON	6
8 A.K.DAVIDSON	22+1/	c EVANS	STATHAM	5
9 R.R.LINDWALL	4+22/	BOWLED	TYSON	8
10 G.R.LANGLEY	0/	BOWLED	STATHAM	0
11 W.A.JOHNSTON	4+12+4/	c EVANS	TYSON	11

WIDES				
BYES				
LEG BYES	4+1+1		TOTAL EXTRAS	10
NO BALLS	1+1 (ALL B+ STON)			
TOTAL				184

FALL OF WICKETS	1 27	2 34	3 77	4 77	5 106	6 122	7 127	8 136	9 145	10 184
BATSMAN	MORRIS	FAVELL	BURKE	HOLE	BENAUD	ARCHER	DAVIDSON	LINDWALL	LANGLEY	JOHNSTON

BOWLERS	RUNS EACH OVER	OVRS	MDNS	RUNS	WKTS
STATHAM		17	6	45	3
TYSON		18.4	1	85	6
BAILEY		6	0	21	0
APPLEYARD		6	1	12	1
WARDLE		4	2	11	0

ENGLAND v. AUSTRALIA
Third Test Match
Melbourne, December 31, January 1, 3,4 5
England won by 128 runs

AUSTRALIA v. ENGLAND   AT MELBOURNE

1ST INNINGS OF ENGLAND

	BATSMEN		HOW OUT	BOWLER	TOTAL
1	L. HUTTON	3243/	c. HOLE	MILLER	12
2	W.J.EDRICH	4/	c. LINDWALL	MILLER	4
3	P.B.H.MAY	0/	c. BENAUD	LINDWALL	0
4	M.C.COWDREY	44223341144114/33412 4444411111411213 432	BOWLED	JOHNSON	102
5	D.C.S.COMPTON	31/	c. HARVEY	MILLER	4
6	T.E.BAILEY	41211242123241	c.MADDOCKS	JOHNSTON	30
7	T.G.EVANS	11111334441/	LBW	ARCHER	20
8	J.H.WARDLE	0/	BOWLED	ARCHER	0
9	F.H.TYSON	3111/	BOWLED	ARCHER	6
10	J.B.STATHAM	12/	BOWLED	ARCHER	3
11	R.APPLEYARD	1	NOT	OUT	1

WIDES BYES	414		9	TOTAL EXTRAS	9
LEG BYES NO BALLS				TOTAL	191

FALL OF WICKETS	1	14	2	21	3	29	4	41	5	115	6	169	7	181	8	181	9	190	10	191
BATSMAN	EDRICH		MAY		HUTTON		COMPTON		BAILEY		EVANS		WARDLE		COWDREY		STATHAM		TYSON	

BOWLERS	RUNS EACH OVER	OVRS	MDNS	RUNS	WKTS
LINDWALL		13	0	59	1
MILLER		11	8	14	3
ARCHER		13·6	4	33	4
BENAUD		7	0	30	0
JOHNSTON		12	6	26	1
JOHNSON		11	3	20	1

AUSTRALIA v. **ENGLAND** AT **MELBOURNE**

1ST INNINGS OF AUSTRALIA

	BATSMEN		HOW OUT	BOWLER	TOTAL
1	L. FAVELL	34·113·4·1·4·4 /	LBW	STATHAM	25
2	A.R. MORRIS	3 /	LBW	TYSON	3
3	K.R. MILLER	2·4·1 /	c EVANS	STATHAM	7
4	R.N. HARVEY	4·1·4·1·4·1·1·1·3·1·1·1·4·2·1·1 /	BOWLED	APPLEYARD	31
5	G.B. HOLE	1·1·1·1·4·2·1 /	BOWLED	TYSON	11
6	R. BENAUD	1·1·1·2·3·1·1·3·1·1 /	c SUB (WILSON)	APPLEYARD	15
7	R.G. ARCHER	4·1·2·2·2·1·4·1·1·1·1·1·1·1 /	BOWLED	WARDLE	23
8	L. MADDOCKS	2·1·2·2·1·2·1·4·3·1·1·2·1·2·2·4·3·1·1·2·1·1·1·1·2·3 /	c EVANS	STATHAM	47
9	R.R. LINDWALL	1·4·2·2·3·1 /	BOWLED	STATHAM	13
10	I.W. JOHNSON	1·1·1·1·1·1·1·1·2·1·1·1·1·1·1·1·2·1·4·4	NOT	OUT	33
11	W.A. JOHNSTON	1·2·1·4·3 /	BOWLED	STATHAM	11

				TOTAL EXTRAS	
WIDES					12
BYES	2·4·1		7		
LEG BYES	1·1·1		3		
NO BALLS	1·1 (BOTH BY TYSON)		2	TOTAL	231

FALL OF WICKETS	1	2	3	4	5	6	7	8	9	10
	15	38	43	65	92	115	134	151	205	231
BATSMAN	MORRIS	MILLER	FAVELL	HOLE	HARVEY	BENAUD	ARCHER	LINDWALL	MADDOCKS	JOHNSTON

BOWLERS	1	2	3	4	5	6	7	8	9	10	11	12	13	14	15	16	17	18	19	20	OVRS	MDNS	RUNS	WKTS
TYSON																					21	2	68	2
STATHAM																					16·3	0	60	5
BAILEY																					9	1	33	0
APPLEYARD																					11	3	38	2
WARDLE																					6	0	20	1

AUSTRALIA v **ENGLAND**   AT **MELBOURNE**

2ND INNINGS OF ENGLAND

	BATSMEN	Runs	HOW OUT	BOWLER	TOTAL
1	L. HUTTON	1111211411141121111112111	LBW	ARCHER	42
2	W. J. EDRICH	132421	BOWLED	JOHNSTON	13
3	P. B. H. MAY	1331221111441112131441122211143134131331114 21	BOWLED	JOHNSTON	91
4	M. C. COWDREY	11212	BOWLED	BENAUD	7
5	D. C. S. COMPTON	21114111221141	c. MADDOCKS	ARCHER	23
6	T. E. BAILEY	4111132112411	NOT	OUT	26
7	T. G. EVANS	2121144412311	c. MADDOCKS	MILLER	22
8	J. H. WARDLE	121144444244412	BOWLED	JOHNSON	38
9	F. H. TYSON	42	c. HARVEY	JOHNSTON	6
10	J. B. STATHAM	0	c. FAVELL	JOHNSTON	0
11	R. APPLEYARD	24	BOWLED	JOHNSTON	6

			TOTAL EXTRAS	7
WIDES	1 (LINDWALL)	1		
BYES	11	2		
LEG BYES	1111	4	TOTAL	279
NO BALLS				

FALL OF WICKETS	1 140	2 96	3 128	4 143	5 185	6 211	7 257	8 273	9 273	10 279
BATSMAN	EDRICH	HUTTON	COWDREY	MAY	COMPTON	EVANS	WARDLE	TYSON	STATHAM	APPLEYARD

BOWLERS	RUNS EACH OVER	OVRS	MDNS	RUNS	WKTS
LINDWALL		18	3	52	0
MILLER		18	6	35	1
ARCHER					
-R-		24	7	50	2
JOHNSTON					
-R-		24.5	2	85	5
JOHNSON		8	2	25	1
BENAUD		8	2	25	1

AUSTRALIA v ENGLAND at MELBOURNE

2nd INNINGS of AUSTRALIA

	BATSMEN		HOW OUT	BOWLER	TOTAL
1	L. FAVELL		BOWLED	APPLEYARD	30
2	A.R. MORRIS		c. COWDREY	TYSON	4
3	R. BENAUD		BOWLED	TYSON	22
4	R.N. HARVEY		c. EVANS	TYSON	11
5	K.R. MILLER		c. EDRICH	TYSON	6
6	G.B. HOLE		c. EVANS	STATHAM	5
7	R.G. ARCHER		BOWLED	STATHAM	15
8	L. MADDOCKS		BOWLED	TYSON	0
9	R.R. LINDWALL		LBW	TYSON	0
10	I.W. JOHNSON		NOT	OUT	4
11	W.A. JOHNSTON		c. EVANS	TYSON	0

WIDES				
BYES	1			
LEG BYES	4441		TOTAL EXTRAS	14
NO BALLS		13	TOTAL	111

FALL OF WICKETS	1	23	2	57	3	77	4	86	5	87	6	97	7	98	8	98	9	110	10	111
BATSMAN	MORRIS		FAVELL		HARVEY		BENAUD		MILLER		HOLE		MADDOCKS		LINDWALL		ARCHER		JOHNSTON	

BOWLERS	RUNS EACH OVER	OVRS	MDNS	RUNS	WKTS
TYSON		12.3	1	27	7
STATHAM		11	1	38	2
BAILEY		3	0	14	0
APPLEYARD		4	1	17	1
WARDLE		1	0	1	0

ENGLAND v. AUSTRALIA
Fourth Test Match
Adelaide, January 28, 29, 31, February 1, 2
England won by five wickets

AUSTRALIA v. ENGLAND AT ADELAIDE
1ST INNINGS OF AUSTRALIA

	BATSMEN		HOW OUT	BOWLER	TOTAL
1	C.C. McDONALD	2144 242111 341133 21314 /	c. MAY	APPLEYARD	48
2	A.R. MORRIS	12212112214 11121 /	c. EVANS	TYSON	25
3	J.W. BURKE	111334 11111 /	c. MAY	TYSON	18
4	R.N. HARVEY	41221142134 /	c. EDRICH	BAILEY	25
5	K.R. MILLER	41111214111111112111311411 /	c. BAILEY	APPLEYARD	44
6	R. BENAUD	14421111 /	c. MAY	APPLEYARD	15
7	L. MADDOCKS	111342221111111313144141112114421114111 /	RUN	OUT	69
8	R.G. ARCHER	61142413 /	c. MAY	TYSON	21
9	A.K. DAVIDSON	212 /	c. EVANS	BAILEY	5
10	I.W. JOHNSON	21121441111114111141141 /	c. STATHAM	BAILEY	41
11	W.A. JOHNSTON	0	NOT	OUT	0

	WIDES					TOTAL EXTRAS	12
	BYES	3			3		
	LEG BYES	3211			7		
	NO BALLS	11	(ONE EACH: TYSON, BAILEY)		2	TOTAL	323

FALL OF WICKETS	1	59	2	86	3	115	4	129	5	175	6	182	7	212	8	229	9	321	10	323
BATSMAN	MORRIS		McDONALD		BURKE		HARVEY		BENAUD		MILLER		ARCHER		DAVIDSON		JOHNSON		MADDOCKS	

BOWLERS	OVRS	MDNS	RUNS	WKTS
TYSON				
—"—	26·1	4	85	3
STATHAM	19	4	70	0
APPLEYARD				
—"—	23	7	58	3
BAILEY	12	3	39	3
WARDLE	19	5	59	0

AUSTRALIA v. ENGLAND		AT ADELAIDE		
BATSMEN	1ST INNINGS OF ENGLAND	HOW OUT	BOWLER	TOTAL
1 L. HUTTON	432111111111111131211333112111111411111112124111112211	c. DAVIDSON	JOHNSTON	80
2 W.J. EDRICH	211111111412H /	BOWLED	JOHNSON	21
3 P.B.H. MAY	1/	c. ARCHER	BENAUD	1
4 M.C. COWDREY	21341141334121314141441141133111134111/	c. MADDOCKS	DAVIDSON	79
5 D.C.S. COMPTON	31413114111342H3111H /	L.B.W.	MILLER	44
6 T.E. BAILEY	212111141111322112111112 1/	c. DAVIDSON	JOHNSTON	38
7 T.G. EVANS	431412541214H1/	c. MADDOCKS	BENAUD	37
8 J.H. WARDLE	611133HH /	c & b	JOHNSON	23
9 F.H. TYSON	1/	c. BURKE	BENAUD	1
10 R. APPLEYARD	4H1	NOT	OUT	10
11 J.B. STATHAM	2/	c MADDOCKS	BENAUD	0

WIDES				
BYES				
LEG BYES	1		1	TOTAL EXTRAS 7
NO BALLS	3 (BOTH BY JOHNSTON)		2	TOTAL 341

FALL OF WICKETS	1 60	2 63	3 162	4 232	5 232	6 283	7 321	8 323	9 336	10 341
BATSMAN	EDRICH	MAY	HUTTON	COMPTON	COWDREY	EVANS	WARDLE	TYSON	BAILEY	STATHAM

BOWLERS	RUNS EACH OVER																				OVRS	MDNS	RUNS	WKTS
	1	2	3	4	5	6	7	8	9	10	11	12	13	14	15	16	17	18	19	20				
MILLER																					11	4	34	1
ARCHER																					3	0	12	0
JOHNSON																								
-"-																					36	17	46	2
DAVIDSON																								
-"-																					25	3	55	1
JOHNSTON																								
-"-																					27	11	60	2
BENAUD																								
-"-																					36.6	6	120	4
BURKE																					2	0	7	0

AUSTRALIA v. ENGLAND at ADELAIDE

2nd Innings of AUSTRALIA

	BATSMEN	Runs	HOW OUT	BOWLER	TOTAL
1	C.C.McDONALD	4·1111·122·113·1·212·111 /	BOWLED	STATHAM	29
2	A.R.MORRIS	2211·11341 /	c & b	APPLEYARD	16
3	J.W.BURKE	311 /	BOWLED	APPLEYARD	5
4	R.N.HARVEY	111121 /	BOWLED	APPLEYARD	4
5	K.R.MILLER	1321142 /	BOWLED	STATHAM	14
6	L.MADDOCKS	2 /	L.B.W.	STATHAM	2
7	R.BENAUD	1 /	L.B.W.	TYSON	1
8	R.G.ARCHER	111 /	c. EVANS	TYSON	3
9	A.K.DAVIDSON	11121·2111·22111·141 /	L.B.W	WARDLE	23
10	W.A.JOHNSTON	111 /	c APPLEYARD	TYSON	3
11	I.W.JOHNSON	111	NOT	OUT	3

			TOTAL EXTRAS	5
WIDES				
BYES	121			
LEG BYES	1	4		
NO BALLS		1	TOTAL	111

FALL OF WICKETS	1	2	3	4	5	6	7	8	9	10	
	21	40	54	69	76	77	79	83	101	111	
BATSMAN	MORRIS	BURKE	HARVEY	McDONALD	MILLER	BENAUD	MADDOCKS	ARCHER	JOHNSTON	DAVIDSON	

BOWLERS	RUNS EACH OVER	OVRS	MDNS	RUNS	WKTS
TYSON		15	2	47	3
STATHAM		12	1	38	3
APPLEYARD		12	7	13	3
WARDLE		4.2	1	8	1

AUSTRALIA v. ENGLAND AT ADELAIDE

2ND INNINGS OF ENGLAND

	BATSMEN		HOW OUT	BOWLER	TOTAL
1	L. HUTTON	32/	c. DAVIDSON	MILLER	5
2	W.J.EDRICH	0/	BOWLED	MILLER	0
3	P.B.H.MAY	2112221243114/	c. MILLER	JOHNSTON	26
4	M.C.COWDREY	4/	c. ARCHER	MILLER	4
5	D.C.S.COMPTON	11112111413222233211	NOT	OUT	34
6	T.E.BAILEY	414123/	L.B.W.	JOHNSTON	15
7	T.G.EVANS	24	NOT	OUT	6
8					
9					
10					
11					

WIDES			
BYES	21		
LEG BYES	13		
NO BALLS			

TOTAL EXTRAS 7

TOTAL 97

FALL OF WICKETS: 1 **3** 2 **10** 3 **15** 4 **49** 5 **90** 6 7 8 9 10 **for**

BATSMAN: EDRICH HUTTON COWDREY MAY BAILEY

5 WKTS

BOWLERS	RUNS EACH OVER	OVRS	MDNS	RUNS	WKTS
MILLER		10·4	2	40	3
DAVIDSON		2	0	7	0
ARCHER		4	0	13	0
BENAUD		6	2	10	0
JOHNSTON		8	2	20	2

ENGLAND v. AUSTRALIA
Fifth Test Match
Sydney, March 1, 2, 3
Match drawn

	BATSMEN	1st INNINGS OF ENGLAND	HOW OUT	BOWLER	TOTAL
1	L. HUTTON	42/	c. BURGE	LINDWALL	6
2	T.W. GRAVENEY	2424311121211132442244432311221112414 14444 1324	c & b.	JOHNSON	111
3	P.B.H. MAY	11144111121123421444211414141213332222/	c. DAVIDSON	BENAUD	79
4	M.C. COWDREY	0/	c. MADDOCKS	JOHNSON	0
5	D.C.S. COMPTON	111111142143111234311213423134444123113/	c & b	JOHNSON	84
6	T.E. BAILEY	4213321421131121111231121111141422211111	BOWLED	LINDWALL	72
7	T.G. EVANS	11211121/	c McDONALD	LINDWALL	10
8	J.H. WARDLE	1211	NOT	OUT	5
9	F.H. TYSON				
10	R. APPLEYARD	DID NOT BAT.			
11	J.B. STATHAM				

				TOTAL EXTRAS	4
WIDES					
BYES	1		1		
LEG BYES	111		3	TOTAL	371
NO BALLS					

FALL OF WICKETS	1	6	2	188	3	188	4	196	5	330	6	359	7	371	8		9		10	for
BATSMAN	HUTTON		GRAVENEY		COWDREY		MAY		COMPTON		EVANS		BAILEY						7 WKTS DEC	

BOWLERS	RUNS EACH OVER	OVRS	MDNS	RUNS	WKTS
LINDWALL —11—		20·6	5	77	3
MILLER		15	1	71	0
DAVIDSON		19	3	72	0
JOHNSON		20	5	68	3
BENAUD		20	4	79	1

AUSTRALIA v. ENGLAND AT SYDNEY

1st INNINGS OF AUSTRALIA

	BATSMEN		HOW OUT	BOWLER	TOTAL
1	W. WATSON	13u2!11212 /	BOWLED	WARDLE	18
2	C.C. McDONALD	631u4 13u 2231 21u4112131132211 31211 /	c. MAY	APPLEYARD	72
3	L. FAVELL	1/	BOWLED	TYSON	1
4	R.N. HARVEY	313141 /	c & b	TYSON	13
5	K.R. MILLER	32u1u23 /	RUN	OUT	19
6	P. BURGE	u222u21 /	c. APPLEYARD	WARDLE	17
7	R. BENAUD	3u /	BOWLED	WARDLE	7
8	L. MADDOCKS	11121u3u1u12214 /	c. APPLEYARD	WARDLE	32
9	AK. DAVIDSON	113114241 /	c. EVANS	WARDLE	18
10	I.W. JOHNSON	2u2111 /	RUN	OUT	11
11	RR LINDWALL	11	NOT	OUT	2

WIDES				
BYES	u213		TOTAL EXTRAS	11
LEG BYES	1		TOTAL	221
NO BALLS				

FALL OF WICKETS	1	52	2	53	3	85	4	129	5	138	6	147	7	157	8	202	9	217	10	221
BATSMAN	WATSON		FAVELL		HARVEY		MILLER		McDONALD		BENAUD		BURGE		MADDOCKS		DAVIDSON		JOHNSON	

BOWLERS	RUNS EACH OVER																				OVRS	MDNS	RUNS	WKTS
	1	2	3	4	5	6	7	8	9	10	11	12	13	14	15	16	17	18	19	20				
TYSON																					11	1	46	2
STATHAM																					9	1	31	0
APPLEYARD																					16	2	54	1
WARDLE																					24.4	6	79	5

AUSTRALIA v. ENGLAND   at SYDNEY

2nd INNINGS OF AUSTRALIA

	BATSMEN		HOW OUT	BOWLER	TOTAL
1	W. WATSON	12 /	c. GRAVENEY	STATHAM	3
2	C.C. McDONALD	2324W·1111211313·1141 /	c. EVANS	GRAVENEY	37
3	L. FAVELL	1W /	c GRAVENEY	WARDLE	9
4	R.N. HARVEY	1 /	c · b	WARDLE	1
5	K.R. MILLER	111112W2W11W41 /	BOWLED	WARDLE	28
6	P. BURGE	3W211111·1	NOT	OUT	18
7	R. BENAUD	1WW1WW·1111 /	BOWLED	HUTTON	22
8					
9					
10					
11					

			TOTAL EXTRAS	
WIDES				
BYES				
LEG BYES			TOTAL	118
NO BALLS				

FALL OF WICKETS	1	14	2	27	3	29	4	67	5	87	6	118	7		8		9		10	for 6 WKTS
BATSMAN	WATSON		FAVELL		HARVEY		McDONALD		MILLER		BENAUD									

BOWLERS	RUNS EACH OVER																				OVRS	MDNS	RUNS	WKTS
	1	2	3	4	5	6	7	8	9	10	11	12	13	14	15	16 . 17	18	19	20				
STATHAM																				5	0	11	1
TYSON																				5	2	20	0
WARDLE																				12	1	51	3
GRAVENEY																				6	0	34	1
HUTTON																				0·6	0	2	1

England versus New Zealand
Test Match Averages

England

Batting	Matches	Innings	Not out	Runs	Highest Score	Average
T W Graveney	2	3	1	86	41	43.00
F H Tyson	2	2	1	43	*27	43.00
M C Cowdrey	2	3	1	64	42	32.00
J H Wardle	2	2	1	32	*32	32.00
J B Statham	2	1	0	13	13	13.00
P B H May	2	3	0	71	48	23.67
L Hutton	2	3	0	67	53	22.33
R T Simpson	2	2	0	44	23	22.00
T E Bailey	2	2	0	18	18	9.00
R Appleyard	2	2	1	6	6	6.00
T G Evans	2	2	0	0	0	0.00

Bowling	Overs	Maidens	Runs	Wickets	Average
J B Statham	58.4	23	91	12	7.58
F H Tyson	49.0	18	90	11	8.18
R Appleyard	36.0	12	80	9	8.89
J H Wardle	76.3	43	116	5	23.20
T E Bailey	33.2	12	62	2	31.00

New Zealand

Batting	Matches	Innings	Not out	Runs	Highest Score	Average
B Sutcliffe	2	4	0	169	74	42.25
J R Reid	2	4	0	106	73	26.50
G O Rabone	2	4	0	61	29	15.25
M E Chapple	1	2	0	20	20	10.00
S N McGregor	2	4	1	26	*15	8.67
A N Moir	2	4	1	17	10	5.67

Also batted

A R MacGibbon	2	4	0	16	9	
H B Cave	2	4	0	13	6	
J G Leggat	1	2	0	5	4	
R W Blair	1	2	0	3	3	
L A Watt	1	2	0	2	2	
I A Colquhoun	2	4	2	1	*1	
M B Poore	1	2	0	0	0	
J A Hayes	1	2	0	0	0	

Bowling	Overs	Maidens	Runs	Wickets	Average
H B Cave	48.0	25	52	3	17.33
J R Reid	56.0	25	76	4	19.00
A N Moir	34.1	4	104	5	20.80
A R MacGibbon	52.1	20	88	4	22.00
J A Hayes	23.0	7	71	3	23.67

Also bowled

R W Blair	12.0	1	49	1	
G O Rabone	2.0	0	4	0	

ENGLAND v. NEW ZEALAND
First Test Match
Dunedin, March 11, 12, 14, 15, 16
England won by 8 wickets

NEW ZEALAND v. ENGLAND   AT DUNEDIN

	BATSMEN	1ST INNINGS OF NEW ZEALAND	HOW OUT	BOWLER	
1	G.O. RABONE		st EVANS	WARDLE	18
2	M.E. CHAPPLE		BOWLED	STATHAM	0
3	B. SUTCLIFFE		c STATHAM	BAILEY	74
4	J.R. REID		BOWLED	STATHAM	4
5	S.N. McGREGOR		BOWLED	TYSON	2
6	L.A. WATT		BOWLED	TYSON	0
7	H.B. CAVE		BOWLED	TYSON	1
8	A.N. MOIR		BOWLED	STATHAM	7
9	R.W. BLAIR		BOWLED	STATHAM	0
10	A.R. MacGIBBON		c EVANS	BAILEY	7
11	I.A. COLQUHOUN		NOT	OUT	0

					TOTAL EXTRAS	12
WIDES						
BYES					5	
LEG BYES					4	
NO BALLS					3	TOTAL 125

FALL of	1	2	3	4	5	6	7	8	9	10
WICKETS	3	63	68	72	76	86	103	113	122	125

BOWLERS	RUNS EACH OVER 1-20	OVRS	MDNS	RUNS	WKTS
TYSON		19	8	23	3
STATHAM		17	9	24	4
BAILEY		12.2	6	19	2
WARDLE		26	15	31	1
APPLEYARD		7	3	16	0

NEW ZEALAND v. ENGLAND   AT DUNEDIN

Lst INNINGS OF   ENGLAND

	BATSMEN		HOW OUT	BOWLER	
1	L. HUTTON		c COLQUHOUN	REID	11
2	T.W. GRAVENEY		BOWLED	CAVE	41
3	P.B.H. MAY		BOWLED	MacGIBBON	10
4	M.C. COWDREY		L.B.W.	REID	42
5	R.T. SIMPSON		BOWLED	CAVE	21
6	T.E. BAILEY		L.B.W.	REID	0
7	T.G. EVANS		BOWLED	REID	0
8	J.H. WARDLE		NOT	OUT	32
9	F.H. TYSON		c McGREGOR	MacGIBBON	16
10	R. APPLEYARD		NOT	OUT	0
11	J.B. STATHAM		DID NOT BAT		

WIDES				TOTAL	
BYES	12			EXTRAS	36
LEG BYES	18				
NO BALLS	6			TOTAL	209

FALL of	1	2	3	4	5	6	7	8		for 8
WICKETS	60	77	101	150	152	152	156	208		Wickets

BOWLERS	RUNS EACH OVER																				OVRS	MDNS	RUNS	WKTS
	1	2	3	4	5	6	7	8	9	10	11	12	13	14	15	16	17	18	19	20				
BLAIR																					8	1	29	0
MacGIBBON																					24.5	11	39	2
REID																					27	11	36	4
CAVE																					24	15	27	2
MOIR																					9	1	42	0

NEW ZEALAND v. ENGLAND		AT DUNEDIN		
BATSMEN	2ND INNINGS OF NEW ZEALAND	HOW OUT	BOWLER	
1 G.O. RABONE		L.B.W.	WARDLE	7
2 M.E. CHAPPLE		BOWLED	STATHAM	20
3 B. SUTCLIFFE		RUN	OUT	35
4 J.R. REID		BOWLED	TYSON	28
5 S.N. McGREGOR		c COWDREY	APPLEYARD	8
6 L.A. WATT		BOWLED	APPLEYARD	2
7 H.B. CAVE		BOWLED	TYSON	1
8 A.N. MOIR		L.B.W.	TYSON	10
9 R.W. BLAIR		BOWLED	WARDLE	3
10 A.R. MacGibbon		BOWLED	TYSON	0
11 I.A. COLQUHOUN		NOT	OUT	1

WIDES / BYES 7 / LEG BYES 10 / NO BALLS — TOTAL EXTRAS 17 — TOTAL 132

FALL OF WICKETS	1	2	3	4	5	6	7	8	9	10
	24	68	75	96	98	103	103	123	126	132

BOWLERS	OVRS	MDNS	RUNS	WKTS
TYSON	12	6	16	4
STATHAM	15	5	30	1
BAILEY	8	4	9	0
WARDLE	14.3	4	41	2
APPLEYARD	7	2	19	2

NEW ZEALAND v. ENGLAND AT DUNEDIN				
BATSMEN	2ND INNINGS OF ENGLAND	HOW OUT	BOWLER	
1 L. HUTTON		c COLQUHOUN	BLAIR	3
2 T.W. GRAVENEY		NOT	OUT	32
3 P.B.H. MAY		BOWLED	MacGIBBON	13
4 M.C. COWDREY		NOT	OUT	0
5 R.T. SIMPSON				
6 T.E. BAILEY				
7 T.G. EVANS				
8 J.H. WARDLE				
9 F.H. TYSON				
10 R APPLEYARD				
11 J.B. STATHAM				

WIDES BYES		TOTAL EXTRAS	1
LEG BYES NO BALLS		TOTAL	49
FALL of WICKETS	1 22	2 47	for 2 wickets

BOWLERS	RUNS EACH OVER																				OVRS	MDNS	RUNS	WKTS
	1	2	3	4	5	6	7	8	9	10	11	12	13	14	15	16	17	18	19	20				
BLAIR																					4	0	20	1
MacGIBBON																					7.2	2	16	1
REID																					4	2	12	0

ENGLAND v. NEW ZEALAND
Second Test Match
Auckland, March 25,26,28
England won by an innings and 20 runs

NEW ZEALAND v. ENGLAND AT AUCKLAND

1ST INNINGS OF NEW ZEALAND

	BATSMEN	HOW OUT	BOWLER	
1	B. SUTCLIFFE	c BAILEY	STATHAM	49
2	J. G. LEGGAT	L.B.W.	TYSON	4
3	M. B. POORE	c EVANS	TYSON	0
4	J. R. REID	c STATHAM	WARDLE	73
5	G. O. RABONE	c EVANS	STATHAM	29
6	S. M. McGREGOR	NOT	OUT	15
7	H. B. CAVE	c BAILEY	APPLEYARD	6
8	A. R. MacGIBBON	BOWLED	APPLEYARD	9
9	I. A. COLQUHOUN	c Sub	APPLEYARD	0
10	A. W. MOIR	L.B.W.	STATHAM	0
11	J. A. HAYES	BOWLED	STATHAM	0

WIDES		4	TOTAL EXTRAS	15
BYES		9		
LEG BYES		2		
NO BALLS		2	TOTAL	200

FALL OF WICKETS	1	2	3	4	5	6	7	8	9	10
	13	13	76	154	171	189	199	199	200	200

RUNS EACH OVER

	1	2	3	4	5	6	7	8	9	10	11	12	13	14	15	16	17	18	19	20	OVRS	MDNS	RUNS	WKTS
TYSON																					11	2	41	2
STATHAM																					4.4	7	28	4
BAILEY																					13	2	34	0
APPLEYARD																					16	4	38	3
WARDLE																					21	19	44	1

NEW ZEALAND v. ENGLAND AT AUCKLAND

BATSMEN	1st INNINGS OF ENGLAND	HOW OUT	BOWLER	
1 R.T. SIMPSON		c & b	MOIR	23
2 T.W. GRAVENEY		c RABONE	HAYES	13
3 P.B.H. MAY		BOWLED	HAYES	48
4 M.C. COWDREY		BOWLED	MOIR	22
5 L. HUTTON		BOWLED	MacGIBBON	53
6 T.E. BAILEY		c COLQUHOUN	CAVE	18
7 T.G. EVANS		c REID	MOIR	0
8 J.H. WARDLE		c REID	MOIR	0
9 F.H. TYSON		NOT OUT		27
10 R. APPLEYARD		c COLQUHOUN	HAYES	6
11 J.B. STATHAM		c REID	MOIR	13

WIDES
BYES
LEG BYES
NO BALLS

12 TOTAL EXTRAS 23
8 TOTAL 246

FALL OF WICKETS	1	2	3	4	5	6	7	8	9	10
	21	56	112	112	163	164	164	201	218	246

BOWLER	RUNS EACH OVER 1 2 3 4 5 6 7 8 9 10 11 12 13 14 15 16 17 18 19 20	OVRS	MDNS	RUNS	WKTS
HAYES		23	7	71	3
MacGIBBON		20	7	33	1
REID		25	10	28	0
CAVE		24	10	25	1
MOIR		25.1	3	62	5
RABONE		2	0	4	0

NEW ZEALAND v. ENGLAND at AUCKLAND

2ND INNINGS OF NEW ZEALAND

	BATSMEN	HOW OUT	BOWLER	
1	B. SUTCLIFFE	BOWLED	WARDLE	11
2	J. G. LEGGAT	c HUTTON	TYSON	1
3	M. B. POORE	BOWLED	TYSON	0
4	J. R. REID	BOWLED	STATHAM	1
5	G. O. RABONE	L.B.W.	STATHAM	7
6	S. M. McGREGOR	c MAY	APPLEYARD	1
7	H. B. CAVE	c GRAVENEY	APPLEYARD	5
8	A. R. MacGIBBON	L.B.W.	APPLEYARD	0
9	I. A. COLQUHOUN	c GRAVENEY	APPLEYARD	0
10	A. N. MOIR	NOT	OUT	0
11	J. A. HAYES	BOWLED	STATHAM	0

WIDES		
BYES		
LEG BYES	TOTAL EXTRAS	0
NO BALLS		
	TOTAL	26

FALL of	1	2	3	4	5	6	7	8	9	10
WICKETS	6	8	9	14	14	22	22	22	26	26

BOWLERS	1	2	3	4	5	6	7	8	9	10	11	12	13	14	15	16	17	18	19	20	OVRS	MDNS	RUNS	WKTS
TYSON																					7	2	10	2
STATHAM																					9	2	9	3
APPLEYARD																					6	3	7	4
WARDLE																					5	5	0	1

Bibliography

Alex Bannister: *Cricket Cauldron* (Stanley Paul, 1954).

Ralph Barker: *Purple Patches* (Collins, 1987).

Denzil Batchelor: *Picture Post Book of the Tests* (Hulton Press, 1955).

Brian Bearshaw: *From the Stretford End. – The Official History of Lancashire County Cricket Club* (Transworld, 1990).

Neville Cardus: *Close of Play* (Collins, 1956).

Colin Cowdrey: *MCC – The Autobiography of a Cricketer* (Hodder & Stoughton, 1976).

Keith Dunstan: *The Paddock that Grew* (Cassell, 1962).

Matthew Engel and Andrew Radd: *The History of Northamptonshire County Cricket Club* (Christopher Helm, 1993).

Alan Gibson: *The Cricket Captains of England* (Pavilion Books, 1989).

Gideon Haigh: *The Summer Game* (The Text Publishing Co., Melbourne, 1997).

Alan Hill: *Herbert Sutcliffe – Cricket Maestro* (Simon & Schuster, 1991); *Bill Edrich* (Andre Deutsch, 1994); *Peter May* (Andre Deutsch, 1996); *Johnny Wardle – Cricket Conjuror* (David & Charles, 1988).

Gerald Howat: *Len Hutton* (Heinemann Kingswood, 1988).

Rev. Malcolm G. Lorimer (Editor): *Glory Lightly Worn* (The Parrs Wood Press, 2001).

Peter May: *Peter May's Book of Cricket* (Cassell, 1956).

K. Miller & R.S. Whitington: *Cricket Typhoon* (Macdonald, 1955).

Patrick Murphy: *The Centurions* (J.M. Dent, 1983).

Don Neely and Richard King: *The Men in White – The History of New Zealand Cricket 1894–1985* (M.O.A Publications, Auckland, 1986).

Jack Pollard: *Australian Cricket – The Game and the Players* (Angus & Robertson, 1988).

Alan Ross: *Australia '55* (Michael Joseph, 1955).

David Sheppard: *Parson's Pitch* (Hodder & Stoughton, 1964).

E.W. Swanton: *Swanton in Australia – With the MCC 1946–75* (Collins, 1975); General Editor, *Barclay's World of Cricket* (Collins, 1986); *Victory in Australia – The Test matches of 1954–55* (Daily Telegraph, 1955).

A.A. Thomson: *Cricket My Happiness* (Museum Press, 1954).

Frank Tyson: *A Typhoon Called Tyson* (Heinemann, 1961).

Crawford White: *England Keep The Ashes* (News Chronicle, 1955).

Contemporary reports in *The Times, The Daily Telegraph, The Daily Express, News Chronicle, Yorkshire Post, Yorkshire Evening News, Manchester Guardian, Sydney Morning Herald, Sydney Daily Telegraph, Melbourne Age, Auckland Star, New Zealand Herald, Jamaica Gleaner, Cricket Today, The Cricketer, Playfair Cricket Monthly, The Cricket Society Journal* and various issues of *Wisden Cricketers' Almanack* have provided the nucleus of printed sources in this book.

Index